Beer, Sociability, and Masculinity in South Africa

Anne Kelk Mager

Indiana University Press

BLOOMINGTON AND INDIANAPOLIS

This book is a publication of

Indiana University Press
601 North Morton Street
Bloomington, Indiana 47404-3797 USA

www.iupress.indiana.edu

Telephone orders	800-842-6796
Fax orders	812-855-7931
Orders by e-mail	iuporder@indiana.edu

⊗ *The paper used in this publication meets the minimum requirements of
the American National Standard for Information Sciences—Permanence
of Paper for Printed Library Materials, ANSI Z39.48-1992.*

MANUFACTURED IN THE UNITED STATES OF AMERICA

Library of Congress Cataloging-in-Publication Data

Mager, Anne Kelk.
  Beer, sociability, and masculinity in South Africa / Anne Kelk Mager.
    p. cm. — (African systems of thought)
  Includes bibliographical references and index.
  ISBN 978-0-253-35449-5 (cloth : alk. paper) — ISBN 978-0-253-22180-3
(pbk. : alk. paper) 1. Beer industry—Social aspects—South Africa—History.
2. Drinking of alcoholic beverages—Social aspects—South Africa—History.
3. Beer—Socal aspects—South Africa—South Africa—History. 4. South
Africans—Alcohol use. 5. Apartheid—South Africa. 6. Masculinity—South
Africa. I. Title.
  HD9397.S52M34 2010
  306.4—dc22
                                    2009039150

1 2 3 4 5 15 14 13 12 11 10

Beer, Sociability, and Masculinity in South Africa

African Systems of Thought

Ivan Karp, editor

CONTRIBUTING EDITORS

James W. Fernandez
Luc de Heusch
John Middleton
Roy Willis

Contents

Acknowledgments

Many colleagues and friends have offered encouragement and support over the several years that I have been researching and writing this book in the gaps between teaching. Inevitably, my debts and gratitude extend beyond the few who can be acknowledged here.

I am particularly grateful to Megan Vaughan, who first suggested that "someone should work on beer" and whose encouragement sustained me throughout the project. Robert Ross and Tim James read the final manuscript and gave me good advice. Ian Phimister, Maanda Mulaudzi, Luise White, Ivan Karp, Tony Bennett, Leslie Witz, Siraj Rassool, Bill Nasson, Debbie Budlender, Joel Krige, Jan Theron, and Shane Godfrey commented on different aspects of the book. Sofie Geschier helped with proofreading. I am most grateful for this support and acknowledge that I alone am responsible for any errors.

Adrian Botha of South African Breweries Limited (SAB) granted me access to selected records and personnel—but only after meeting me at Forries (then a tied house) and making sure that I was not a teetotaler. For some at SAB, independent research was an intrusion. Others put their skepticism aside and did their best to explain how things worked in the real world of beer. These men, passionate about SAB and its product, taught me a great deal. For this, I thank them. If I have not produced the story they wanted, I trust that they will accept that historians have a job to do too.

I am very grateful to those who helped me with legal material. Advocate Joel Krige guided me patiently through the law reports, and Glynn Williams of Chennels Albertyn generously gave me access to the legal record. Attorneys at the patent, trademark, and copyright firm Adams and Adams tracked down an unreported case for me.

My thanks are due to Barbara Charles and Robert Staples for access to their archive and for their generous hospitality in Washington, D.C.

Thanks are also due to Alex Lichtenstein, who pointed me in the direction of reports on SABMiller in the United States and Niel Krige who kept me informed of Norman Adami's movements.

Librarians Lubabalo Booi at the Law Library at the University of Cape Town, Kate Hunter at the University of Cape Town's Graduate School of Business, and Laureen Rushby in the Government Publications section of Chancellor Oppenheimer library at the University of Cape Town always made time to search for material. Their help is much appreciated. Finally, Andrew Ball and Richard Maguire helped me track down sociologist and T-shirt collector Chris Bolsmann, who brought the Bafana jersey for the cover from Birmingham, UK. I owe them a very big thank-you. Photographer Collin Albertus produced the cover image with professional enthusiasm.

The National Research Foundation of South Africa provided support in the early stages of the project, and the University of Cape Town's Research Fund kept me going over the longer term.

Beer, Sociability, and Masculinity in South Africa

Introduction

Since the advent of democracy in South Africa in 1994, the alcoholic beverage industry has been the focus of considerable public interest in this country. The Truth and Reconciliation Commission discussed the relationship of the industry to the apartheid state after a major brewing corporation declared that instead of benefiting from apartheid, the business of beer had experienced unfair discrimination at the hands of the Afrikaner nationalist government. In 2002, an official of the Competition Tribunal declared that a century of state intervention in the wine and spirits sector had benefited "narrow private interests rather than the public interest" in a way that was "possibly unparalleled in its breadth and intensity."[1] Comparing the mentality of those in South Africa's alcohol sector to the mentality of the robber barons of the U.S. oil industry in the late nineteenth century, he added, "The alcoholic beverages sector represents to competition folklore in South Africa, what, we imagine, the oil industry represented to those concerned with competitive markets in the USA at the turn of the last century."[2] At the same time, national and provincial legislatures grappled with the task of regulating the illicit industry, which included some 200,000 dealers. While dealers demanded licenses, other members of the public demanded stricter controls and the Medical Research Council warned that alcoholism levels in South Africa were dangerously high.[3] This preoccupation of public institutions with issues related to alcohol production and consumption highlights the significance of the study of alcohol, and beer in particular, for South Africa's past and present.

Racial ideas permeated colonial attitudes toward addiction to alcohol in the final decade of the nineteenth century, when the colonial trade in alcohol was robust. Two sets of beliefs prevailed in this period and extended into the mid-twentieth century. The first view held that a strong alcohol industry was good for the colonial economy because it generated taxes, profits, and jobs. The second view saw alcohol as a threat to the colonial project. Proponents of this view saw blacks as individuals of "weak character" who were unable to cope with alcohol and were prone to theft and idleness. This discourse emanated from the fears of whites about their own safety. Stemming from racial phobia, it led to a preoccupation with fixing "the African character" in relation to alcohol use and abuse and closed off any attempts to understand indigenous traditions of sociability in relation to alcohol.

By 1889, alcoholism had become a serious enough problem for colonialists that it warranted a commission of inquiry. The Cape of Good Hope Liquor Laws Commission compared indigenous and white attitudes toward drunkenness. For whites, the commissioners claimed, drunkenness carried "a stigma of disgrace" that moderated behavior. In contrast, intemperance among blacks generated "no feeling of shame." The "condition of the native mind" was the result of "a low state of civilisation."[4] "Thieving," "idleness," and "drunkenness" were part of a pathological condition of the "native character."[5] Colonial control meant introducing measures that would ensure sobriety among blacks. As in other parts of the colonial world, selective prohibition became the state's chosen instrument.[6] It would prohibit the sale of "European liquor" to blacks only; Coloured farm workers in the Western Cape, many of whom were descended from freed slaves, were deemed a separate category. Colonialists believed that Coloureds were motivated by and could be controlled more effectively through a regular supply of crude wine than through higher wages. Thus, they would not be subjected to prohibition.[7]

And of course, whites were not included in this prohibition. Regulation of alcohol gave colonialists an instrument for according privilege to chiefs and a handful of missionary-educated blacks while at the same time maintaining a regular supply of sober workers for farms and mines.[8] In this racist discourse, colonialists believed that because whites were imbued with Protestant ideas about discipline, restraint, and the value of hard work, they would be able to overcome any character weaknesses that led to alcoholism. These ideas persisted into the twentieth century and led to the extension of selective prohibition across all provinces in 1928.[9]

From the first decade of the twentieth century, municipalities following the initiative of the city of Durban acquired a monopoly on the brewing and sale of sorghum (millet) beer so that they might derive revenues for the administration of black African life in cities and towns. Indigenous black people in South Africa have been officially designated "native," "black," or "Bantu" by different colonial administrations. The 1950 Population Registration Act divided the population into four "races": black, white, coloured (i.e., mixed race), and Asian. This book uses African for "indigenous black." Municipal beer was sold to African men in cavernous beer halls in urban townships; mining houses provided similar facilities in workers' compounds. These beer halls were not popular. These men objected to the unpalatable brews served as slops in bleak concrete sheds, while women were angered by the greed of a state that denied them the right to brew at home. Beer halls took men's earnings and robbed home brewers of incomes from the sale of beer. In defiance of restrictions on home brewing, women set up illicit drinking houses, or shebeens, where men (and a few women) with a bit of cash found convivial, sociable drinking.[10] Highlighting these interventions of the colonial state and the way people responded to them, early histories focused on alcohol as a site of oppression and African resistance.[11]

Moving beyond these concerns, this book is concerned with the growth of the commercial beer industry, including its form, its character, and its links to leisure activities in the second half of the twentieth century. It can be read both as an economic history of bottled beer and a social history of beer drinking under apartheid. Underlying this interdisciplinary approach is the assumption that while alcohol occupies an ambiguous space in society, straddling economic, social, and cultural production, a distinction can be drawn between sociable and unsociable drinking.[12]

To qualify as a leisure activity, sociable drinking requires autonomy.[13] Drinking that takes place under official government control is not leisure activity. But just as the meaning of leisure and the link between leisure and autonomy are contextually bound and change over time, sociability also is not static. As capitalism advanced in the late twentieth century, leisure was increasingly subjected to the power of commercial interests. As Ken Worpole put it, leisure became "much more amenable to the rhetoric of enterprise and business than to the age-old dream of free association, rest from work, play, and a feeling of community and the creation of art and culture."[14] While the producers of alcohol were not the entity in South Africa that controlled who might drink what, where they might drink it, when and with whom they might drink, they made it their business to link consumer desire to particular brands and to guide consumer choices. As an arena of consumption, sociable drinking became an aspect of the market. This did not imply an absence of autonomy so much as the ability of the market to constitute consumers as social agents.[15] How drinking as a leisure activity was marked both by changing alcohol regimes and by the effects of powerful marketing strategies is a central theme of this book.

In the colonial discourse of South Africa, a distinction was made between sorghum beer ("kaffir beer") and malt beer (clear beer), between "uncivilized" and "civilized" drinking. It was assumed that control over the supply of liquor in South Africa was consolidated in the Liquor Act of 1928. A key provision of the act prohibited the sale of European liquor to blacks— that is, all nonindigenous liquor, including malt beer, wine, and spirits, whether produced locally or imported. This racially inspired prohibition remained in place until 1961. A handful of educated black men were granted permits exempting them from prohibition, reflecting the assumption that drinkers of sorghum beer and other beverages fermented from African grains and fruits (opaque beer) would progress by degrees to the "superior" beverages of their colonial masters. Colonial discourses implied a ladder of development and assumed that transition to drinks of a higher alcoholic content required the discipline of "European" lifestyles. Africans should be introduced to the white man's liquor gradually. Expedient colonial practice often meant that this paternalist discourse gave way to the desire for revenue or political gain.[16] In Ghana, for example, imported gin provided revenue needed to administer the colony, and in Nigeria, colonialists used liquor to win allies among chiefs.[17] In several postcolonial contexts, political power and the liquor business enjoyed close proximity.[18]

Consumption of "European liquor" did not take place outside of African meaning systems. As scholars have shown, alcohol consumption in Africa was a significant site for the production of power outside of governments and state institutions. As urbanization increased in many parts of the continent, drinking became more widespread and a broader range of intoxicating drinks became available. Social change tended toward more dispersed notions of power, often generating anxieties about appropriate drinking behavior. Nostalgic narratives constructed by older men blamed the availability of commercial liquor for the demise of respect and authority conferred through beer. In their view, young men flush with cash simply ignored structures of authority and respect.[19] In contrast, young urban drinkers immersed in popular understandings of power and authority developed their own ways of exercising it. As Emmanuel Akyeampong demonstrates, new drinking cultures in Ghana became the loci of new understandings of power.[20] In South Africa, working-class cultures fashioned in shebeens were associated with innovative social forms such as musical performance, social parody, and disdain for the law.[21] In other contexts, drinking rituals drew on continuities at the same time that they acknowledged discontinuities. Suggs shows that in southern Botswana villages, young and old men who drank together made an effort to accommodate change because both needed to achieve a renewed sense of belonging.[22] While new drinking cultures were constantly introduced, they brought new pressures. In Justin Willis's words, the "ambiguity of power" was never far away.[23]

Anthropologists Ivan Karp and Juha Partanen remind us that beer drinking provided the possibility for sociable interaction. "Pure" sociability, they suggest, can be understood as playful pleasure freed from substantive, objective goals, allowing individuals to engage in commensal, reciprocal social interaction.[24] The world created by sociability is artificial; it has no ulterior motives and provides the most fulfilling form of social relationship, "a feeling for, a satisfaction in" associating with others and a sense that "the solitariness of the individual is resolved into togetherness, a union with others."[25] Here the "pleasure of the individual is always contingent on the joy of others" and talk has no objective other than as an end in itself.[26] Sociability becomes a game "played in society" in such a way that "people actually play society."[27] Karp and Partanen argue that individuals crave the kind of social interaction that provides drinking pleasure that is temporarily free of social hierarchy.

In sub-Saharan Africa, sociability through beer drinking arose because of a willingness to participate in reciprocal beer drinking as a "fundamental part of the definition of the sociable person."[28] As a sociable experience, drinking brought men together in commensal ways; it was a form of "social communion, a commensal sharing in which persons who participate are stripped of the capacities in terms of which they interact in non-beer drinking contexts."[29] Camaraderie created an artificial mode of interaction with beer serving as a lubricant of equal "social communion." While sociable drinking in its ideal form assumed a momentary equality, it did not imply an absence of social inequality in everyday life. In practice, social communion was constructed in cultural contexts that were far from equal.[30] In some instances, sociability was inflected with deep memories of the meaning of respectability associated with authority and drinking decorum; in others, the past was less present. The type of beer, the circumstances and purposes for which it was brewed, whether it was sold or given, and the environment in which it was consumed influenced the meaning of sociability. Imbricated in these brews were the hidden effects of unequal power relations and the changes they underwent over time.

Capitalist commerce, too, impinged on sociable interaction and disrupted proper drinking behavior. Commercial brewers made it their business to understand local drinking practices and the local meanings of power and status. They were keen to learn who drank with whom, where they drank, and how and under what circumstances they drank so that branding and advertising could tap into and redefine meanings for commercial purposes. As Paul Morris suggests, producers tried to commodify local meanings and establish universal drinking values.[31] Consumers sometimes bought into these commodified meanings. Susan Diduk's study of drinking in a group of Cameroonian villages shows that in line with commercial marketing, men's preferred beer brands and drinking habits became powerful signifiers of status, following closely on established age and marital status as markers of hierarchy.[32] But commercial power had its limits and often failed in its efforts to claim authority; brewers frequently pulled back unsuccessful advertising commercials and drinkers sometimes parodied commercial prescriptions in imitative and creative ways.[33]

Anxieties about leisure as unstructured free time led to the introduction of the idea of recreation. In the early decades of the twentieth century, colonial authorities grew concerned about how workers spent their time away from work and explored the possibility of introducing recreation as an adjunct to labor. In South Africa, the American Board of Missionaries made a case for providing recreational facilities for Africans: "Proper and adequate provision for native recreation would mean better workers, keener mentally and physically, better citizens less likely to be criminals, better neighbours, less likely to be anti-white, more likely to possess a true sense of community values."[34] Sport, the missionaries implied, would keep men away from alcohol. In support of this view, the Johannesburg City Council provided a soccer field, a tennis court, and a clubhouse at the Bantu Sports Club in the center of the city.[35] These facilities would help Africans use sport as a conscious means of self-betterment, "an instrument of improvement and assimilation."[36] Yet despite the intentions of colonialists, spectator sports in Africa very quickly became associated with drinking.

For the mass of greater Johannesburg's poor, games were about participation and revelry rather than about social uplift. Soccer in particular became everyone's game: it was rough, informal, and wildly entertaining. The location of municipal beer halls and illicit brewers next to soccer fields ensured that much drinking occurred. Heavy drinking deepened the risks and pleasures associated with the game, increased the exuberance of spectators, and marked the identity of players. Nicknames suggested a positive association with liquor: one hero was dubbed "Waqafa Waqafa" (heavy drinker) and another, whose play allegedly drove sorrows away and brought enjoyment to the crowd, was called "Scotch Whiskey."[37] Peter Alegi tells us that journalist Rolfes R. R. Dhlomo reported that rowdy players drank *skokiaan* (a home-brewed alcoholic concoction with a strong kick), smoked an unnamed substance wrapped in brown paper, and rubbed their legs with *umuthi* (medicine to ward off evil) to make themselves "brave and fearless."[38]

By the 1940s, the soccer crowd had become notorious for its exuberance, enthusiasm, rowdiness, and heavy drinking.[39] For blacks, playing soccer under a segregationist government did not provide opportunities for social advancement. After the National Party came to power in 1948, government policy shifted away from providing recreational facilities for black Africans. In the 1950s, a strong contingent of the black elite was caught up in political work rather than sporting activity, and by the 1960s, much of this educated layer of the population had bled off into exile. With little formal support, young black Africans continued to play soccer for pleasure, developing a unique style and marking the game as a space for masculine heavy drinking.[40] Sponsorship began to trickle in after 1961, when the ban on the sale of "European liquor" to blacks that had been in force since 1928 was lifted. Despite the fact that the law mandated that alcohol be distributed through the Urban Bantu Councils, liquor producers began sponsoring sports events for blacks to promote their products. Sponsorship encouraged new forms of sociability and fostered new values that linked sport, beer, and masculinities. Over the next two decades, black soccer developed an association with commercially brewed brands of clear beer.

Among white English-speaking South Africans, rugby rather than soccer was the main vector for conferring masculinities associated with beer drinking. Rugby, a constituent element of "muscular Christianity," was introduced into elite all-boys' schools in the late nineteenth century. By the 1920s, Afrikaners had come to embrace rugby. Imbued with a settler spirit and still smarting from the Boer War that ended in 1902, sons of the Afrikaner elite at Stellenbosch University perceived rugby as a "collective sport of combat," a space for "conquering barbarism."[41] Sponsored by brewers and supported by beer drinkers, rugby became a national sport. White beer-drinking sociability became central to the very spirit of rugby.[42] Conversation at rugby stadiums, in dressing rooms, and in pubs revolved around how much beer a man could drink, and excessive drinking became a sign of masculine prowess. Drinking rituals were fused with the cultural and political meanings of rugby.[43] By the 1970s, rugby sociability had brought English and Afrikaner men together, generating a less antagonistic notion of settler manhood than had been possible in the early decades of the twentieth century.[44]

At the heart of this male-centered culture of mass spectator sport was what Clifford Geertz called "deep play." Geertz identified the manifestations of deep play in his description of Balinese cockfighting. He saw cockfights as an arena where male behavior was imagined, performed, and celebrated. Men bonded as meanings of masculinity became tied up with the risk, desire, and competition that cockfighting generated in Balinese society. At stake for spectators and players alike were "esteem, honor, dignity, respect," all critical elements of status.[45] It was through "deep play" that Balinese men constructed a sense of themselves as gendered beings in society.

In South Africa, soccer and rugby both became sites for deep play. In general, while soccer developed as a site of deep play for black men, the game of rugby drew white men into a masculine camaraderie of deep play.[46] Both games centered on public ritual, mass team support, masculine sociability, and beer drinking. Male competitive sport as deep play acquired a cultural power akin to that of religion; sporting contests became occasions where men came together under conditions of "heightened excitement" and experienced "moments of ecstasy."[47] Sports rituals provided moments for men to affirm deeply held, shared beliefs.[48] As spectators, men bonded exuberantly over the physicality and skill of the players; they roared and cheered as they were pulled into the game through identification with their own childhood involvement in sport. This was the substance of men's sociability, and it provided a lifelong focus. "You meet people, you make lifetime buddies together, you recall these stories over and over again," one enthusiast said.[49]

Forged through mass ritual activities that defined themselves in opposition to women and femininity,[50] stories about sports and the culture they reinforced incorporated women as trophy girlfriends and willing participants in sex and drunkenness. Masculine camaraderie re-created primary bonds of friendship between men and reinforced men's exclusive access to power and authority over women. For Canadian feminist Varda Burstyn, the male exclusivity of mass sport stemmed from a gender division of labor in which men did not have direct responsibility for maintaining and caring for people. This meant that men in general enjoyed relatively more leisure than women.[51] Mass spectator sports became homosocial environments that generated a language of "erotic, heroic, masculine idealisations." Male sports culture enabled this "master-narrative of hypermasculinity" to thrive. Burstyn argues that violent sport became an expression of the tension between men's attraction for other men and the need to "discharge" that attraction.[52]

From a less oppositional perspective, male interest in violent sport can be seen to stem not only from men's attraction to other men but from men's relationship to femininity and the desire for the approval of other men. Pierre Bourdieu argues that men are under great pressure to take up the challenge of "pursuing glory and distinction in the public sphere," at the same time demonstrating prowess in the sexual and reproductive sphere. This "exaltation of masculine values" is constantly threatened by the "fear and anxiety aroused by femininity," generating a vulnerability that "leads to sometimes frantic investment in all the masculine games of violence, such as sports in modern societies, and most especially those which most tend to produce the visible signs of masculinity."[53] Men are caught up in this exulted masculinity. As Bourdieu points out, manliness "must be validated by other men," and individual men may behave in ways that spring from "the fear of losing the respect or admiration of the group."[54] Manliness was also constructed "against femininity, in a kind of fear of the female, firstly in oneself."[55]

Beer drinking and deep play was not the only form of masculinity available to men in South Africa. However, because masculinity was constantly remade by men who promoted beer, drank beer, and participated in the ritual of male spectator sport, a robust beer-drinking masculinity was readily available to large numbers of men who were racially separated by sporting codes or segregated stadiums. Individual men did not necessarily experience beer-drinking deep play in the same way, nor would anyone have identified exclusively with a single masculine form. Individuals were likely to embrace more than one discourse of what constituted appropriate behavior.[56] Nonetheless, ideas generated by deep play were powerful in the world of beer, where they permeated sociable interactions, business practices, and labor relations.

From the mid-1950s to the beginning of the twenty-first century, the economic history of South African Breweries Limited, producers of well over 90 percent of the country's bottled beer throughout this period, became intertwined with the cultures of masculine beer drinking. By ensuring that beer became the most popular alcoholic beverage in the country and by repeatedly affirming a masculinist beer-drinking culture, SAB became a powerful agent in the shaping of social values. SAB promoted bottled beer as the lubricant of masculine sociability and deep play, building these values into brand personalities and beer advertising. When prohibition was lifted, SAB supplied clear beer to the townships initially through the Urban Bantu Councils and later to shebeeners. Moving ahead of the general public, SAB used advertising commercials to cast male sociability as multiracial.

Masculine deep play also permeated the way the brewing giant engaged its competitors in the marketplace. SAB acquired a reputation for a robust, masculinist style of doing business. Over time, its corporate culture came to mirror the tight, disciplined action of sportsmen on the field. In the 1950s, brewers occupied the highest pinnacle of status at SAB and dominated corporate culture, the mystique of successful brewing according them special status. Twenty years later, in the intensely competitive environment of the 1970s, marketing executives became all powerful; their maxim that "until a sale is made, no economic activity has occurred" created a new company ethos. As turnover increased in the 1980s, accountants became increasingly powerful, developing new systems and tightening lines of responsibility. Their influence was later displaced by brand managers. As apartheid collapsed and SAB began redesigning its manufacturing operations, workplace designers came to prominence.

Workers in the brewing industry in South Africa were overwhelmingly male, predominantly black African, and, relative to other workers in the manufacturing sector, more skilled and better paid. Employed almost exclusively by SAB, these workers began to organize themselves into a trade union in the mid-1980s. Trade union organization—the shopstewards' committee in particular—provided a locus for the construction of a new masculine identity centered on the values of an anti-apartheid, anti-exploitation ideological assertion. When this masculinist militancy overreached itself in the late 1980s, the union's shopstewards reined themselves in and worked within the framework of annual wage negotiations. But when their employers sought to lead the union into world class manufacturing—the new business ideology of globalizing manufacturers—the shopstewards led an intense onslaught against this new frontier of capitalism. Ultimately, workplace restructuring at SAB redefined the space for the making of masculinity and recast its meaning. Identities for the highly skilled workers of world class manufacturing cohered not so much around collective militancy but around performance and career path.[57] In 1999, SAB was listed on the London Stock Exchange and it moved onto the global stage. Three years later, SAB plc acquired a major North American brewing company and became SABMiller plc. From the global perspective, masculine beer-drinking sociability was set to encompass the universe. Back in South Africa, SAB Ltd began to manage its corporate identity as a brand characterized by a covenant between the corporation, the nation, and its people.

Beer, Sociability, and Masculinity in South Africa explores how masculinities were constructed in and through the interplay of sociability, beer, and commerce in South Africa from the mid-1950s. It examines the relationship of brewing companies to the illicit liquor trade, the apartheid government, and the racially configured consuming public. It follows the game plans and competitive strategies of rival brewers and deconstructs their advertising and marketing strategies. It looks at the ways brand identities both drew on and reconfigured masculinities that tapped into popular understandings of power and sociable drinking. It explores how elements of deep play entered into the character of sociability and into competitive business strategies. Throughout this book, the spotlight constantly refocuses on SAB as a powerful economic force and a dynamic actor in the performance of social values.

Concerned with production and consumption, agency and representation, this book does not follow a singular approach. Rather, it transgresses conventional disciplinary boundaries in an attempt to construct the social and economic history of a commodity and its effects on society. The questions it raises are informed by a fascination with the interrelationships of economic power, social values, and behaviors, while the narrative follows a kaleidoscopic vision, foregrounding areas where economic, cultural, and social issues converge, overlap, and become commingled. The book's purpose is to track the history of an alcoholic beverage, the principal producer of that beverage, and the men (and women) who consumed it. In so doing, it provides a window onto competitive practices, masculinities, and sociability in South Africa under apartheid and beyond.

Beginning in the mid-1950s, chapter 1 shows how bottled beer became a popular element of sociable culture, augmenting the illicit liquor trade and contributing to the National Party government's decision to lift prohibition. Chapter 2 charts the rise of SAB as a de facto monopoly and explores the deep play of its competitive strategies, while chapter 3 discusses gender and sociability as key elements of SAB's advertising. Chapter 4 explores antisocial drinking and alcoholic excess as the flip side of sociability. Chapter 5 highlights contestations over power and masculine beer culture in the context of antiapartheid resistance. In chapter 6, the focus is on the efforts of corporations and entrepreneurs to configure heritage and reconfigure drinking cultures in the transition toward democracy. Chapter 7 examines how SAB retained its competitive advantage at a time of intense global competition; it also discusses how powerful managerial strategies influenced conceptions of the postapartheid man. Finally, the epilogue outlines how relations between local and global brewing influenced the meaning of sociability in South Africa in the first decade of the twenty-first century.

one

Illicit Drinking, Prohibition, and Sociability in Apartheid's Townships

While urban black drinking cultures had been associated with shebeens, prohibition, and illicit liquor at least since the 1920s, three developments in the mid-1950s set in motion a new trend. First, the thriving illicit liquor trade was overcoming the resources of the police. Illicit drinking spots, or shebeens, were increasing in popularity.[1] Shebeens thrived both because of and despite the 1928 prohibition on the sale of "European liquor" to Africans. Second, the National Party government remained at a loss as to how to handle the illicit trade. Wine farmers and distillers regularly lobbied the government to give them access to the black market, and by the 1950s, the regime was beginning to entertain the possibility of lifting prohibition.[2] Third, changes in the brewing industry added impetus to the move toward liquor liberalization. South African Breweries, a regional brewer, merged with two others in 1955 to form a single national brewer responsible for the production of 95 percent of the country's malt beer.[3] These developments came together in the 1950s to set in motion a series of dramatic changes in African drinking cultures over the next fifty years.

After prohibition was imposed, urban black drinking cultures were bound up with illicit economic and social behaviors. By the 1950s, shebeens had become a ubiquitous feature of city life. "Johannesburg is thick with shebeens" wrote a *Drum* magazine journalist in 1951.[4] *Drum*'s booze columns (regular features by writers who celebrated drinking) were filled with tales about "highbrow" shebeens that sold exotic imported spirits to professional men and women and their rough counterparts who plied homemade intoxicating brews laced with harmful substances such as tobacco juice or paraffin to the poor. Almost all shebeens were run by enterprising shebeen queens, many of whom employed Coloured runners, or mailers, to purchase "European liquor." Although such premises were often located in the front room of a township house, the overhead was high; it included protection money for corrupt police officials, fines for illicit liquor dealing, inflated fares for taxi owners who transported the contraband alcohol, and payment for "lookouts" and bouncers, who monitored the behavior of patrons and kept an eye out for the police.[5] In 1956, approximately 600 people a day were convicted for the illegal possession of liquor. *Drum* journalists decried this attack on sociable drinking and repeatedly called for an end to prohibition.[6] But their readers were divided on this issue. A "referendum" conducted by the magazine in 1954 indicated that 183 were in favor of ending prohibition while 153 were opposed.[7]

Famous as spots where musicians confined to racially demarcated townships came together, shebeens were foremost places of drink. Shebeen drinking cultures centered very strongly on the type of liquor consumed, the character of the shebeen queen, and the class of patrons attracted to her establishment. Bloke Modisane, whose mother brewed *skokiaan* and *mbamba* (both adulterated alcoholic drinks) in a Sophiatown backyard, observed that those who drank these concoctions had only one purpose—to get drunk: "It was in the manner they drank the skokiaan, in the way they paused almost to feel the drink take effect; I felt that for them getting drunk was a purposeful destruction of the pain of their lives, a drowning of themselves in orgiastic expenditure."[8] Barberton was a quickly brewed concoction of bread, yeast, and sugar. It was known to cause the skin to peel, and it turned long-term users into "raging madmen, especially in fights."[9] *Skokiaan* and barberton drinkers escaped from themselves into the noise that was both part of the effect of the concoctions and "part of themselves."[10] These were not sociable drinkers. In contrast, Can Themba describes the scene at Little Heaven, a highbrow spot in Sophiatown where the room was well furnished, brightly lit, and crowded with men and women sitting in groups of three or four, listening to the hottest jazz, and drinking bottled beer.[11] In the 1950s, beer was not as popular among elite black drinkers as *mahog* (brandy) and sherry; spirits were more easily transported and more effectively intoxicating than clear beer.[12] Most of this "European liquor" was locally produced.

Each shebeen was characterized by what Jacky Heyns calls its particular "aunty tradition," a mythology constructed around the figure of the shebeen queen. This lore centered on the masculine physicality of the shebeen queen, who was typecast as a tough heavyweight capable of packing a punch that would "make a Kalahari caveman wince."[13] It was promoted by, among others, *Drum*'s journalist and photographer Peter Magubane, who caught a shebeen queen thrashing an unwanted patron as her bemused regulars looked on.[14] The image of the tough, oversized shebeen queen was paired with that of the protective mother who conveyed "unyielding female authority."[15] A third element of this idealization was that all shebeen queens were single mothers who "accommodated the hazards" of the drinks trade in order to provide for their children.[16] Casey Motsisi's "two hundred pound weight" fictitious Aunt Peggy, who wobbled her way across the floor, her "beefy right arm" held out, calling "Money on the table first . . . or else," was the archetype maternal figure who was devoted to her patrons.[17] Jacky Heyns's "Aunt Rose," on the other hand, was preoccupied with her own sexuality. Aunt Rose "thumped her way through the drinking lounge" in red, rabbit-eared slippers and liked to have a younger man about her. When a toy boy "could not stand up against the wind anymore," she packed him off. His place was taken by a "brand new Chippendale," and Aunt Rose replaced her slippers with "high-heeled red suede shoes and disappeared into the bedroom for three days."[18] At the same time, shebeen queens claimed respectability for themselves, invested in their children's education, and attained a standard of living that would have been impossible in the formal job market for black women.[19] While *Drum* journalists celebrated the performance of these independent women, they derided the feminine wiles of shebeen molls—young, attractive women who were often employed by the shebeen queen to lure men into their custom. Molls flirted, wheedled free drinks, and generally played on the vulnerability of men who patronized shebeens.[20] For select shebeen patrons, sociable drinking meant consuming prohibited "European liquor" rather than homebrew and it meant selecting a drinking spot and ordering a drink, activities that required discernment and information. Knowing what to do and how to do it in a respectable shebeen was part of what it meant to live in a city. Drinking was a smart thing to do; it demonstrated worldly familiarity and the power that came with it.

By the end of the 1950s, the escalating scale of the illicit liquor trade was such that the police admitted they could no longer curb its growth.[21] At the bottom end of the trade, home brewing was out of hand. By 1961, more than 13,500 gallons of illicit liquor were brewed daily in informal settlements such as Cato Manor near Durban, which had an estimated population of 80,000 to 120,000.[22] In that same year, there were 30,000 bootleggers in the Western Cape, more than 10,000 shebeens in Soweto, and over 300,000 prosecutions for the illegal possession of liquor in the nation as a whole.[23] At the top end, administration of the permit system introduced by the 1928 Liquor Act had become impossible. In terms of this act, black men in the Cape Province and Natal who were formally educated or owned property were deemed sufficiently "civilized" to be permitted to consume limited quantities of "European liquor." Permits were conditional on two years of good behavior under the Liquor Act, a clean criminal record, and permanent employment. Permit holders were limited to eight bottles of malt beer and four bottles of natural wine or two fortified wines and one bottle of spirits per month.[24] Most of them drank at home. Those without permits drank illegally. Even the police recognized the dangers of prohibition. As one senior official explained, "The Native gets drunk because he swallows whatever quantity of liquor he has obtained as quickly as possible so as not to be caught with it in his possession."[25] It also encouraged a disregard for the law. Prohibition, which was undermined by the inability of the police to cope with enforcing the law, was leading to contempt for the law in general.[26] The police also acknowledged that shebeens provided an atmosphere of congenial companionship. Many blacks preferred them to the crowded, impersonal municipal beer halls that had more in common with prisons than places of conviviality. One high-ranking police official argued that black drinking habits might be "normalised" if prohibition was lifted.[27]

Parliamentary debates on lifting restrictions pertaining to liquor were constructed in relation to whites' racialized perceptions of the character of persons in society.[28] The National Party government recognized that prohibition had placed a crippling burden on the police and judicial system. It had also kept profits on sales of "European liquor" out of white hands. The government appointed a commission of inquiry to look into the effects of prohibition and the possibility of removing the system. In 1960, Avril Malan, chair of the commission, reported that prohibition was a political problem that was causing much "irritation" to blacks.[29] Native resentment was spilling over into a "country-wide rebellious reaction" to the law, the police, and the white man. Recommending that the injustice of prohibition be removed, the commission declared that it was unfair to discriminate against men whose tastes in liquor had changed "irrevocably" as a result of urbanization. "European liquor" was the choice of people in the city, regardless of color, Malan reported. A mere 50,000 of 9 million Africans had permits in 1960. The commissioner argued that the liquor market could be expanded incrementally by extending the number of permits issued.[30]

While Afrikaner members of parliament saw prohibition and the 1928 Liquor Law as the initiative of missionaries and the pro-British temperance movement, they did not adopt Avril Malan's recommendations uncritically. In a confusing mixture of fear and envy, they berated prohibition for nurturing an evil trade in liquor and fostering "terrifying breeding places of trouble and violence." At the same time, prohibition had made it possible for "swanky shebeens" to flourish, giving blacks enormous profits.[31] Moreover, since illicit sales constituted 60 percent of the national liquor trade, it was clear that white producers of alcohol were supplying the shebeeners. The National Party government believed that it was unfair to expect the alcoholic beverage industry to ignore the black market, and the minister of justice proposed lifting prohibition to prevent the illicit trade in "European liquor" from becoming a blot on the new republic.[32]

D. L. Smit, a United Party spokesman on native affairs, had been the main advocate for prohibition in the debates of the early 1960s. Son of a missionary, Smit had been a magistrate and had served as the minister of native affairs in the second administration of Prime Minister J. C. Smuts (1939–1948). His objections to lifting prohibition revealed a colonial fear of what freedom of the market would bring to black societies.[33] People "emerging from primitive barbarism" should not be given uncontrolled access to European liquor, he maintained, because it would loosen the hold of indigenous custom on individual behaviors.[34] The "privilege" of access to European liquor would be misconstrued. "Immature" people would undoubtedly see it as conferring "an improved status." Moreover, Smit argued, black men coupled an irrational preference for strong liquor with an inability to "take" their drink. Echoing one of the perennial fears of white colonialists, he warned that uninhibited drunkenness and the self-perceptions it induced would lead black men to commit acts of sexual violence against both black and white women.[35] Others argued that South Africa's "success with colonialism" would be jeopardized if drink were supplied to "our 360 000 mineworkers away from the controlling influence of tribe, wife and family."[36] This discourse echoed the belief of colonialists that rampant "expression of individual desire, of licence and passion" would surely follow the lifting of controls on the market.[37] The prohibitionist logic was that if children were forbidden to drink intoxicating beverages in all civilized societies, then "immature" black people should be treated similarly. This logic was shared by members of the temperance movement and religious organizations who feared the deleterious effects of liquor on "under-developed peoples."[38] For these groups, paternalism underpinned the principle of white trusteeship in colonial society; to ignore it was to go against western civilization.

The all-white Parliament voted to end prohibition in 1960, not gradually, as the Malan Commission had proposed, but "in full." Coloureds would be given the same privileges as whites, while blacks would be restricted to purchasing "European liquor" (that is, all alcoholic beverages not indigenous to Africa) from outlets run by municipalities in the black townships.[39] While the shebeen-patronizing journalists of *Drum* magazine celebrated, many people of color did not. As four African men stood outside Parliament with placards protesting, "Now shebeens will thrive" and "The wine people will now become rich and our children will become hungry," Dr. Richard van der Ross, prominent educator and leader in Cape Town's Coloured community, said, "The liquor concessions are being played up as equality with the Europeans. This is rubbish."[40] Prominent black leaders, including Chief Albert Luthuli of the African National Congress (ANC) and Dr. R. T. Bokwe, medical officer of health for Middledrift in the Eastern Cape, condemned the new dispensation, pointing out that rapid social change necessitated tight control over liquor.[41] Other black leaders, including clergymen, supported a minority liberal position that upheld the freedom of the market and the economic rationality of blacks over missionary paternalism and white interests.[42] This view was also adopted by the South African Institute of Race Relations, a nongovernmental organization, and a few black businessmen who welcomed the lifting of discriminatory legislation.[43] The shebeeners themselves, who were neither legal nor organized, were not drawn into this public discourse. Without a voice, they could do little other than adopt a wait-and-see attitude.

Market-driven interests also reflected Afrikaner thinking on prohibition. The act of becoming a republic in 1961 had led to South Africa losing its preferential trade status in the Commonwealth, posing a major threat to exporters of wine and spirits.[44] Anxious wine farmers and liquor producers wanted to expand the market for liquor. Also, the apartheid regime saw an opportunity to gain revenues from taxes on wider sales of liquor to blacks. Liberalizing black access to alcohol would draw attention away from apartheid's repressive controls. Prohibition was lifted in 1961 soon after a state of emergency was imposed following police shooting of protesters against the pass system in Sharpeville in March of that year. The relaxation of prohibition laws also came in the wake of the banning of African nationalist organizations. The state promoted the new system as an act of generosity and hoped that it might distract critics from the slew of apartheid laws passed in the 1950s and the silencing of African political voices. "Freedom" of access to alcohol complemented political repression; the closure of political space was replaced by the opening of drinking spaces.

If legitimating African demand for nonindigenous alcoholic beverages was one key objective in ending prohibition, another was the apartheid government's desire to obtain revenue from the sale of "European liquor." Some municipalities had enjoyed a monopoly on the production and sale of sorghum beer since 1908. All municipalities were now required to produce and sell sorghum beer and distribute beer, wine, and spirits. This meant that municipalities were required to build and run bars and bottle stores as well as beer halls.

A second piece of legislation followed on the heels of the revised Liquor Act. The Sorghum Beer Act (Act 63 of 1962) reaffirmed the government's monopoly in the production and distribution of sorghum beer, forbade the sale of home-brewed beer, and empowered local authorities to forbid home brewing altogether.[45] In accordance with apartheid nomenclature, the act also renamed sorghum beer as Bantu beer. The change was necessary, the deputy minister of the Department of Bantu Administration and Development explained, since "kaffir beer" was derived from the "people once called kaffirs," not from "kaffir corn" (sorghum). Since it was government policy to use the term Bantu rather than "native" or "kaffir" and since the beer brewed contained as much maize as sorghum, it should be known as Bantu beer.[46] Perplexed by this new language, members of parliament asked what was to happen to terms such as "Boerkaffer," used for a black person brought up "in the ways of the Afrikaner people and although he was black was regarded as good as a white man."[47] This disquieting racist discourse, which evoked considerable mirth in the House of Assembly, implied that if blacks and their drinking habits were to be kept apart from whites and *their* drinking habits, in-between identities had to be suppressed and erased from memory.

The Nationalist government reaped the benefits of lifting prohibition and constructing more beer halls with adjacent bars. Sorghum beer production increased from over 20 million gallons in 1953/54 to nearly 61 million gallons in 1961/62.[48] At 15 cents to 20 cents a gallon, the profit margin for producers was often over 100 percent. Revenues from "European liquor" sold in municipal bars augmented the income from beer-hall sales of sorghum. SAB had sold approximately 18 million gallons of clear beer to Africans in 1960, and demand was likely to increase.[49] Regulations stipulated that the urban Bantu Affairs Administration Boards retain at least 20 percent of the profits on liquor sales for the development of township amenities; surplus profits were to be transferred to the Department of Bantu Administration and Development head office for the financing of the homelands.[50]

Preparation for the end of prohibition was frenzied. While the new legislation gave local government a monopoly on the distribution of and revenue from the sale of alcohol, neither the municipalities nor the Bantu Affairs Administration Boards had any experience in retailing beer, wine, and spirits. The physical infrastructure was set up in the townships on the Witwatersrand, where bars and bottle stores were built alongside the beer halls that supplied sorghum beer to working men. For management skills, local government turned to SAB, which, through the South African Brewers' Institute, had hastily established a training school in liquor retailing in a storehouse at the old Ohlsson's Brewery in Cape Town.[51] Here groups of thirty or forty municipal staff spent a week learning how to run a bottle store. The trainers were selected from among SAB's reps whose experience in the South African Defence Force had taught them "the scientific way" of conducting courses.[52] Deepening cooperation with the authorities, SAB appointed Dr. Frans Cronje, a United Party Member of Parliament who had served on the Liquor Commission, to its new African sales division.[53] SAB was convinced that bottled beer would soon become the preferred drink of Africans.[54]

The new law went into effect on 15 August 1962, six months after it was announced; officials hoped this would give everyone enough time to prepare for the anticipated orgy of drunkenness.[55] The government and the police were "very, very worried at what might happen," said a senior SAB man.[56] White fears mounted as the moment of free access to alcohol approached. The press carried notices advising that paydays at the ends of weeks and months were "danger days." For some whites, blacks with money in their pockets were simultaneously a threat and a source of revenue. Since the streets brought blacks and whites into close proximity, drunkenness on the roads and sidewalks was a primary concern of local governments. The Road Safety Council advised the public to take "precautionary action against traffic hazards arising from accessibility of liquor to Bantu."[57] Motorists were advised to look out for drunken cyclists between 6 and 8 P.M.[58] Pamphlets distributed in African languages throughout the townships by the Department of Information called for moderation. They offered such advice and information as "Go slow with the new liquor"; "The law will punish drunkards severely"; "Too much liquor is bad for your kidneys"; and "Everything you conceal is revealed if you drink too much of the new liquor."[59] Radio Bantu broadcast warnings on the hazards of drink and the effects of alcohol on "judgement and the senses."[60] More paternalistically, the Federale Vroueraad and the National Council of Women were asked to warn their domestic servants against the dangers of drink.[61]

"So what did happen?" I asked a master brewer of "European beer." "Nothing," replied the brewer, who knew "a lot" about African drinking habits from his experience as brewer on the Zambian Copperbelt in the 1950s.[62] "It was all a big panic."[63] In the Cape, most bottle stores had very few customers.[64] On the Rand it was a different story. A Johannesburg newspaper reported shebeeners looking gloomy as they watched their patrons buy liquor from the township bottle stores. One journalist apparently overheard a "beer baron" mutter out of the corner of his mouth, "I give them a month and they'll all come back to me."[65] A more phlegmatic shebeener named Aunt Lilly said, "If I know the drinkers, they'll finish all their bottle-store drink on the way home and they'll be knocking at my door."[66] Curiosity led at least one black man to hover in the doorway of a bottle store. "I don't want to buy," he said, "I just want to see what it looks like inside."[67]

In Cape Town, the response took on a gendered tone when fifteen members of the Federation of South African Women, an organization aligned with the African National Congress, marched on city bottle stores, blocking access to the newly constructed separate entrances marked "non-European off-sales"; that is, bottle stores. They carried babies strapped to their backs, shook their sticks at male onlookers, and shouted at would-be customers: "Kaffir beer, yes, but liquor, No!" Angered by the fact that the new bottle stores would take household income out of the hands of African men, they chorused "They cannot even pay *lobola* [brideprice], how can they afford liquor?" "We want food, money, freedom—not liquor."[68] A few days later, Lennox Mbokwana, a resident of Langa township, responded to the women's protest. Men's failure to pay *lobola* was due to low wages and the high cost of spirits in shebeens run by women, he said. The "mammas" of the Federation of South African women should be happy that men were "now coming home early on Fridays without going home from work to the shebeens and with more money in our pockets."[69]

That people went about their business as usual brought little surprise to blacks, great relief to most whites, and disappointment to brewers.[70] In anticipation of great demand, SAB had invested in new bottling plants and built massive warehouses ("hangars, huge in every direction") alongside their Johannesburg plants where glass bottles were stacked to the ceiling. "Everything suddenly became millions instead of hundreds of thousands."[71] But when the big day came, there was virtually no change in demand. "We threw a lot away because it got stale," lamented a top brewer. Why had SAB misjudged the market? "It was an easy explanation—we hadn't worked it out. What had been happening was that long before the law was changed the beer was going from white bottle stores and was finding its way to black shebeens. There was no way for us to know. All our numbers were really wrong. We thought the white trade was drinking a certain number of litres per head when in fact they weren't. And so all our calculations were based on: if that's what the whites drink they don't drink as much as the blacks do in terms of beer and we can expect huge numbers. And the police believed it as well."[72]

Free access to alcohol did not mean the same thing across the country. Unlike Durban and Johannesburg, where local government administrations had run beer halls from the first decade of the century, the municipalities of Cape Town, Port Elizabeth, and East London had opposed the introduction of beer halls.[73] They looked upon the new dispensation with dismay. In 1957, the Cape Town city council had opposed constructing beer halls in the black townships under its control. In mid-1959, when the first beer hall in the Cape region was opened at Mbekweni, adjoining the town of Paarl in the wine region of the Boland, the city of Cape Town feared that it would be instructed to follow suit. The Cape Town city council was all the more vulnerable because it was responsible for only two of the three African townships in the area—Langa and Nyanga West. The third, Nyanga East, fell under the Nationalist-controlled Divisional Council.[74] In order to prepare for engaging with the national government and to gauge the views of its black residents, Cape Town's city council conducted a referendum. "Do you want liquor to be sold in your townships?" they asked 25,000 "permanent" residents in Langa and Nyanga West.[75] Permanent residents were those who met the requirements of the influx control legislation, principally the Native Law Amendment Act (1952).[76]

The referendum elicited a clear "no": 11,167 were against the sale of alcohol and a mere 2,916 were in favor of beer halls and bars. The council claimed that 66 percent of residents opposed the sale of alcohol in their townships.[77] The referendum was a complicated exercise, however. Not only did the Nationalist government want to suppress the result but also some 8,000 ballot papers were not returned.[78] This was partly due to opposition to the referendum. African political activists, many of whom were sympathetic to the African National Congress, the Pan-African Congress, and the Communist Party, all of which had recently been banned, called for a boycott of a referendum in which their organizations could not have a voice.[79]

Others believed the referendum was the first step in the marketing of alcohol in the townships.[80] Several organizations formed a deputation to the city council. Mrs. Mafu spoke for the National Council of African

Women: "If a beer hall is established the men will spend more money and there will not be sufficient money to pay the rent." She added, "My own son who drinks is very troublesome and he will be worse if there is a beerhall." Anxious that the council should keep its hands clean, Rev. Kok of the Methodist Church of South Africa urged that the government be left to "do its own dirty work."[81] In a later submission to the Council, Mr. G. G. Ndzotyana, a Grand True Templar wrote, "We implore the Council not to force liquor down one's throats—We have other grievances of vital importance which could be attended first. What my people need is better wages not bars."[82] African prohibitionists were supported by organizations outside the townships. Mrs. J. M. Maurice of the Templars of Wynberg, a mixed-race suburb of the city, expressed the view that blacks did not want liquor as they had seen it bring Coloured people to their knees.[83]

Resolving to respect "the wishes of the people," the city council informed the Department of Justice that the council had no authority to "sell liquor to Natives."[84] But its protest fell on deaf ears; the Department of Bantu Administration and Development instructed the council to "provide facilities for the on- and off-consumption of liquor by the Bantu in the Bantu residential areas" under its control.[85] Notice of the council's application for authority to sell liquor was published in the press in October 1961. It ended twenty years of opposition to selling intoxicating spirits to residents of housing provided by the city council in black areas. In the meantime, the city council expressed alarm at the "gold rush" created by whites applying to sell liquor to blacks.[86] But it was not particularly in favor of black businessmen entering the liquor trade. Nor was there a great clamor from blacks and Coloureds who wanted to be liquor dealers. The number of blacks engaged in business in Cape Town was small. In Langa, Cape Town's oldest African township, only a handful of butcheries and general dealer stores and a single fish shop were owned by blacks. These proprietors struggled to pay their rents and were always in danger of being shut out of the premises.[87] Only one "infuriated African" demanded to know why black businessmen should be kept out of the liquor trade and why black consumers were denied the freedom to exercise their purchasing power as they chose. In contrast, the African Chamber of Commerce in Johannesburg sent a memorandum to the Department of Justice insisting that blacks should be given the opportunity to compete with city councils as purveyors of alcohol.[88]

In Port Elizabeth, as in Cape Town, the city council had voted against building bottle stores and becoming the publican of New Brighton and Kwazakhele, two of the city's townships. But the national government, intent on using liquor sales to raise revenue for black township administration, forced its hand.[89] The unease of liberal councils that opposed Nationalist policies was not alleviated until 1971, when the national government wrested township administration from municipal control by establishing Bantu Affairs Administration Boards in urban areas. The functions of these new boards included producing "bantu beer," distributing all forms of liquor, managing beer halls and bars, and policing shebeens.[90]

The Cape Town city council's first attempts at brewing Bantu beer (i.e., sorghum beer) and retailing bottled beer and other types of "European liquor" were messy. Twelve months after the end of prohibition, a pilot brewing plant went into production alongside a Langa men's hostel, where a former dining room was converted into a makeshift beer hall. Here 600 gallons of instant Bantu beer produced from a dry power and allowed to ferment were consumed per day by migrant men.[91] But the pilot brewery operated well below capacity; its Bantu beer was not popular, and patrons needed time to adjust to the strange taste of the instant brew.[92]

At the same time, the city council had plans for luxurious lounges and a beer garden called Jabulani (a word that means let us rejoice/have fun) made of concrete structures that were softened with wood-veneer paneling, wall-to-wall carpeting, piped music, and upholstered furniture. Patrons were to be served by male stewards trained by the Brewers' Institute. Gender and dress codes were to be strictly applied: women would be permitted to enter only in the company of a man, and laborers in overalls would be confined to the adjacent beer halls.[93] Despite some fascination with the newly built lounges, shebeens did not disappear and the council had difficulty asserting its monopoly over liquor distribution. Commercial vans were seen driving around the townships hawking liquor, while individual consumers were said to be clubbing together and ordering weekend supplies from bottle stores outside the township. Divisional Council officials urged the Cape Town city council to speed up its building of liquor outlets in Nyanga East and looked to the central state for amendments to tighten up the law.[94]

By the end of 1966, the first bar lounge in Cape Town's Langa township was ready to serve sixty-eight white-collar drinkers in genteel surroundings. In the adjacent beer hall, seventy-two blue-collar workers could drink their Bantu beer seated on benches and another 157 could imbibe the brew standing in the courtyard. The council reported that sales of "European liquor" in Cape Town's townships yielded "dramatic revenues," increasing over 500 percent in seven years, from R498 000 in 1963 to R4,869,000 in 1971.[95] In contrast to the national state's language of panic and fear, the Cape Town city council reported that black self-control was the order of the day. Both the beer hall and the bar lounge were doing well, and "Africans bought only what they could afford and knew exactly what they wanted."[96] Choices were determined by the size of consumer pockets: brandy was the choice of those with a bit of money and bottled beer was a favorite on pay-days. Many resorted to cheap wine at the lean end of the week. Since they had heard no complaint from black "housewives" that "any of their menfolk had been spending excessive amounts on liquor," pro-government voices on the council claimed that black opposition to liquor had been dispelled.[97] Others, aware of disquiet among many blacks, continued to monitor the sale of liquor in townships.[98] Cape Town's city council also held out against pressure from the provincial government to allow liquor licenses in or close to council housing in Coloured areas.[99]

The end of prohibition changed the day-to-day work of running a she-been. Shebeen queens spent less time brewing sorghum (or other grain) beer and distilling "concoctions" in drums in their backyards and more on arranging for the storage of commercially bought liquor. Many employed black runners (*gwevas,* in the argot of the illicit liquor trade) to purchase liquor from township bottle stores. The new dispensation also reshaped the gendered character of the illicit trade. While women still constituted the overwhelming majority of shebeeners, the number of men running drinking establishments increased steadily.[100] Men who entered the she-been trade tended to enter at the top end, using savings from formal jobs. Dan Moeketsi worked as a piano tuner for an established piano house before turning to shebeening.[101] Jeff Mkhwanazi ran a popular shebeen in Soweto's Tladi section after being forced to give up his coffee cart business when the center of Johannesburg was cleared of black informal traders.[102] Mandla Radebe ran a disco at Emanzini in Emdeni township, while "Big Mike" Sedikwe, who started shebeening after "retiring" from the Young Americans gang and returning home from prison, ran a jazz house in Soweto.[103] "People of all respectable classes drink at my cook-dladla," said "Big Mike." He explained the importance of a distinctive and convivial ambience: "But I certainly do not allow the rude and rough characters to enjoy the facilities which my spot offers to the decent clientele who always buy and settle for their drinks here. Yes, I do not give the tsotsis any double-up in my cook-dladla."[104]

The resourcefulness and resilience of shebeeners made for successful entrepreneurship and substantial profits in some instances. Cash purchases of beer amounting to 5,000 cases of quart bottles per month were not uncommon for Soweto shebeeners in the early 1960s; these figures grew enormously over the next five years.[105] By the end of 1969, Sowetans were spending R16 million a year on bottled beer—four times the rent collected in the township.[106] But shebeening was also a risky business, and entrepreneurs lived in fear of "going down." Tales of Soweto shebeeners who had fallen on hard times carried implicit warnings: when Storey's shebeen became too popular it lost its status as an elite joint, and Rocks Machaba's place in Pimville went down when it lost its reputation as "the real spirit of e'spotini."[107] (Shebeen owners often used "espotini," slang for "at the choice spot," rather than the less descriptive "shebeen.")

By the 1970s, Soweto's shebeens had filled the gap left by the demolition of the inner-city black freehold area of Sophiatown in the late 1950s.[108] As one journalist put it, Soweto's "spots" (shebeens) provided a "cordial, genial, homely atmosphere in suitable surroundings" with "hot, vibrant, crazy pop music and specialised discoteque [sic] numbers" so that patrons could have "real fun, township style." A good time was to be had when a shebeen provided the right kind of "'woza woza' stuff which never fails to rock the madly yelling and whirling cats into oblivion."[109] While the character of a shebeen was shaped by its patrons and changed over time, shebeens were generally sustained by the customers' desire for sociability, "a feeling for, a satisfaction in, the very fact that one is associated with others and that the solitariness of the individual is resolved into togetherness, a union with others."[110] In many ways, shebeen culture had become a key element of what it meant to be a sociable person in a South African township.

The lifting of prohibition generated new tastes. Within a year of the new legislation, clear beer accounted for over 80 percent of drinks sold and 53 percent of revenue from government bottle stores and bars in Soweto. But these figures underrepresented black consumption of clear beer. While the Bantu Affairs Administration Boards recorded a sale of 885,235 quarts of beer in the first twelve months, vendors (most of whom were from outside the township) returned over 2 million empty quart bottles to bottle stores in Soweto.[111] Shebeeners were clearly continuing to purchase much of their supply illegally from bottle stores outside the township. This strategy helped them avoid detection but also enabled them to shop around. In greater Cape Town, where wages were lower, Cape brandy and crude wine regularly outstripped demand for clear beer, but as soon as a little more money became available, beer sales shot up dramatically.[112] By 1968, blacks spent about 8.5 percent of disposable income on alcohol (including sorghum beer and other forms of alcohol) while whites spent 4.1 percent and Coloureds 9.6 percent of their disposable income.[113] Drunkenness increased too. Whereas in 1959, less than 4 percent of blacks were convicted for the offense of drunkenness, this figure had risen to 27 percent by 1968.[114] At the same time, concerned social workers began to draw attention to the problem of alcohol abuse among blacks in all the major urban centers. The South African National Council on Alcoholism (SANCA), which had served white and Coloured communities since its inception in 1956, opened a treatment center for black alcoholics in Durban in 1969. This was the first public acknowledgement that excessive liquor consumption was also a black problem.[115]

Buoyed by the massive increase in black demand, SAB acquired the license to brew Carling Black Label in 1966. A high-alcohol brand, Black Label was identified with "a tough, macho man's-kind-of-man," a brand personality intended to appeal to black drinkers.[116] SAB congratulated itself on "keeping pace with the nation."[117] As the volume of beer handled by the shebeens increased, SAB felt obliged to violate apartheid laws and service the illicit trade, especially retailers who handled large volumes of bottled beer. This was no simple matter. The illegal status of shebeens prevented consistent servicing, and many lost refrigerators and liquor stocks along with their cash takings in police raids.[118] White owners of bottle stores also conducted business with shebeen owners. Offering "a cent off here, two cents off there," shebeen runners promoted these "bargains" by word of mouth.[119] Business at these stores was a shady affair:

> It's 15h00 on a Thursday. The small bottle store near the city centre has its windows uninvitingly painted over. Inside is a long queue of blacks. No-one waits long. It's a mamma and pappa store: Pappa wraps substantial purchases with dexterity while Mamma tends the till. Where's all this liquor going on a Thursday afternoon? Ssh . . . this is the shebeen trade. Strictly wholesale. Some shebeeners buy 2 000 cases of beer a month. But it wouldn't do to send a truck, would it? The store has a monthly turnover of R100 000 and works on 8% mark up. It sells more in half an hour than many stores sell in a day. Not bad? "Yes," agrees the proprietor, "but there are certain expenses."[120]

SAB serviced these and countless other liquor outlets. The shebeen trade and its direct and indirect relationship with SAB led to a shift away from sorghum beer toward bottled beer in Soweto in the latter half of 1969.[121]

Black consumption of alcohol gave the Nationalist government much to celebrate. Both through direct profits for the Bantu Administration Boards and through excise tax on the producers of bottled beer, the state's coffers were substantially augmented by the consumption of both sorghum and malt beer.[122] The sales of "European liquor," including spirits, malt beer, and wine, rose from R168 million to R427 million between 1963 and 1971, while sales of Bantu beer climbed from R16 million in 1964 to R67 million in 1971.[123] The vast increases in liquor revenues meant that city councils could contribute substantially to the government's efforts to set up administrations in the "native reserves" now called homelands.[124] From 1968, "surplus bantu beer profits" were diverted to the homelands while local Bantu Affairs Administration Boards operated largely on profits from European liquor.[125] Yet the promise of improving amenities in urban areas gave way to implementing grand apartheid designs through pouring resources into bureaucracies that might lead to the homelands becoming self-governing states.[126] African consumers were unwittingly drinking themselves into deep structural apartheid.

Despite the lifting of prohibition, black sociability continued to be constructed within the frame of illicit drinking. Shebeeners survived police raids and competition from bar lounges because of sheer tenacity and the conviviality of their spots as "watering holes." But more important, shebeeners survived because they met a demand.

SAB helped make it possible for shebeeners to meet demand. By sending their representatives to talk to shebeeners, it provided support and acquired commercial intelligence. This information was haphazard and piecemeal in the 1960s, but by the 1970s SAB was acquiring more systematic and accurate data, a fact that placed it ahead of its competitors. As consumers became more discerning, SAB introduced brands that became signifiers of status. Consumed in increasingly large quantities, bottled beer shaped new drinking cultures and lubricated the process of becoming a sociable person. While the government might have preferred greater demand for products of the wine industry, in its excise regime the financial benefits from beer production were considerable. If lifting prohibition had not ended the illicit trade, it had increased government revenues.

"If You Want to Run with the Big Dogs": Beer Wars, Competition, and Monopoly

From the mid-1950s, the brewing industry became an arena of contestation between Afrikaner and English interests. Afrikaner entrepreneurs wanted to break the English domination of the industry. Spurred on by deep historical tensions, they did not share the liberal ideas of their English rivals and believed that the state had a responsibility to intervene in the market.[1] But the National Party government struggled to align the dual objectives of boosting Afrikaner interests and building an economy dominated by large conglomerates . Only when competition turned to strife did the state see fit to intervene.[2] This conflict between English and Afrikaner interests and the state's role in it had far-reaching effects on every aspect of the brewing industry, the culture of beer, and the beer-drinking public.

In the mid-1950s, South African beer was produced by three regional breweries—Ohlsson's Cape Breweries Ltd had 26 percent share of the market, South African Breweries Ltd had 64 percent, and Chandlers Union Breweries had a small share. A fourth brewery, Stag, had a "tiny little bit" of the market. Over 80 percent of Ohlsson's and SAB's shareholders lived in the United Kingdom, and 50 percent of Chandlers Union Breweries was owned by the British brewer Courage. Ohlsson's and SAB in particular were "rigorously controlled from London." Each brewing company sold its products through a system of tied houses owned by producers of alcoholic beverages that were made up of hotels—described as "small, drab and dreary" by one chairman of SAB—and managed houses (bars) owned by the brewers and leased to tenants.[3] Since tied houses could sell only the owner's beer, brewers were constantly trying to increase their number. Competition between SAB, Ohlsson's and Chandlers was intense, and the business of these three brewers involved endless property deals that often attracted the interest of non-brewer parties.

In 1956, SAB, Ohlsson's Cape Breweries, and Chandlers Union Breweries merged to create a single dominant producer. SAB has in its archives a note on the merger written by Stephen Constance, a British barrister who had immigrated to South Africa and was chairman of the newly appointed South African SAB board of directors. In the note, Constance recalls how he was sitting at the bar in the Bulawayo Club with the managing director of Rhodesian Breweries, a subsidiary of SAB, when "a tall chap, very drunk" staggered up to him and slurred, "Watch out, Sam Glazer has asked for a list of Ohlsson's shareholders." Glazer, a property dealer and "one of the original clients of Volkskas," an Afrikaner bank, was "quite well in with the government." Constance believed that Glazer's plan was to acquire Ohlsson's, sell the brewery to Afrikaner entrepreneur Anton Rupert, who was known to be interested in the brewing industry, and make a fortune selling off the remaining assets. This scenario spelled disaster for "the entire British brewing industry in South Africa." So Constance rushed off to the coast of Scotland, where Ohlsson's chairman, Geoffrey Dent, was holidaying, in order to warn him.[4]

Constance's account of his meeting with Geoffrey Dent is colorful. Dent had married a daughter of a prominent British brewing family who did not welcome Constance as he entered the hotel after the long trip from Bulawayo. Constance claims that the Dents regarded him as a "jumped-up-petty-fogging attorney" who had not been to Eton, a "traitorous little bastard" who had emigrated to South Africa and knew nothing about the brewing trade. Dent was out shooting woodcock when Constance arrived, dressed for the South African summer. Mrs. Dent loaned Constance a weatherproof jacket and sent him in search of her husband. In the jacket pocket Constance found and read a telegram warning Dent not to trust the SAB chairman. At dinner, Dent declared that he was not interested in doing business with SAB or the "Jew from Lithuania" (Glazer) whom he had on a previous occasion "kicked down the stairs."[5]

This was bad news. Aware of the intense antipathy in some quarters toward English investors in South Africa, Constance feared that Dent's attitude would fire Glazer's determination. Constance headed to London, where he learned not only that Glazer had obtained capital from the Bank of America but also that a second syndicate comprised of Union Breweries and Pepsi-Cola was planning to make a bid for Ohlsson's. The SAB chairman moved to block the second deal by asking the Courage family to sell 50 percent of its interest in Union Breweries to SAB. After a lengthy dinner and much red wine, Col. John Courage agreed. Constance then approached the Bank of England for loan capital. When his application was turned down after a three-week waiting period, Constance went back to the Courage family and proposed that the cash deal be turned into a share deal. The Courages agreed to accept one SAB share in exchange for every five Chandlers Union Breweries shares. Guided by the Courage family, Union Breweries abandoned its syndicate. That left Sam Glazer. When he was unable to outbid Glazer, Constance made a deal to establish a joint company with him: once they had taken over Ohlsson's, they would split the properties. Constance sent the SAB property manager to the Savoy Hotel, where Glazer was staying, and for two weeks Glazer put the SAB man "through the wringer." But the deal did not go through. Neither the SAB Board nor Chandlers Union Breweries, now a subsidiary of SAB, would allow it. Glazer was furious; he was determined to go for Ohlsson's.

Glazer confirmed Constance's fears, and Constance opted to make a "contested bid" for Ohlsson's. As a first step he had to acquire 10 percent of Ohlsson's' shares with which to block Glazer. Then he had to find the capital to make an offer. Barclays and Standard Bank gave permission for SAB to use its overdraft facility of £1.5 million to buy Ohlsson's shares. Constance flew to London to consult with Dent and found that Glazer had gotten there ahead of him. But Glazer had annoyed Dent by declaring that "he couldn't stand [him] or the English establishment, or the British brewing industry" and would outbid any opponents and break up Ohlsson's. By the time Constance arrived, Dent was willing to draw up a deal with SAB on condition that Ohlsson's non-executive board members received compensation and that Ohlsson's would be guaranteed three seats on the new board. Although Dent was concerned that the South African government would not accept the monopoly about to be created by the merger, Constance believed that the Afrikaners would tolerate it and discussed the issue with Senator Ditt van Zyl, a Nationalist Member of Parliament whom he had strategically placed on the SAB Board. Van Zyl arranged an audience with the minister concerned, who assured SAB that the merger would be allowed.[6]

Two more hurdles remained. While the boards of Ohlsson's and Chandlers Union Breweries were in favor of a deal, SAB wanted 100 percent of Union Breweries and Ohlsson's in order to facilitate rationalization and investment in research and development. As Constance worked on the documents to be sent to the respective shareholders, Sam Glazer arrived in London to make a cash bid for Ohlsson's. With no time for consultations with shareholders or the board, Constance publicly announced that SAB's offer was unconditional. Sam Glazer withdrew. Seven days later, key shareholders signed acceptance of the merger. Sam Glazer was reputed to warn, "Never do business with Constance, he doesn't slam the door in your face, he puts your balls in it and slowly squeezes."[7]

The official SAB version of the merger differs from that of its chief architect in one key respect. SAB claims that merger was an "inevitable" consequence of the nationalist government's practice of basing excise on volume produced rather than on absolute alcohol content. This practice, SAB claimed, forced prices up and made economies of scale necessary.[8] "Nothing could be further from the truth" declared Constance, long after he had been dismissed as SAB's chairman. According to Constance, SAB's reglossing was a strategic myth, a rhetorical counter to the apartheid government's favoring of wine over beer. The excise tax on beer was increased after the merger, while the excise on wine, which was represented by powerful political interests, was nominal and in some categories wine producers were exempt.[9]

SAB responded to the discriminatory excise against beer by expanding into wine.[10] In 1960, SAB took over the Afrikaner-owned Stellenbosch Farmers' Winery and in 1966 established the Stellenbosch Wine Trust as the holding company for Stellenbosch Farmers' Winery.[11] This move upset Anton Rupert, doyen of Afrikaner capital. Rupert's Rembrandt Group Ltd (Remgro) and its subsidiary, Oude Meester Group, controlled the wine and spirits industry through its ownership of the Ko-operatiewe Wijnbouwers Vereniging van Zuid-Afrika, Beperkt (KWV).[12] Rupert was incensed at SAB's entry into the wine industry.[13] His Oude Meester company declared that SAB had broken a "gentleman's agreement" by competing directly with them; this breach was a sign, he believed, that "SAB would in time also be able to establish a monopoly over the wholesale marketing of wines and spirits."[14] Oude Meester appealed to the courts, which found that SAB's takeover of Stellenbosch Farmers' Winery infringed the Liquor Act. SAB was required to reduce its holding of Stellenbosch Farmers' Winery to 33 percent. Then, to affect a compromise, the South African Parliament intervened, amending the Liquor Act to accommodate SAB's new position in the wine industry.[15] By ratifying SAB's crossing of the divide between English and Afrikaner capital, the government allowed an upset in the established order of the liquor industry.

At the same time, SAB rebuffed Afrikaner attempts to enter the brewing industry. SAB closed all the gaps in the white market so that Corrie Schoeman's attempted resuscitation of the defunct Stag Breweries in 1962 collapsed. One year later, Afrikaner entrepreneur Anton Rupert's franchise agreements with Whitbread and Heineken fared no better, as these brands could not get a foothold in the SAB-dominated market, and in 1967, SAB took over the franchise of Old Dutch.[16] The Nationalist government responded to SAB dominance by imposing a tax that calculated excise on a sliding scale based on volume produced by a single brewery. This tax was directed at SAB's recently established Isando plant where 120,000 gallons (545,520 liters) of beer were produced per day.[17] Isando boasted state-of-the-art automated technology. Forklift trucks loaded 400 empty bottles a minute onto a conveyor belt and into a washing machine; once cooled, bottles were electronically inspected. In the filling process, an ultrasonic beam set up a vibration so that foaming beer bubbled to the top, eliminating air before corking.[18] The plant represented SAB's commitment to efficient technology and economy of scale. But the government was not impressed. Its punitive measures helped increase natural (unfortified) wine's share of the market and reduce the share of beer.[19] While SAB's appeal against the tax on large plants failed, the corporation did not deviate from moving toward automated megabreweries. It believed that large-scale scientific breweries would provide a competitive advantage over the long term. Excise levies (13 cents on a bottle of lager beer as against 0.1 cent on a bottle of wine) reduced SAB's profits from R7,306,000 in 1966 to R5,894,000 in 1967. The company's strategy to protect itself against drops in share prices included diversifying its interests.[20] Venturing into the capital goods sector, SAB acquired a 24 percent stake in a giant engineering corporation and took control of food, furniture, footwear, paints, and aircraft companies. SAB also expanded its investments in bottle stores, nonalcoholic beverages, and the hotel industry.[21]

In the meantime, the apartheid state's pariah status helped SAB achieve a more South African profile. By SAB's seventy-fifth anniversary in 1970, nearly 80 percent of its shares were in South African hands and the company enjoyed the support of powerful personalities in the National Party. P. W. Botha, Member of Parliament for the district of George, was on the board of SAB Hop Farms Pty Ltd, and liberal Afrikaner Dr. Frans Cronje was chair of the SAB board.[22] SAB was also becoming more deeply embedded in the South African farming economy; increasing quantities of its barley, two-thirds of its malt, and one-fifth of its hops requirements were grown locally.[23] But SAB still could not shake off its image as an uitlander.

SAB's domicile in London was perceived to be "bad for business." But its request to the English Parliament for permission to change its domicile to South Africa was rejected.[24] The House of Lords refused permission. Defeated, SAB approached the South African cabinet to request an amendment to the South African Companies Act so that the transfer of domicile could be implemented. SAB's solicitor's encounter with a state official during this process confirmed the company's view that the government was prejudiced against it:

> We got a somewhat chilly reception and the official said in no way would the cabinet do anything to the benefit of SAB. However, when I explained that the amendment would benefit not only SAB but any foreign company which wanted to change its domicile to South Africa, he sprang alive and shouted "Japie." In came a rather timid clerk who was told to put the suggestion as a special item on the agenda for the next cabinet meeting. He said success was certain.[25]

In 1979, SAB was incorporated in South Africa. But excise taxes continued to rise. Prospects for growth in the beer market looked good. In 1971, clear beer represented only 9 percent of the total alcoholic beverage market; sorghum beer dominated at 49 percent, natural wine followed at 14 percent, brandy at 10 percent, and malt beer at 9 percent.[26] However, SAB, like other brewers, believed that "clear beer" was the drink Africans aspired to, and from this perspective, the scope for expansion was enormous.

Recognizing that brewing had prospects, Louis Luyt, a fertilizer magnate who was a former rugby player, wanted to move into beer. In 1972, Luyt approached Anton Rupert, his partner in the fertilizer company. Both men had grown up as poor Afrikaners and were driven by a hunger for wealth and power. But Rupert was not interested in Luyt's new idea. "Quietly seething inside," Luyt found capital in the United States and established a brewing company.[27] With his eye on the market, Luyt appointed Alec Sabbagh, SAB's onetime regional marketing man, as managing director.[28] Fired up after a trip abroad, Sabbagh claimed there was strong international support for the new venture. "Like us, they're tremendously attracted by the thought of taking on virtually only one competitor in what they regard as a good long-term market," Sabbagh reported.[29] He speculated that SAB would spend "close on R10m" on discounts, preferential displays in retail outlets, and topping up salaries to prevent sales staff from going over to the opposition.[30] Dick Goss, SAB Group CEO, positioned himself for battle against Louis Luyt Breweries (LLB) by resigning his partnership in Triomf Fertilizer and asking Louis Luyt to divest himself of his SAB shares.[31]

As LLB was floated on the Johannesburg Stock Exchange, enthusiastic support from the press—and a little cunning—enabled Luyt to sell all of the stock in the new company despite the depressed economic climate. The financial editor of the *Star* described "the eye-catching emblem" on LLB's bottles as "the Luyt family crest dating back centuries in Prussian history." But, laughed Louis Luyt, there was no such crest; the labels were the invention of the advertising agency. The senior *Star* journalist must have been taken in by the lavishness of the launch the night before, he said.[32] Boasted Luyt, "Die Vaderland pictured me as the white knight who was to help restore faith in the stock market." As he gleefully noted, the reality was more prosaic. The South African government had encouraged him to close the share offering a month early, he said, creating the impression that "it was already fully subscribed."[33] Press reports egged on the opponents with headlines such as "Breweries Battle Fermenting," "Throwing Down the Gauntlet" and "Beer—A Storm Brewing."[34] They also diagnosed SAB as "showing signs of fat round the heart," weighed down by "too many senior executives and brands unable to earn their keep," and speculated that SAB would not be able to withstand the challenge.[35] The *Star* dramatically inflated Luyt's goal of 7.5 percent market share in the first year to 30 percent.[36]

Anton Rupert, too, was drawn by the media hype and saw in LLB an opportunity to keep SAB from expanding further into wine and spirits.[37] Rupert made Luyt a proposition: Luyt could have shares in his Oude Meester brewery in exchange for shares in Luyt's beer, fertilizer, and aircraft companies.[38] When Luyt declined, Rupert played the Afrikaner nationalist card, pointing out that together they would build a strong new conglomerate that combined fertilizer and liquor. The prospect of "forming an alliance against established English interests" won Luyt over.[39]

The battle for the South African market was on. In the first round, competition centered on breweries, brands, bottles, and spies. LLB established a brewery at Krugersdorp (Chamdor) and began building a second plant at Bloemfontein. Luyt planned to launch three brands in the first six months.[40] The media celebrated the sophistication and tight budgeting of LLB, indirectly providing advance publicity for its brands. Luyt, who described himself as a "beer-drinking street fighter," claimed that a new frenzy gripped "SAB's war room," which dispatched many spies to his Chamdor brewery.[41] To fool these informers, he "ignited the furnaces in a feigned production exercise at Chamdor in full sight of their omnipresent spies."[42] The ruse worked: SAB was six weeks early in its launch of the first of its new brands intended to offset the novelty of Luyt's beer. When Luyt

Lager was launched, SAB was empty-handed. Farmers loyal to Luyt fertilizer began to drink Luyt Lager, and some South African Defence Force canteens, keen to support an Afrikaner brewer, replaced all SAB stock with Luyt Lager.[43] According to the press, white barmen were bribed to sell rival products at room temperature or claim that they were out of stock.[44] Rumors of fighting in white pubs were confirmed when an LLB employee had his jaw broken in a brawl with a SAB loyalist.[45] In the townships where the brewers vied for the illicit shebeen trade, "one side," according to Luyt, "would immediately snitch on the other when it got wind of a new delivery, usually with the help of well-planted spies."[46] "Tough guy" Godfrey Moloi, shebeen king and ardent Luyt supporter in Soweto, began calling himself Godfrey Louis Luyt Moloi.

Conflict over bottles and advertising led SAB to embark on litigation. While it was common practice in the beverage industry to buy used or returned bottles, SAB asked the court to stop Luyt from taking in large quantities of SAB-labeled bottles.[47] While the court ruled that Luyt should desist from buying SAB bottles, sorting "empties" and removing labels was so labor intensive and inefficient that it was almost impossible for either side to avoid ending up with the other's bottles. So Luyt and SAB's Dick Goss called a truce. But, as Luyt recalled gleefully, the bottles for his Madison Lager were very similar to those for SAB's Carling Black Label with a slightly longer neck: "Much to our delight they jammed SAB's bottling plants, causing costly stoppages."[48] Although SAB complained that Luyt's advertising of Madison Lager as an old American brand was misleading, the Advertising Standards Authority ruled that Madison was a new local brand. However, Luyt admitted that the idea of "Madison" as a name for one of his beers had occurred to one of his executives as he was crossing Madison Avenue in New York. The case and its outcome imposed considerable costs on LLB, and Luyt's admission that Madison Lager's "heritage" had been invented was another blow to the brand.

In August 1972, Anton Rupert applied for an interdict to restrain SAB from using Master Brew as a trademark. Distillers Corporation (SA) Ltd declared that the name "Master" infringed on its registered trademark of "Oude Meester."[49] In response, SAB asked the court to expunge Distillers Corporation trademarks for "beer, ale and porter" since they had been used exclusively for wine and spirits. When the judgment favored Distillers, SAB appealed to a higher court.[50] Three years later, the Supreme Court of Appeal overturned the ruling, leaving Distiller's Corporation to pick up the costs of the case.[51] Trademark law in South Africa was considerably advanced by the appellate division's judgment in the Master Brew case, which established that "the particular circumstances" for registering a trademark had a bearing on the intended uses and "monopoly right" to the trademark.[52] Ultimately, however, the market was the final arbiter. And the market's verdict was that Master Brew was too bitter. SAB moved swiftly to launch a sweeter German-style beer.[53]

In the meantime, Louis Luyt and Anton Rupert fell out. Luyt was furious with Rupert for not consulting him before buying the Kronenbräu brand from Germany and the Highland Brewery in Swaziland. He was annoyed that Rupert's Western Province Cellars retail chain was not providing marketing support for LLB brands. And, he alleged, Rupert was using his tobacco salesmen as spies.[54] There was clearly not enough space for two Afrikaner bulls in one camp. By the end of 1974, Rupert had bought out Luyt's beer shares, registered a new company, Intercontinental Breweries (ICB), and replaced Luyt Lager with Kronenbräu. Rupert was determined to gain a substantial share of the 200-million-rand-a year beer market.[55]

The retail trade provided the arena for much of the second round of the beer wars. SAB's subsidiary Solly Kramer and Rupert's Western Province Cellars Ltd were locked in a bitter price war. Retail profit margins were drastically reduced as prices were slashed by between 6 and 14 percent.[56] Rupert believed that the retail industry was eating out of SAB's hand. SAB sidestepped the Liquor Act's stipulation that retailers stock the brands of competing producers by providing generous incentives for retailers that stocked and sold large quantities of SAB products. Opposition brands were "frozen out."[57] A major obstacle for Rupert was that this kind of price war was facilitated by the structure of the retail industry.[58] After the tied-house system was abolished in 1957, four major companies came to control the liquor trade: Stellenbosch Wine Trust (SAB) owned 131 bottle stores, Oude Meester (Anton Rupert) owned 180 stores, independent merchant Union Wine (Jan Pickard) owned 23 stores, and Gilbeys Distillers & Vintners owned 38. Together these four controlled 85 percent of the liquor trade and drove the large-scale price wars.[59] Another 15 percent of the legal liquor trade was made up of licensed restaurants and twelve bar or pub licenses. Both SAB and Rembrandt (Anton Rupert's holding company) relied on their nonliquor interests as sources of cash flow and profit.[60]

In November 1973, Rupert threw out a challenge to SAB by announcing that he would relinquish his retail outlets in the interest of "an unfettered retail structure, free of any interference or pressure by breweries or other liquor producers."[61] But talks with SAB failed. Acutely aware that Rupert's Oude Meester had been the biggest owner of bottle stores in South Africa since 1965, Goss was not about to trust Rupert's announcement. Instead, he argued that discounted liquor was in the public interest. Rupert responded by engaging in a price war more aggressively, acquiring new bottle stores and converting an established chain into discount stores.[62] Rupert's more than 200 stores and SAB's 150 stores continued to battle for domination of the liquor retail industry, which was valued at R210 million by 1975.[63]

By this stage, producers' penetration of the retail trade was hobbling independent retailers, who were unable to access loans or benefit from discounts. Parliament intervened, publishing draft legislation forbidding performance discounts, or price discounts to retailers who sold large volumes. Anxious to avoid regulation, the liquor giants preemptively negotiated with each other to prevent the bill from reaching a second reading. SAB reported that it had met with the minister of justice and agreed to remove discounts based on volume.[64] In addition, the National Liquor Board drew up a "factor points system" as a tool for limiting the number of liquor outlets any one producer could own, control, or hold an interest in.[65] Points were also allocated for loan financing. Frank Moodie, the SAB-appointed chair of Solly Kramer's liquor store chain at the time, described the loan system as "the ultimate wheeling and dealing," a process that required "close personal friendships." Beyond the Solly Kramer subsidiary, SAB granted loans to independent retailers, the size of the loan depending on market performance or volume. There was no single set of rules, as loans were advanced in a "host of permutations and combinations." SAB's strategy was to tie the independent retailers to itself. The result, as Moodie put it, "was that we had a huge thrust, most of the critical outlets in the country were supportive to SAB and in fact Rupert could never understand why his products could never really establish greater market share."[66] In some instances, loans were very large and their benefit to the discounters was enormous. Sammy Linz of the Rebel liquor chain allegedly borrowed R2.5 million at low interest from SAB.[67] Although these loans ran counter to the Liquor Board's attempt to reduce the hold of producers over retailers, they did not end the beer giant's quest for control of the liquor retail sector. The points system was too complex to administer and fell into disuse after a little more than twelve months.[68] Competition for control of the retail industry continued.[69]

Although ICB's smaller breweries meant that they paid a lower excise (ICB paid an average of 10.15 cents per beer compared to SAB's 11.44 cents per beer in 1973), Rupert's brewing venture was in trouble.[70] Losses were mounting. A loss of R4.8 million in 1974 was followed by a loss of R4.3 million in the first half of 1975.[71] ICB's brands—Beck's, Kronenbräu, and Heidelberg—were apparently unable to make inroads into the dominance of SAB brands in the market. Castle Lager continued to hold 60 percent of market share and Lion Lager had 20 percent. In addition, Schafft Lager had found a new niche among black consumers. Press sympathy continued to lie with the underdog; journalists lamented ICB's apparent inability to break through SAB's "stranglehold" over the market for black consumers, then 60 percent of the total beer market.[72] SAB had erected powerful barriers to entry, and ICB's strategy of buying its way into the 520-million-liter beer market was proving extremely costly.[73] But there was no relief from the competition.

ICB's launching of new brands kept the public engaged with its products. In 1977, it launched Culemborg Lite with "lower residual carbohydrate" and a calorie count of "below 100," taking on SAB's Hansa Pilsener, which had a calorie count of 122.[74] But when ICB acquired Colt 45 from the United States, SAB's Beer Division was quick to respond. Marketing Director Peter Savory decided to use Stallion, a trademark the company had registered a decade earlier, to preempt the Colt 45 brand. A stallion is older than a colt, and age was a useful feature in an industry that used heritage and manhood to create brand identities. SAB's initial idea was to substitute "Stallion" for "Colt," but Dick Goss felt that this was "sailing too close to the wind." Lying in the bath one morning, SAB's senior marketing man Peter Savory hit on the idea of an inverted 45: SAB's brand would be Stallion 54 with an alcohol content of 5.4 percent, some 1.5 percent stronger than Castle or Lion lager.[75] With Goss's blessing, two marketing men approached "a one man ad agency and swore him to secrecy," engaged a one-man printer, and worked with a single brewer to produce Stallion 54 in a week. Surprised and delighted, SAB's sales force "went out there with a sense of power" as the ICB's Colt 45 brew was still in the tanks, waiting to be bottled.[76]

ICB took SAB to court, claiming that SAB had infringed on their trademark. Stallion 54 was designed to "deceive and cause confusion," ICB claimed, and had rendered the launch of its own brand unviable.[77] The court confined itself to the issue of the identity of the trademarks, and the judge ruled that there could be no confusion between a stallion and a colt. "A stallion conjures up the idea of an uncastrated horse and is normally suggestive of vigour and virility. A colt . . . conjures up the idea of a young horse," the judge said.[78] ICB appealed, only to receive a more dismissive judgment. The judge ruled that a court of law could not censure a competitor who "through diligence and foresight" had stolen a march on its rival. The judge further ruled that the courts "should not be converted into a market forum."[79] One SAB manager jubilantly summed up the verdict: "If you get caught with your pants down, don't come to the courts for restitution."[80]

Still Rupert did not give in. In September 1978, Rembrandt bought out minority shareholders in ICB and Oude Meester acquired 49 percent of Gilbeys, at a cost of over R43 million.[81] Apartheid was at its height, and sentiment in the white market continued to lie with Rupert. As SAB's corporate rating began to fall below the average rating of the rest of the industrial market on the Johannesburg Stock Exchange, it embarked on an even more aggressive expansion into the retail sector, building twenty new Solly Kramer's stores at a cost of R7 million.[82] A few months later, SAB attempted to take over Union Wine and Picardi Hotels, the only vertically integrated liquor groups outside the Rembrandt and SAB stables. These acquisitions would have given SAB twenty-eight hotels, twenty-seven hotel bottle stores, and twenty-nine other bottle stores. SAB applied to Minister of Justice Jimmy Kruger for government sanction for these acquisitions, but Kruger refused permission. The matter had to wait for the government's report on monopolistic conditions in the supply and distribution of liquor, he said.[83] Officially blocked, SAB called off the deal.[84] "It's patently unacceptable," seethed Dick Goss. "Here we have a situation where things are made unequal—and on ministerial discretion."[85] SAB, after all, had been "forced" to negotiate with Jan Pickard to keep Rembrandt out, as Pickard confirmed.[86] Nor did Rembrandt deny its intentions. "What do you expect—we're fighting for our survival," a spokesman responded.[87] Government, he alleged, had favored SAB by granting bottle store licenses to hotels at a time when they owned 300 hotels. (He did not add that most of these were small and were subsequently sold.) Further, SAB had been allowed to change its domicile without changing its legal persona, enabling the company to retain valuable contracts. Said Rupert, "All allegations of favoritism by the government and its officials [are] unjustified and [constitute] to my mind an improper effort to influence public opinion at a time when the matter should really be considered sub judice."[88] He was adamant. "We're certainly not going to stop," he asserted proudly, "and we have enough funds to see this thing through. As long as SAB wants to continue competing in the wine and spirit sectors, there'll be a battle royal. In the meantime, the battle is not helping the smalltime retailer, and I feel bad about it. But we did not start it. It was a bad day for us all when the [South African] Breweries went into wine."[89] SAB was not prepared to leave the fray either. "We can't simply sit back and let Rupert's boys have their way. The race goes to the swiftest. No one has any divine right to a share in the market," said Dick Goss, SAB's CEO.[90]

Watching Rupert pour R40 million in three years into advertising and promoting beer proved too much for fellow captains of Afrikaner capital.

Professor Fred du Plessis, chair of Senbank, stepped in to broker a deal between SAB and Rembrandt.[91] This proverbial "walk in the vineyard" yielded an agreement that du Plessis claimed "went through the cabinet untouched" and astounded economic commentators. An announcement on 13 November 1979 handed ICB to SAB lock, stock, and barrel. In exchange, Rembrandt, SAB, and KWV were to form a new company, Cape Wine and Distillers (CWD), in which each would hold a 30 percent stake. The remaining 10 percent went to the public, principally farmers. SAB gained full control of the beer industry—at that point R600 million a year—and maintained a stake in wine and spirits. Through the merger of three major wine and spirits companies—Stellenbosch Farmers' Winery, Distillers, and Castle Wine—CWD would control 75 percent of the wine and spirits sector. Producers would determine prices with the government acting as a watchdog. SAB and Rembrandt agreed to withdraw from the retail trade and dispose of their bottle stores over a period of twelve years at a rate of 7.5 percent over the first five years and 10 percent for the next seven years, removing vertical integration from the liquor industry. CWD would not own any bottle stores or hotel liquor outlets.[92]

While ICB's managing director Gerhard Steinmetz believed that with 14 percent of the beer market, Rupert should have held out, Rupert turned his back on beer and moved to secure deeper control of wine and spirits.[93] Within days of the "new deal," Rembrandt and KWV announced that they had pooled their interests in CWD to form a 60 percent holding company. Rembrandt and KWV now had joint control over CWD, which controlled 90 percent of wine and spirits production. As journalist Michael Coulson observed, "Any group controlling 90 percent of any market is a monopoly, whether it behaves like one or not."[94] SAB was reduced to a minor player in the wine and spirits sector of the alcohol beverage industry. The liquor industry and its watchers were taken by surprise. Speculation was rife as to how KWV, a producers' (that is, farmers') cooperative, had financed its entry into CWD. Some suggested that Rembrandt's overseas interests had provided a loan, implying that SAB had been double-crossed.[95] The move was cunning; Rupert saved face and his supporters retained their pride despite the devastating blows of the beer wars.

For its part, SAB was satisfied that competition had been good for beer. Between 1972 and 1979, per capita consumption of beer rose from 13.18 liters to 22.90 liters per year, while wine consumption fell from 11.00 liters to 8.74 liters.[96] SAB's marketing director believed that it had outperformed the opposition. "I think it is safe to say in a tactical and strategic sense that they [ICB] did not do one single thing first; SAB had closed the gaps. That was our strategy—close the gaps and any gap perceived—be it a product type, brand, image area like the German one and pricing gap, packaging gaps. We shut them off, turned the taps off and ICB woke up too late."[97] Size gave SAB the ability to squeeze ICB's profit margins. "For them to have to sell anything at all they had to match us which meant that their margins were appreciably lower, especially as they were spending three or four times as much per hectoliter on advertising and selling as we were because of our volume," said SAB marketing director Peter Savory.[98] SAB used its close relationship with the free (white) trade and the illicit (black) trade to keep Rupert in a vice grip, "graunched on the one side by the guys in the shebeens and the black market" and "confined to his own directly controlled outlets in the white market" on the other.[99] Moulton argues that SAB's competitive edge was due to management ensuring that the beer "[was] on stream at the right price." This professionalism enabled SAB to "throttle competitors; their controls are so good."[100]

Retailers were displeased at the creation of two near-monopoly producers and remained unimpressed by promises that vertical integration would offer them some relief. Natie Matisonn, chairman of the Hotel, Liquor and Catering Association, complained that the deal "bristle[d] with inequities," creating "two mammoth monopolies." The formation of Cape Wine and Distillers created a "complete cartel," Matisonn argued, because the retail trade remained unprotected against control by producers.[101] His fears were not unfounded. It soon emerged that Jan Pickard, son-in-law of Eben Donges, one of the National Party's most generous supporters, had obtained permission from the government to increase his bottle-store holdings from 75 to 129. Pickard formed a group with supermarket magnate Natie Kirsch, a move that positioned Pickard's Union Wine to become the dominant player in alcohol distribution. This drive for closer links with supermarket chains flowed from the structure of the white retail industry, which was characterized by a large number of bottle stores and a small number of pubs. While black-owned retailers (illicit shebeens and distributors) accounted for two-thirds of beer sales, they did not have a political voice and were dependent on the support of SAB.[102]

In a bid to respond to retailers' complaints, the National Party government launched an inquiry into monopolistic conditions in the liquor industry.[103] The Maintenance and Promotion of Competition Act of 1979 appointed a Competition Board, whose role was to investigate restrictive practices and monopolies and make recommendations to government ministers. Before the Competition Board released its report, leading financial journalists called for less government interference. "It boggles the mind that government should be party to a deal" that created a monopoly in the wine and spirits sector, wrote one journalist, who called for a return to the market.[104] Another journalist felt that government needed to break with the Puritan ideology that justified state control of liquor distribution, imposed a restrictive licensing system on whites, and refused to grant licenses to blacks.[105] Some felt that the Liquor Act itself should be changed. "Like going out, collar and tie in the midday sun, SA's Liquor Act is one of the more disagreeable legacies of British colonial rule. . . . It is narrow minded, restrictive and paternalistic and administered by bureaucrats trained in the maintenance of law, order and security rather than in the promotion of a free market operation."[106]

When the Competition Board finally presented its report late in 1982, it sliced into the 1979 agreement the cabinet had approved, declaring that the establishment of CWD was a "restrictive practice" and that the merger between Oude Meester and Stellenbosch Farmers' Winery should be terminated along with KWV's 50 percent share in CWD. The board recommended that the Liquor Act be amended to remove restrictions on retail licensing and that the limitation that producers could own no more than five bottle stores, as recommended in 1979, be revoked. Further, the board argued that vertical integration by producers and retailers should be deemed unlawful.[107]

An amendment to the Liquor Act in 1981, ostensibly to allow more competition in the retail trade, clearly favored the wine industry, since grocers, including supermarkets, were permitted to sell wine but not beer.[108] This coup for the wine industry was followed by another, two years later, when the Competition Board ruled in favor of CWD acquiring 300 new bottle stores while insisting that SAB sell all its retail outlets. The National Party government had effectively overruled the terms of the 1979 settlement in favor of one party over the other. SAB was furious. "Had we known that CWD would be permitted to acquire 300 bottle stores while SAB could have none, we would never have gone along with the agreement," said Ken Williams, chair of SAB's beverage division.[109] The state's intervention appeared to reflect the Competition Board's contradictory and ambivalent interpretations of the value of competition in the economy. While the board viewed concentration as an inherent tendency of capitalism, it was ambivalent about the value of concentration in the South African economy. It could not decide whether mergers and acquisitions were a consequence of superiority in the market or an abuse of power. The board also tended to conflate the notion of public interest with national interest.[110] Without clear direction about how to handle competition, the cabinet appears to have dealt with the problem as a conflict between businessmen. In so doing, the cabinet believed it was acting in the national interest. Industry watchers angered by the government's failure to deal with the issue of competition declared the cabinet's intervention a betrayal of the government's duty to the public.[111]

Both Rembrandt and SAB denied that they behaved as monopolies. The chairman of KWV and CWD claimed that Oude Meester, Stellenbosch Farmers' Winery, and Henry Tayler & Ries (Rembrandt's importing agency) competed against each other and against independent wine estates and cooperatives.[112] Observers also questioned whether SAB would want to continue holding a minority share in CWD, over which it had "little say," and remarked that with distribution to blacks still in the hands of the Bantu Affairs Administration Boards, the CWD could not be the "final stage in the evolution of the liquor industry."[113]

While denying that it sought monopoly status, SAB defended its status as the "single supplier" in the malt beer industry. "We competed as hard as we could in a tough market. If we've landed up with a monopoly, that's hardly our fault," commented Dick Goss.[114] Following a massive increase in beer volumes in 1980–1981, SAB was anxious that the market should view their monopoly status as good for the public.[115] The brewing giant pointed out that despite the fact that it controlled 94 percent of the beer market, it had not behaved monopolistically in terms of pricing and strove to keep costs and prices as low as possible.[116] It cited the Competition Board's confirmation that SAB had not used its monopoly in malt manufacturing to block supplies to ICB.[117] Moreover, SAB asserted, it did not have the ability to behave monopolistically.[118] The major determinant of beer pricing was government excise, a factor entirely outside of its control. This claim was not entirely accurate. Indeed, in 1978, malt beer, with a 4.5 percent absolute alcohol content, was taxed R6.34 per liter in 1978 while wine, with a 10.5 percent absolute alcohol content, was taxed a mere 38 cents, and fortified wine with an absolute alcohol level of 20 percent was taxed a mere R3.50.[119] However, figures showing the relationship between excise duty and real beer prices after 1958 indicate that excise was increasing while the price of beer was coming down.[120] Nonetheless, excise increases continued to be based on market share by volume rather than on absolute alcohol content, a trend that showed no sign of conforming to international practice.

Beer accounted for 38 percent of alcoholic beverages in South Africa in 1981; in that year, beer provided 39 percent (R400 million) of total excise income, spirits 31 percent, natural wine 21 percent, and fortified wine 9 percent.[121]

When the government proposed an increase in wine excise, wine farmers protested loudly. In 1982, 2,000 wine farmers and KWV board members in Paarl petitioned against a 23 percent increase in the excise on fortified wine and brandy. They berated the finance minister and threatened to unseat the MP for Piketberg if government did not show more support for wine farmers. The government hastily published a notice reducing the duty on fortified wine and brandy by 5.43 cents per 100 liters, a saving of some R10 million for the producers.[122] The apartheid government capitulated to the wine farmers, leaving black consumers, who constituted 70 percent of the beer market, to bear the brunt of excise increases.

SAB also claimed that economies of scale were beneficial to the consumer. Said Williams, "We have all conceivable major types of product and pack: lagers, ales, pilseners, stouts. Conventionally capped bottles, screwtop bottles, cans. We always behave as if we have competitors looking over our shoulders." And, he went on, "The consumer doesn't think SAB, he thinks Lion or Castle. Our products compete with each other, so there are no real areas where consumer needs are not met." Nor was SAB courting market control, he claimed. "Being a monopoly per se has no particular attraction to us. In a long term sense it's better to have competition than not. But we think we have a good track record as a monopoly. We will not behave irresponsibly or against the public interest."[123] Peter Savory, director of marketing, added that SAB welcomed competition. "When we say we would welcome a competitor, people laugh out of the sides of their mouths. But it's true: life isn't the same. Not having a competitor takes some of the spark out of life, takes away some of the sheer desire to do better. It gets boring after a while. Like a boxer who spends all his life punching the bag, there is nobody to compare yourselves with. It does not matter what you do, people say it's because you are a monopoly."[124] Dick Goss said that fear of complacency made his job tougher. "My challenge is to find meaningful goals to keep us in trim. I cannot manufacture a competitive situation, but I enforce the condition that our planning assumes we have a competitor in three years time. And we work to a formula which keeps our price increases below inflation."[125]

Under Goss's leadership, mergers and acquisitions became SAB's daily business. By the early 1980s, diversification had become, in Goss's words, "a bit of a buggers' muddle." Although "selling is often seen as a defeat. A cock up by someone," he planned to refocus SAB Group.[126] But Goss was caught off guard in 1983 when three major corporate shareholders—Anglo American, Johannesburg Consolidated Investment Company Limited, and Liberty Life—supported the establishment of a new holding company—the Premier Group—with a 34 percent stake in SAB.[127] The hostile move took place without consultation with SAB. To be controlled by a milling company that produced dog biscuits was the ultimate insult felt board member Mike Rosholt; SAB had become "a subsidiary of a dog food company."[128] His pride wounded, Dick Goss resigned, and Meyer Kahn, a self-styled "boykie from Brits," took over the helm.

Dick Goss later described the 1970s as "an era of fierce, perhaps vicious competition" that was "rough and tough and demanding," particularly at the "front line." But it was also highly enjoyable. He and his executives at 2 Jan Smuts Avenue, Braamfontein, SAB's headquarters, had fostered a robust corporate culture that demanded deep loyalty, teamwork, driving ambition, and absolute commitment to the product.[129] This was a culture developed by men for men; it had "rubbed off" from one generation to another and over time had acquired an aura of historical depth.[130] Careful selection of staff brought "like people together, people with shared values and beliefs"; those who "went beyond a certain code of conduct, did not belong."[131] As the leader, Dick Goss was "one of the toughest" and "quite a disciplinarian. If you did not perform you were at risk that you might be out."[132] Goss, the product of a rugby school, saw tough, macho camaraderie as compatible with "an openness among managers, among staff to express an opinion," so long as it was conducted with controlled self-discipline.[133] High demands were placed on employees, who were expected to show "perfectionism and high standards of achievement."[134] They were to demonstrate ability in "beating off attacks" and "immobilising the opponent."[135] A successful corporate culture in the beer industry meant running in front with the big dogs or becoming the carcass the winners fed on.

In sum, concentration occurred in the context of apartheid policies on liquor distribution, heavy excise taxes on beer, and intense competition between Afrikaner and English capital in the alcoholic beverage industry. As a de facto monopoly since 1955, SAB developed a repertoire of strategies to ensure that it retained dominance in the market. First, SAB combined aggressive competition with takeovers of breweries that had been knocked out in the process of competition. Second, SAB secured vertical integration through ownership and control of retail outlets. Third, SAB kept abreast of distribution to the illicit liquor dealers in apartheid's black townships. Fourth, SAB constructed large-scale breweries with scientific technologies in order to keep production cost and prices down. Finally, and perhaps most important, SAB developed a corporate culture that both created and reflected the values of masculine domination. This culture was honed during the beer wars of the 1970s.

three

Beer Advertising: Making Markets and Imagining Sociability in a Divided Society

Advertising became a key element of the South African brewing industry as ideas about marketing and building brands evolved. But the South African market presented particular challenges. Although advertising always portrayed beer brands as something consumers should aspire to, the limits of that aspiration were racially circumscribed: low wages in the black market and conservative Calvinist values in the white market set boundaries for configurations of sociable interaction. Long periods without serious external competition meant that advertising was driven by competition between brands within the SAB stable. Brand managers and advertising agencies exercised prudence as they looked for ways to extend the market while reflecting everyday sociable interactions connected with drinking beer. Those commercial messages that stood out from the 1960s until the end of the 1980s kept abreast of social change, both anticipating and promoting softened gender stereotypes and the possibility of multiracial sociability.

Following the lead of the brewing industry in developed economies, SAB began to take advertising seriously in the 1960s. In the industrialized economies of the north, the idea of marketing brands rather than products had led to massive changes in business practices. Branding was evolving into a sophisticated sub-industry for every consumer-oriented manufacturer. Brand identities were created for particular products through packaging and media advertising.[1] How a brand took on a particular configuration of the past (or of masculinity) was the creation of designers' readings of social values so they could rework them and sell them to the consumer as signs.[2] Branding changed the character of marketing. Brands competed in the advertising arena, which provided a structure through which goods and consumers became interchangeable. Advertisements worked by enticing consumers to consume the signs rather than the product, thus consuming their own imaginings.[3] Beer advertisements encouraged drinkers to consume symbols such as status, powerful male physicality, or reward for success as they consumed the product, beer. They were a means through which men (and to a lesser extent women) come to imagine themselves as individuals or members of communities.[4] Regular consumption of symbolic values boosted sales and demand for the brand.

The early 1960s was a period of dramatic change within SAB. Until then, the company had been "totally production oriented . . . with no enthusiasm for modern marketing." Promotion was crudely associated with sportsmen—"a phalanx of reps—ex-rugby and wrestling Springboks, over-the hill sports stars with cauliflower ears and other sports types who traipsed around the pubs buying rounds of drinks on the company. Their main challenge was to stay erect."[5] Marketing took little account of brand difference. "Here's a beer, take it" was the sales technique, rather than "What kind of beer do you want?"[6] The end of prohibition in 1961 heralded a new era. If beer was to establish itself ahead of other beverages among black consumers, it needed a new image. "As a matter of principle, we had to take beer out of the kitchen and put it in the living room," said Peter Savory, SAB marketing director. Since American advertisers were adept at using "positioning concepts" to turn products into brands linked to the values, lifestyles, and perceptions of the target market, SAB sent Savory to Harvard Business School to study marketing. On his return, Savory established new ground rules for SAB branding. He wanted to portray sociability as the prime reason for drinking and focus strongly on men's sporting activity.[7] Together with the earlier guideline that brands should reflect "respectability, brand heritage and perceptions," Savory's rules constituted the blueprint for SAB advertising for the next three decades. Emphasis on branding raised the status of marketing within SAB. "Don't talk to me about people being your main asset," Savory said. "Your main asset is your brands."[8]

Brand personalities were rendered recognizable through their character profiles and insignia. The ideological constructs of masculinity and heritage became the identifying markers of SAB brands. Men and masculinities were central to the SAB imaginary. "Beer," Savory said, "is a very important part of a man's life. If you want a fight, tell a man his beer is piss."[9] A man should be able to identify his brand; this confidence was a critical element of the meaning of beer for a man. Savory explained: "If you go into a bar with two or three friends, you have to know what brand you want. You must be seen calling for it, putting your hand in your pocket and taking out hard-earned money. Then you put it in your mouth, taste it and swallow. In swallowing, the beer causes a change in your personality. If [a beer purveyor] break[s] that chain with, say, a hot beer or an oily glass, then god help [him]."[10]

In the context of marketing, heritage was functional and invented, creating a mythical past for commercial ends. SAB came to understand that strategically conceived, heritage "reinforces the knowledge and expertise of prior success; it builds on nostalgia and relies on a mystique bigger than personality."[11] From this perspective, heritage enabled a brand to move beyond the parochial to claim universal values, creating a sense of reliability, permanence, and security, the timelessness of an Arcadian fantasy. A beer without a heritage was bricolage, of no lasting value, an "instant" brew, as kitschy as an engagement ring with an imitation diamond.

For SAB, the first stage in the process of building brands was achieving consistency in characteristics such as the color and taste of the beer and uniformity in the shape, size, and color of the bottle. A "packaging improvement programme" produced revamped labels centered on heritage insignia that signaled prestige and power—castle turrets, lions, and gold ribbons. Signatures described the beer and stressed its quality and nourishment—"golden good . . . rich with flavour," "good health in every glass"—and linked these qualities to male ingenuity and status with the phrase "Brewmaster approved."[12] Advertising, the second stage of SAB's brand building, was precipitated by the need to fend off competing brands such as Louis Luyt's Kronenbräu 1308 lager. Luyt had gone to great lengths to create this brand, buying a fourteenth-century brewery in Bavaria, inventing a name with a ring of heritage, dating it 1308, and putting a beer dray, "an image loaded with apparent heritage," on the label.[13] The association of place with brand signature signaled German culture and announced Luyt's intention to counterpose ICB's imagery with the perceived "Englishness" of SAB's heritage symbols.

The second stage was advertising. "Beer advertising," said Peter Savory, "is only an adjunct to male social interaction and social enjoyment. If this is depicted well—credibly, aspirationally—that's what you are getting in the bottle."[14] Laying down firm parameters, he insisted that "manly advertising must address the largely male beer drinkers." What constituted manliness was strictly set down and gay men were precluded from configuring brand identities. "We didn't allow any queers on the brewers' account. Could you imagine two Springbok lock forwards leaving the field and saying, 'Let's have a glass of that cheeky red wine.'"[15] Powerful physical masculine attributes characterized all brand personalities; the more rugged the masculinity, the higher the alcohol content. Tampering with a brand's characteristics was risky. In the 1960s, Lion Lager, a high-alcohol-content beer associated with rugby, was SAB's leading brand. Lion Special, introduced so that Lion lovers might have a light alternative, failed "because it was perceived to be weak and 'manly' men were not prepared to be seen drinking weak beer in public."[16] In contrast, Rogue, a strategic brand introduced to take advantage of a government reduction on excise in the late 1960s, was successful in pairing low alcohol content with a strong masculine image. The large bull elephant added "symbolic strength to the appearance" of the brand, explained Savory.[17]

Promoting beer as "the beverage of the people," SAB advertisements followed a format: "Beer goes with the crowd to the beach, the braai [barbecue] and the picnic spot. It follows the races, attends prize fights and test matches: accompanies the fisherman to sea and awaits him in the coolness of the spring."[18] But these experiences were segregated. Apartheid regulations and values controlled social environments and the imaginative space of advertising. Divisions along racial, cultural, gender, and ideological lines limited opportunities for advertisers to configure sociability in innovative ways. By the late 1970s, formulaic renditions of white male outdoor social interaction had become tedious. Muscular men posing as hunters under the caption "Down a lion . . . feel satisfied" or in sports clothing ("I like my sport. I like my beer. Hansa is the answer") or after a rugby game ("Castle Lager. The beer of your life") were standard.[19] Bored with this formula, one journalist called for an end to ads that relied on "a gang of intrepid explorers schlepping through the bush to rub two sticks together, roast some crocodile liver and wash it down with beer to the accompaniment of the most melancholy jingle this side of the Marche Funebre."[20] The journalist's alienation pointed to the emptiness of the masculine identities portrayed and echoed weaknesses in beer advertising globally.[21] But SAB's response to the charge of "dour, earnest, humourless—and deadly dull" advertisements was defensive. "If Mr Howard can tell us how he could be funny to the cultures of Afrikaans, English, Hindu, Moslem, Tamil, Coloureds, and nine major African language groups all at the same time and still maintain a central brand image, would he please do so."[22] Notwithstanding this public outburst, the SAB marketing director promptly "banned all braais" in beer ads.[23]

Expansion in the white market meant including white women in print advertisements. In the late 1960s, SAB embarked on a cautious campaign to draw women into the orbit of masculine sociability. Marketing to women meant finding a way round the moralistic femininity of Calvinist ideology and the confinement of white women to ladies' bars.[24] To overcome these ideological barriers and introduce the idea that female drinking was acceptable, SAB produced a series of "educational" advertisements aimed at turning social anxiety about female drinking into desire. Women drinkers were positioned in the home in spaces that overlapped with those of men (the swimming pool and the patio) in a way that reinforced femininity as an adjunct to male sociability. They displayed companionship, intelligence, and feminine self-control. The series consists of three line drawings of attractive, self-assured women in their thirties facing the camera and sporting a full glass of beer. Qualified by a disclaimer ("Issued in the interests of a better understanding between the sexes by the brewers of Lion beers"), one caption reads:

> Everything a man wants! Plays it cool. Never at sea, wherever she is. Doesn't chatter. Does communicate. Can say more with one long-lashed glance than any doll since Cleopatra. And she likes beer! Thinks "two beers" is the friendliest call. And she's right! Beer is traditionally the companionable drink. . . . No wonder more and more women are joining the men for a beer or two. What more could a man want![25]

Women could acquire this "look" by consuming beer and men could aspire to it by allowing women to do so.[26] In these images, women drank for men's pleasure, under male control. By adding a complementary white middle-class femininity to existing brand images, the new advertisements avoided uncoupling beer and masculinity and implicitly dispelled fears of uncontrolled female drinking in public bars.[27] There was no middle-class coyness in SAB's in-house magazine, however. Advertisements for new packaging showed a topless woman with long hair and a hat pulled over her eyes promoting "man-size," "long tom," and "king" beer cans, which were stuffed under her belt. In this image, the female body was paired with beverage packaging, inviting male consumption of both contents.[28]

It was not only SAB's cautious promotional advertising that drew white women into the beer-drinking community at the height of apartheid. A travelling game show sponsored by the Castle Lager brand attracted thousands of white women over a three-year period in the late 1960s. The Castle Lager Key Game, a live quiz show conducted by presenters Adrian Steed and Beatrice Reed on Springbok Radio, gripped the imagination of suburban South Africa on Wednesday nights. In the Germiston city hall on one such night:

> So up they roll to share in the Castle Key Game—a thousand honest, sober citizens with babes in arms and granddads bringing up the rear and pretty girls on their boyfriends' arms and even the Mayor and Councilors . . . all arriving to egg the contestants on, to bellow advice, to groan over misfortune, to rejoice over a major killing. . . . The crowd hangs breathless on the turn of fate, then screams as the tension mounts. It's self-identification. Call it, if you like, emotional strip-tease.[29]

This emotional release in the whites-only hall not only provided entertainment but secured loyalty for the sponsoring brand as Mrs. Brown Eyes chose the key to the right box and won a car.[30] Gender stereotypes in the journalistic discourse reflected the dominant values of the East Rand locality and pervaded beer-inspired representations of women in everyday discourse. Although these family events took beer out of the kitchen, they did little for women's status. But they did contribute to the growth in the white female beer market.[31]

When SAB began targeting black townships in the late 1960s, its representatives advised that the market would not respond well to brand differentiation. Shebeeners, they said, tended to hook on to "the dominant brand in the market because they knew they could turn that brand around," said Bruce Starke, SAB's senior marketing manager. They directed customers to that brand and created "a barrier to entry for other brands."[32] Township drinkers understood that the shebeener was "doing customers a favour by taking the risk of purchasing and providing liquor and risking the law." They apparently accepted the absence of choice as circumstantial. "Imagine trying to be individual in that situation—'Now really chaps, I'd prefer Hansa Pilsener!'"[33] Drinking practices were shaped by culture, context, and circumstance. Since beer drinking in shebeens was usually communal, quart bottles were preferred to pints. "Arrivals would pool money and the shebeener would load the table."[34] SAB marketers saw continuity as well as circumstance in the meaning of beer for Africans. The quart bottle was the equivalent of the gourd passed around in a rural homestead, the symbol of "a huge heritage for a long drink among Africans."[35] This undifferentiated view of blacks was fraught with difficulty, however, since it rested on a stereotype of blacks as "traditional," non-individualized, and "unknowing," as Timothy Burke put it.[36]

In the mid-1970s, SAB changed its strategy and looked for ways to introduce brand differentiation into "the African market." The shift was less a consequence of the company developing a more complex view of people than of its need to foster competition between brands. SAB feared that a smart competitor could exploit the vulnerability generated by single brand dominance. Because it was a monopoly producer, its ideal scenario was for three house brands to vie for market share at any one time. To fabricate this competition and to see if anyone "could crack the dominant brand," new brands needed to be introduced from time to time.[37] At the same time, SAB was anxious to find a brand with an acceptable image. One way around this problem was to import a lager whose brand identity was wholly un–South African. In 1966, SAB obtained a license to brew Carling Black Label, "America's lusty, lively beer." A high-alcohol-content beer that was advertised as having "extra strength," Black Label could be promoted to black consumers without the taint of apartheid attitudes; it also fitted neatly with the view that trendy blacks preferred a strong beer and looked to North America for cultural images.[38] "Carling's extra-strength brew" was sold in quart bottles and pop-top cans packaged in twin sixpacks.[39]

Expanding the beer market in the townships meant moving beyond Soweto to places where urban black communities were distinguished by different consumer habits. In the townships of Port Elizabeth and East London, for example, sherry was the favorite drink after sorghum beer.[40] In the early 1980s, SAB sent Frank Moodie, a man with university training in psychology and management, to promote a culture of clear beer in this market. Initially, his efforts to introduce Lion Lager met with little success, largely because "there were too many social issues in the way."[41] He found a way of linking beer to the alleviation of local problems so people would identify Lion Lager with caring for the community. The cost of schoolbooks was an important issue to black consumers, particularly since white school-children were supplied with free books. So Moodie devised a scheme for Lion Lager to subsidize books. Two cents for every bottle of Lion Lager sold in the township went toward the purchase of schoolbooks. The government backed the initiative and agreed to contribute 0.5 percent of the cost, its support stemming from the long-established practice of using profits from alcohol consumed by blacks for township services.[42] The Books from Beer Fund took off, financing the purchase of hundreds of schoolbooks and even the construction of several school buildings. Beer sales in the townships soared, increasing to 50 percent of market share in the region within three years. The Port Elizabeth townships became Lion Lager territory. "Books from Beer" associated the brand with goodwill, enabled Lion Lager to deliver "values other than liquor," and earned the brand a following.[43] By

1983, 79 percent of the township of New Brighton's drinkers preferred Lion Lager, while only 27 percent hung on to sherry.[44]

By the early 1980s, as blacks accounted for 80 percent of beer sales, SAB began testing the limits of advertising under apartheid.[45] Zimbabwean independence led to heightened anticipation of political change in South Africa. Despite some anxiety over losing the white market, SAB was encouraged by the experience of U.S. brewers, who had demonstrated that masculinity and sociability were more powerful than skin color in beer advertisements. SAB believed that sport would appeal to all viewers and that as a nonverbal means of communication sport images would avoid potential communication difficulties.[46] Sport was the principal social activity for most young whites and an increasing number of black people. A wide range of sporting activities and tournaments enjoyed some form of SAB sponsorship. When the same advertisements were beamed to segregated television audiences tuned into channels that were differentiated by language and content, viewers responded favorably. Market analysts Nick Green and Reg Lascaris celebrated the innovation: "By using the unspoken language of sport, Castle and Lion, the country's top beer brands[,] build up favourable associations without exhortation and without explanation."[47]

This experiment was followed in the mid-1980s by images of multiracial sociability in beer advertisements. In a pathbreaking television series, SAB constructed SAB founder Charles Glass as a bridge to an imagined future.[48] Advertisements positioned Glass, colonial brewmaster and purveyor of beer to miners on the Witwatersrand, as a genius, a master of the craft of brewing, a man with deep knowledge of and commitment to the country and its people. His brew, Castle Lager, is the beer with the longest and proudest heritage in South Africa. In a series of commercials, the Charles Glass myth was used as a vector for imagined multiracial pub sociability. As the brewmaster of the Witwatersrand, Charles Glass played host to men of all hues, welcoming them into the colonial drinking scene and accepting their toasts. Glass entertained upper-class English settlers, taught Afrikaners and miners how to drink respectably, and hosted visiting cricket players and the press. Recasting colonialism itself as inclusive, a Castle Lager anthem helped viewers cross into a world where black and white drinkers enjoyed camaraderie.

> When we drink Castle
> We fill with admiration
> For Charles whose brewing class
> Won fame across the nation.
> When we drink Castle

We draw our inspiration
From Charles' brew and
How it grew upon our reputation!

The men raise their glasses "To Charles!" in drinking scenes that were entirely invented yet "legal and almost credible," like scenes from weddings or graduations, where the ceremony, at least, might be multiracial. At the same time that they constructed a heritage for a brand, these images imbued SAB's slogan ("Making beer, making friends") with a new multiracial meaning. "This was not apartheid South Africa," explained an SAB marketing man, "it was the projection of people into a future."[49] Intrigued, the Christian Science Monitor phoned SAB's Peter Savory to find out if this sort of socializing was indeed occurring, while local journalists scoffed, "We can't drink like this in South Africa."[50] Asked why the apartheid regime did not respond to these multiracial scenes, Peter Savory ventured a guess: "Deep down they saw the end of apartheid coming, and it eased their burden when they were challenged publicly."[51]

By the time the African National Congress was unbanned in 1990, the single token black in a Castle Lager ad had grown into a pub half-filled with black drinkers. The Castle Lager market was recast as the "Charles Glass Society," signified by a colonial icon, a beer brand, and multiracial masculine sociability. "My beer will rank with the finest in the world," vows Charles Glass in these advertisements, "or I will seek alternative employment."[52] Lisa Glass, the actual brewer, is not present in the advertising narrative. Charles, her husband, is portrayed both as brewer and purveyor of beer on the Rand. In eliminating Lisa Glass from the narrative and in obliterating the gender division of labor in this colonial brewing story, the advertising copywriter was freed to construct a male icon and a myth of a master brewer. The Charles Glass story, like the wider SAB heritage narrative, is a discourse for men about men. Women are out of place in this world of male sociability.

The trope of entrepreneurial success, too, is almost purely fictional. "Glass's beers grew in fame and stature," SAB's Centenary Centre brochure records, "taking their identity from the symbol of regal pride and heritage that graced the labels." However, it is evident that Glass's brewing career was short. It was also marred by domestic violence and constant bickering with his brewer wife. In 1890, after only "a couple of years" of successful production, Glass sold Castle Brewery and left for England, returning later to set up in (failed) competition with Castle.[53] The advertisers' rendition of Glass's physical image and sensuous personality sits uneasily with the historical evidence of an irascible hustler of beer in the mining town.[54]

"Colonial entrepreneur" might be a more appropriate characterization than the SAB's slippery trope of "brewer for the nation." Glass is unmistakably British. The empire rather than the nation presented him with opportunity. His market was the English miners on the Rand, and when he did not make enough money, he sold his brewery and went home to the metropolis. While his presence affirms the place of bottled beer in the wider culture of colonial exploitation and domination, his role in the colony was a far cry from the multiracial socializing of the Charles Glass Society.[55]

Did soaring sales in the 1980s mean that black drinkers bought into the myth of brewmaster Charles and raise their glasses "to Charles"? Unlikely. One interviewee was quick to point out that blacks are accustomed to negotiating "a heritage imposed on us, a heritage that we have inherited rather than being part of its formation." Township beer drinkers did not ask "to what extent we identify with Charles Glass, but whether we like the taste of the beer." Skeptical of the notion that advertising directly molded opinion, this observer did believe that advertisements stimulated interest in beer brands more generally.[56] Ultimately, Charles Glass simply anchored the meaning and personality of the brand through association with generic notions of male bonding. The success of the advertisements was in the pairing of "loyalty, trust and spirit of comradeship" with images of "socialising in sophisticated style, untainted by officialdom."[57] As apartheid began to crumble, the idea of multiracial sociability and a world beyond racial divisions became a fascinating prospect.

By the late 1980s, SAB advertising had begun to respond to increased social stratification in black society and concomitant changes in buying power. Image makers sought a deeper understanding of black consumers and needed more "hooks" to encourage them to switch brands. Configuring aspiration appropriately was key. As Green and Lascaris explained, "A blue-collar white artisan drinks lager for one set of reasons and a black clerical worker for another. It's an up-market choice for the township resident. He pays a premium in comparison with sorghum beer, and the positioning takes him further from his roots. He becomes a metro swinger. The targets are different and so are the triggers to brand preference."[58]

South African marketing experts urged their colleagues to deconstruct catchall phrases such as "black market" and "the township resident" and reconstituted them as "niche markets" or "fragmentary identities."[59] This shift in approach made it possible to hook new consumers into brand images. Initially, SAB experimented with smaller brands and explored new forms of subjectivity as racial and gender orders showed signs of fluidity. Ohlsson's Lager advertisements in the *Sowetan* were directed at a "new generation" drinker.[60] Inviting change, the ads presented alternative forms of masculinity that were less securely positioned in the society than sporty, muscular men. Under the banner heading "How to say goodbye to your old beer," a sophisticated young black man seated alone at the bar stares at an old quart bottle. The caption reads, "Just say that now you've grown up, you simply prefer Ohlsson's distinct but somewhat more subtle flavour."[61] A month later, a new Ohlsson's advertisement explains "how to introduce your old friends to your new beer." Four men—two white, two black—are seated at the bar. Three are blindfolded. A white man, perhaps the one who has introduced these men to new ways, watches as the blindfolded men guess the brand. "Beers don't change. People do. As we grow up, we outgrow things. Our taste matures. And we start looking around for a replacement."[62] The only man in a collar and tie is black. Somewhat pensive, a little playful, perhaps a trifle cynical, and definitely male and multiracial—these are the markers of the sociability of the new generation.

Two years later, Ohlsson's advertisements identify a new masculinity for this generation—sensitive, artistic, brooding. Consecutive issues of the *Sowetan* carry full-page portraits of a black university student, a black musician, and a white youth conveying the individualism of serious, talented young men who feel alienated from the mainstream. "They said I wouldn't make university. They said the old beers are best. They were wrong both times," reads one caption. "They say my music is too heavy. They say my beer is too light. They don't understand either," reads another. "I've got a great understanding with the older generation. They don't drink my beer, and I don't drink theirs," said a third.[63] In this campaign, the new generation sought to construct its heritage by distancing itself from the past. The targeted niche market was more wished for than achieved, however. The consumer community did not cohere around the alternative masculinities projected by the advertisements.[64] By the end of the 1990s, Ohlsson's Lager, one of the original brands in the SAB stable, had been discontinued.

The marketing of a brand as nonconformist was more successfully taken up by Hansa Pilsener advertisements. Aimed at a trendy, relatively affluent urban niche market, Hansa advertisements depicted accountants, medical students, golfers, men in black ties, and lovers of jazz—men who did not want to be one of the flock, preferred a lighter alcohol content, and enjoyed a bit of fun. A Hansa Pilsener television commercial in the mid-1990s set up pub/tavern sociability as heterosexual and mediated by humor—a significant step in SAB advertisements. The marker for the brand is playful nonconformity, a sophisticated silliness. A blindfold device is used to great effect as glamorous black women cover their men's eyes with white handkerchiefs. One black man asks, "Is this a woman thing?" "No, it's a man thing," comes the reply from the sensuous black woman tying the blindfold. Playing along, the men pretend to identify the brand by "the kiss of the Saaz hop" but laughingly confess that the shape of the glass is the giveaway. As they lick the foam from their upper lips, the men roll out a string of descriptors evocative of wine tasting—"bracingly crisp, refreshingly different, distinctly dry," with "full malt taste and a clear golden colour" added on.[65] Unlike the identity-crisis theme of the young men in the Ohlsson's campaign, the Hansa man is sure of himself; he enjoys his new status and the pleasures it brings.

Amstel, brewed under license from Dutch brewer Heineken, remained SAB's biggest moneymaker in the premium market.[66] Its cosmopolitan image contrasted sharply with the Afropolitan thrust of the Hansa campaign. Amstel advertisements played on cosmopolitanism, deploying symbols of classical upper-class European masculinity as value signs for the lager. Amstel signified heritage. In one campaign, the masculinity of the European "connoisseur" was featured through handcrafted collectors' items—flintlock pistols, a carriage clock, an acoustic guitar, a piano, a goblet, and a fishing rod. The timeless quality of classical craft reinforced the brand's character as mellow, "slow brewed, extra matured."[67] Another Amstel heritage series that stressed the superior quality of the product centered on classical European images of the ingredients of beer and the brewing process—barley fields, deeply burnished copper, and bright green trellised hops.[68] SAB management apparently instructed that this "expense account" brand was to be associated only with symbols; no images of people were permitted.[69] When the designers "ran dry" on still life and rural landscapes, they compelled their bosses to relent and permit images of appropriately elitist social behavior.[70] The result was an Amstel television commercial set in the private gambling suite of an exclusive hotel carrying the legend "Because Amstel is a premium beer it has often been regarded, unjustly, as a bit snobbish. This of course is entirely untrue when one considers how well it goes down with chips."[71] The play on the word "chips" might reflect SAB's concern about competition from casinos in the leisure and consumer markets in the 1990s. As a premium brand, Amstel was positioned to draw the postapartheid "traveling elite" who tracked between townships, suburbs, metropoles, and casinos.

The formal ending of apartheid in 1994 boosted the mainstream lager market. Beer advertisements promoted sociability as part of an all-embracing national identity imagined as a "deep, horizontal relationship" in which race and class were obliterated.[72] Castle Lager, a brand that had long been associated with sport sponsorship, was now identified with multiracial nationalism in sporting arenas.[73] As soccer was pulled out of the margins and placed at the center of the new nation's sporting activity, Castle Lager's continued sponsorship enabled the brand to draw on new images of masculinity as it created spectacles of emotional nationalism. In one advertisement, the supremely fit and honed bodies of black soccer stars were offset by their nonconformist hairstyles such as dreadlocks or bleached curls. Painted across the faces of supporters, the national flag submerged signs of race beneath those of nation. Crowds packed the stadiums, chanting the slogans of a new common identity and pride in the first national soccer team. "From the biggest supporters of soccer in South Africa to the biggest supporter of soccer," Castle Lager commercials rang out:

> One nation, one soul, one beer, one goal.
> Let the nation pull together
> Let's celebrate our soccer today.
> The beer of the people is with us,
> With us every step of the way.

This advertisement signs off with the announcement "Castle Lager. Proud sponsor of Bafana Bafana" as national exuberance reaches a climax and bubbles over, like the head of a foaming beer.[74] Soccer advertisements celebrated the new nation—"When all the colours and textures of soccer come together—Laduma! Let's celebrate good times! Come on!"[75] Castle Lager sales soared, providing 2 percent of South Africa's GDP in 1995 and enabling SAB to continue its massive sponsorship.[76]

Rugby and cricket advertisements, like their white supporters, were more cautious in their embrace of change. But President Mandela's blessing of the players at Newlands in the 1995 Rugby World Cup symbolically cleansed rugby of its racist past and enabled the Springbok team to be reborn as the amaboko-boko (the boks) of the postapartheid nation.[77] Sharing the podium with, among others, the managing director of South African Breweries, President Mandela instilled pride and dignity in the national team. For over a decade, South Africa's victory at the World Cup and the pride of the nation was deeply significant in the forging of a new South African identity, enabling black and white to embrace each other.[78] The moment reinforced the relationship between sport, beer sponsorship, and masculine sociability as supporters lingered in pubs reliving the highlights of the game. It also provided SAB with a magnificent photo opportunity that the company has used again and again in television commercials and in print media.

Multiracialism and nationalism were kept farther apart in cricket advertisements. During the 1996 international cricket series against India, only two years after South Africa's first national elections, Castle Lager advertisements used Indian nationalism as a spur: the slogan "Support your team. We do" accompanied images of Indian supporters watching the South African game. A year later, SAB advertisements included parodies of Australian national images—corks hanging on hat brims to repel flies and references to baahmen (men who bleat like sheep)—that invoked stereotypes of sheep farmers and constructed an "other" against which commonality among South African viewers might be generated. These advertisements achieved a mild form of patriotism in keeping with ruddy-faced players daubed in white sunburn protection and crowds swaying in a wave. Cricket, the gentleman's game, failed to generate the same intensity of passion that robust contact games such as rugby and soccer achieved. Even the overflowing beer mugs were captioned with restraint:

> It seems there's no containing our national pride.
> Time to steer one down the gulley.
> Just a reminder, keep a good run rate.
> During the break, snatch a few singles.
> Time to bring on the great South African All Rounder.
> Castle Lager.[79]

Fortuitously for SAB, the character of the game did not signal restrained consumption: five-day matches generated great thirsts and kept the pubs full long enough for advertisements to achieve a fusion between the brand and the game.

Although the place of sport in the intensely emotional experience of social change in South Africa generated powerful commercial messages, it did not subvert the formula of linking beer brands with sport and masculine sociability. However, there was a shift to advertisements clearly aimed at black consumers and a move away from conventional pub sociability. SAB commissioned HerdBouys, the agency that "best understood the milk stout user"—predominantly Nguni men from the eastern coastal regions of the country perceived as "slightly conservative and blue collar"—to produce a television commercial that would satisfy the core market, move large quantities of beer, and attract younger men to the brand.[80] HerdBouys strategic director Dimape Seremanye put an idea on the table: HerdBouys would couple traditional African dance with Castle Milk Stout, the most physically masculine brand in the SAB stable. The agency would produce an advertisement "different from all other beer ads," derived not from sports stadiums or British pub sociability but from an African culture of recreational drinking, sociability, and masculinity.[81]

The result was a sensuously choreographed version of the Ndlanu, a triumphant Zulu war dance. Performed after sunset in a dusty township yard, the dance takes place in front of a wood-and-iron house; there is no hint of the tainted mining compound. Bonding within and between the all-male audience and the muscular performers is palpable. Images of the dance are fused with images of milk stout so that "the strength and power of the dance is synonymous with the strength and power of the beer."[82] Heavy crates of milk stout are passed over the flames and frosty milk stout runs into the sweat of beautiful black bodies. The Castle Milk Stout man, a familiar icon in the brand's advertisements, is both an individual and "the essence of a stout drinker who has modernised over time, who hasn't forgotten his cultural traditions, has been successful in an urban environment and continues to prosper."[83] This brand personality, "an element of both worlds—where we come from and where we are going to," embraces the ambiguities present in the target market, which in turn echo those of other postcolonial identities.[84]

The Ndlanu advertisement followed conventional brand rules. The body parts associated with the muscular power of the working class and on which earlier milk stout advertisements relied—strong arms, big hands— remain the icons of the milk stout man. In the HerdBouys commercial, he sports a rugged watch on a bold wrist and wears khaki trousers, signifying an outdoor job. He drives a "bakkie" (small truck). A big, bold masculine glass is the brand's signature, while the dark beer and creamy head highlight the beer's characteristics. Finally, the description of milk stout as "the black and beautiful beer" transposes 1970s Black Consciousness rhetoric into advertising discourse and seals the elements of culture, politics, and masculinity in the identities of black working men.

Unashamedly ethnic in conception, the Ndlanu milk stout advertisement sought not to reinforce a narrow ethnicity but to construct a black heritage for bottled beer. HerdBouys director Dimape Seremanye saw in milk stout's relatively homogenous market a unique opportunity to celebrate previously unrecognized meanings of sociability and drinking practices. Through the Ndlanu advertisement, he demonstrated that clear beer was as much part of African sociability as it was of any other beer-drinking culture. He challenged the view that there were two authentic African drinking cultures—a rural, customary tradition of sorghum beer and an urban culture of bottled beer quaffed in shebeens. The Ndlanu advertise-ment broke down this binary division and confirmed that authenticity and modernity were compatible in the lived experience of African culture.[85]

In the late 1990s, advertisements for mainstream beer brands reflected the choice that confronted the new generation of postapartheid men—take advantage of opportunities in the global economy or build the democratic nation by staying home. Castle Lager developed a series of diasporic ad-vertisements that showed young middle-class South African men in the cities of the world going to great lengths to locate their favorite brand. At the same time, SAB corporate advertisements depicted strong men working together to build a national economy. Both series drew on the emotional power of nationalism to demonstrate the power of brand loyalty. A popular Castle Lager advertisement shot on top of a New York penthouse showed homesick South African men roasting sausage on a barbecue and singing the Castle Lager jingle with their hands over their hearts. Nationalist nos-talgia permitted the reinstatement of the braai in beer advertisements and provided a bridge to the celebration of SAB's own expansion abroad. The advertisement implied that South Africans were tied to each other and to the nation through sociability and brand loyalty. Playing to the lifestyle of the new elite, nationalist sentiment was configured through internation-alism.

Imaginings of a single nationalism did not put an end to the idea of a dual market, and marketing discourses continued to build on racial assumptions about the character of persons. The advertising industry's leading advisers, Green and Lascaris, described the growing African elite as dizzied by a mix of "money, envy, greed, ambition, snobbery and cov-etousness."[86] In this discourse, newcomers to wealth and power were out of control, overcome by their eagerness to "indulge a taste for extravagant as well as conspicuous consumption."[87] The discourse naturalized blacks as conspicuous consumers in much the same way as women were seen as attracted to luxury in nineteenth-century Europe.[88] Established white marketing experts advised business on how to attract the disposable in-comes of the new elite and projected a fear of "the other" onto this market. "The nouveaux riches are notoriously sensitive to the least slight or snub," cautioned Green and Lascaris, who recommended that advertisers looked to nationalism as a means of engaging the new big spenders.[89] "Love of country may initially be expressed as the challenge of building a new South Africa," they advised, adding that "emotions connected with that concept will be strong." The challenge for communicators was to "harness those feelings" to promote consumption.[90]

Manipulating emotions proved complex; not all beer advertisements that played on "love of country" generated positive responses. One advertising designer was distressed when his television commercial fell flat. His depiction of returning black exiles buying land for a community football field got the politics wrong; from the perspective of national liberation, the state should provide sporting amenities for all. Nor did the experimental signs of "responsibility" and "give back" fit well with the established signs of heritage, masculinity, and nationalism. Advertisers who did not "fit a brand into existing values" and sought to influence the market did so at their peril. As advertising designer Juan Scott put it, "The people who drink these brands are so sure what they want to be, you try to reflect this sentiment."[91] Ultimately, sociability was more important than patriotism for black drinkers. "You have to show that Castle means friendship. That's what works. Castle drinkers spend a lot of time getting their mates into a shebeen and they want to stick with them."[92] This did not mean that nationalism could not work for black consumers—effective portrayal meant finding the right mix of masculine physicality, sociability, and nostalgia and linking this to nationalist sentiment.

As SAB invested large sums in advertising—the share of its advertising budget devoted to beer amounted to R85 million per year in the early 1990s—opposition to advertising for alcoholic beverages began to mount.[93] While social critics condemned marketing discourses for reifying consumer values, those opposed to the advertizing of alcoholic beverages decried the artificial relationships and invented spaces of beer advertisements. These protesters argued that commercials that inverted the reality of lived encounters were highly dangerous.[94] Communist Party official Jeremy Cronin objected to Castle Lager's fictional Charles Glass Society and its celebration of consumer values.[95] Researchers at the South African Medical Research Council objected to SAB's sponsorship of national sports teams, complaining that violence, rowdiness, and underage drinking at sporting events were a consequence of liquor advertising. Others argued that outside a commercial's framing, the bonhomie of liquor advertisements gave way to racial tension and domestic violence.[96] These critics drew parallels between ravages on the social body and consumerism's devastating impact on the environment, lamenting the broken glass, mangled tin, discarded packaging, and disintegrating brand symbols that littered the landscape. At its most extreme, this discourse equates form with content and the material of consumption with its waste.[97]

To counter the potential effects of this subversion, SAB constantly provided educational material on responsible drinking, advertised the dangers of driving under the influence of alcohol, and funded research into fetal alcohol syndrome. The beer giant also invested in recycling initiatives and conducted campaigns to remove litter from strategic sites on the landscape. Its efforts were designed to protect both the corporate image and its product from the disruptive power of waste. But this message was not always successfully conveyed. In South Africa, as elsewhere, some drinkers remained more interested in "a calculating hedonism, a hedonism in which the individual strategically moves into and out of control, enjoying the thrill of the controlled suspension of constraints."[98] For consumers who saw beer as a "drug food," appeals to moderation had little impact.[99] In the context of a society ravaged by the effects of migrant labor, racist legislation, and lives confined to urban ghettoes, drinking to excess provided an escape from disappointment.[100] Such chemically, socially, or ideologically conditioned drinking patterns were likely to be more successfully prevented than corrected. These objections raise the difficulty of the enormous symbolic power of advertising for a transitional society with vast gaps in income, education, and standards of living.

While SAB avoided responding to the general anti-alcohol discourse, it was quick to defend attacks on the integrity of its brands. In 2001, Laugh It Off, a small T-shirt company in Cape Town, lampooned SAB's advertising of Carling Black Label. Laugh It Off recast the slogan, "Carling Black Label Beer: America's lusty, lively beer, enjoyed by men around the world" as "Black Labour, white guilt: Africa's lusty, lively exploitation since 1652, no regard given worldwide" and printed it on a T-shirt in the layout and colors of Carling Black Label's brand insignia. Its purpose was to offer critical comment on a marketing strategy that in its view had exploited the misery of black people in South Africa. Significantly, Laugh It Off did not make fun of the "lusty, lively" masculinities of the advertisement; this possibility was precluded by the proximity of the brand's masculinist values to its own style of humor. SAB was not amused and took the matter to court, charging that the parody cast aspersions on the integrity of the brand. SAB also claimed that the T-shirt company was making money with its trademark. Both the Cape High Court and the Supreme Court of Appeal ruled in favor of SAB, but the Constitutional Court ruled against the brewer. The T-shirt company was not competing in the beer market, said the court, but was instead selling an "abstract brand of criticism" and generating humor. Laugh It Off had used trademarks in a way that was both "original and parasitic, simultaneously creative and derivative."[101] The two-man company was exercising its right to freedom of expression in a democratic country. Also, the judges pointed out, SAB had failed to demonstrate that the satire had caused economic harm. Members of the media hailed the ruling. In their view, the court had both demonstrated an understanding of popular culture and acted to safeguard the space it provided for critical social comment. The judgment was a victory for the people, a win for David over Goliath.[102] The reason SAB needed to defend its brand was expressed most vividly by a company stalwart who was distressed by the Constitutional Court's verdict. "Our trademark law has gone to pot," he raged. "What will the rest of the world think of us? Nurse [the CEO of Laugh It Off] is a mommy's boy."[103] While the case was a mere tempest in a teapot for some, others accepted that SAB had an obligation to defend its brand.

SAB had invested heavily in brand identities recognized by their characteristic masculinity, sociability, and heritage conveyed by insignia, color, and packaging. Muscular configurations of masculinity provided experience and emotion, while sociability and heritage provided a story for the brand. SAB advertisers believed that tampering with these features was extremely risky. Beer advertisements responded to social changes without disrupting the character of brands or the identification of beer with masculine sociability. When SAB advertising targeted white women in the late 1960s, they introduced a femininity that complemented masculine sociability. When the company introduced images of multiracial drinking, it brought in brewing icon Charles Glass as a bridge to an imagined sociability. In the mid-1990s, advertisements asserted that multiracial nationalism was an intrinsic element of South Africa's beer heritage. Postapartheid corporate advertisements positioned SAB as the brewer to a powerful, hardworking nation ready to embrace the world.

four

"Tomorrow Will Also Be a Hard Day": Antisocial Drinking Cultures and Alcoholic Excess

Narratives of excess drinking in South Africa do not necessarily implicate beer drinkers, nor do they tell us much about bottled beer. However, bottled beer cannot be dissociated from stories that come from cultures of drink. Tales of intemperance arise in medical discourses, the polemics of social reformers, psychologists' reports, and government statements. As narratives of consumption, they tell us how people inside and outside of government tried to understand the abuse of and dependency on alcohol. They convey different social understandings of excess. For those in power, the notion of alcoholism and the meanings of excessive drinking were inflected with colonial understandings of "race," "character," and "disease" and of the state's responsibility to rehabilitate out-of-control drinkers.

In 1949 the World Health Organization's (WHO) committee on mental health acknowledged that alcoholism was a public health issue.[1] The discourse of mental health cast alcoholism as an individual problem, defining an alcoholic as someone whose drinking habits deviated from accepted social practice. The implication was that society needed protection from the deviant behavior of "mentally ill" individuals. In South Africa, this view sat comfortably with missionary and state perceptions that prohibition was a necessary protection for society. Since blacks who imbibed "European liquor" "lost control," they should be prevented from gaining access to it.

In contrast, social welfare professionals sought institutional state support for the care and rehabilitation of white alcoholics.[2]

In 1952, the WHO changed its definition of alcoholism from mental illness to disease.[3] But this modification was contested because the debate on the etiology of alcoholism was inconclusive. One perspective held that defining alcoholism as a disease placed the blame on the consumer and absolved purveyors of all responsibility.[4] Another argued that the discourse of disease provided social welfare professionals with a rhetorical tool for lobbying the government to support rehabilitative treatment.[5] While it did not quite remove the stigma of drunkenness, the idea of alcoholism as a disease invited social benevolence rather than censure.[6]

The apartheid regime viewed the notion of alcoholism as a disease with skepticism. In 1950, the Work Colonies Act provided a framework for treating white and Coloured alcoholics in institutionalized retreats that combined discipline and physical labor with medical treatment.[7] A year later, the National Council for Mental Health accepted the WHO's definition of alcoholism as a disease.[8] The council recommended that alcoholics enter mental hospitals for treatment by mental health professionals.[9] In 1963, the government set out a comprehensive approach to alcoholic rehabilitation in the Retreats and Rehabilitation Centres Act. At the same time, a National Alcoholism Advisory Board was established to keep the minister of social welfare and pensions informed of developments in the field of alcoholic research and rehabilitation. Legislation did not immediately lead to enhanced services, however. Whether or not an alcoholic was admitted to a state retreat depended, in the bland discourse of apartheid bureaucracy, "to a large extent on the availability of trained social workers and suitable treatment centres in the community."[10] Resources were allocated by race: whites were well provided for, but few state resources were devoted to rehabilitation programs for Coloureds and none were devoted to blacks.[11]

Meanwhile, the incidence of alcohol abuse was increasing. In 1965, a psychiatric study in the Cape estimated the incidence of alcoholism among Coloureds at 22 percent, purportedly the highest for any racial group in the country.[12] Alcohol abuse was described as endemic on wine farms where wages were partly paid in cheap wine, a practice known as the tot system. Farm workers began and ended their day with a tot (a tin can of varying size) of crude wine supplied by the farmer.[13] In the cities and towns, the popularity of wine among Coloured people was ascribed to the ready availability of cheap rough wine. Substance abuse in poor Coloured areas was also associated with the smoking of *dagga* (cannabis). Inhaled through a red-hot bottleneck, *dagga* smoke scorched the mouth and throat. *Dagga* smokers reputedly consumed large quantities of beer from shebeens to cool their throats.[14]

White panic over the extent of Coloured drunkenness in the 1960s and 1970s generated much public interest. Whites who took a hard apartheid line argued that Coloureds should take responsibility for their own reha- bilitation. Since the number of teetotalers among the Coloured population outnumbered the alcoholics, they said, teetotalers should put their "liquor consciousness" to use by taking greater responsibility for Coloureds who abused alcohol.[15] An even more paternalistic view held that government intervention would save Coloured people from themselves. In this view, Coloured people had not attained the moral standards required to tackle the problem of excess use of alcohol. Professor Muller of the University of Port Elizabeth held that laborers, and by extension all people of color, had failed to develop a set of "controlling norms" that might regulate their drinking behaviour.[16] An economics professor at the University of Stel- lenbosch added that since 40 percent of Coloured people lived below the poverty line, many were caught up in "a subculture of poverty," a "patho- logical pattern of life" that could be broken only through state interven- tion.[17] A third perspective perceived alcoholism as a cost to the economy. The government had a duty to intervene to ensure an adequate supply of sober workers for agriculture and industry. Its intervention should be seen as economic rather than moral, proponents of this perspective argued. Moreover, said one researcher, since "95% of criminal acts" committed by Coloureds were related to alcohol consumption, government intervention to reduce alcoholism would also reduce crime.[18]

Yet the government was slow to respond. In 1967, the first state-run outpatient clinic for "non-whites" was established at Livingstone Hospi- tal, Port Elizabeth. The South African National Council on Alcoholism (SANCA), an organization that employed social workers dedicated to pre- venting and treating alcohol dependency, was given a state subsidy. Ten years later, as a government commission found that "drinking was the only way [Coloureds] knew of passing the idle, empty hours during the weekend," the Avalon Treatment Centre was established in Cape Town.[19] Limited though they were, these efforts indicated some commitment to confronting alcohol abuse in selected Coloured communities.

While alcohol abuse by Coloureds and whites was recognized as al- coholism, a strongly social Darwinist discourse constructed all blacks as "naturally heavy drinkers" who were largely "immune to chronic alcohol- ism." Proponents of apartheid constructed black alcohol consumption as another means of reinforcing a discourse of racial difference.[20] A belief that black Africans were different from Coloureds provided the justification for the Department of Bantu Administration and Development's dismissal of the need to support blacks with a dependency problem.[21] In the meantime, medical practitioners and social workers drew attention to the problem of increasing alcohol abuse among black Africans, a problem that was no less serious for this group than it was for other South Africans.

Medical practitioners identified alcohol-related problems and malnutrition among African men who drank large quantities of state-brewed sorghum or maize beer. The beer sold in government beer halls was not the nutritious drink that home-brewed grain beer was, they noted.[22] Under apartheid, mass-produced grain beer was steadily stripped of its vitamin and nutritional content by the substitution of maize grits for whole-grain sorghum; in a bid to cut costs, the amount of sorghum in the state's recipe was reduced from nearly 5 percent in 1953–1954 to less than 1 percent by the end of the decade.[23] Maize was cheaper than sorghum; it was also easier to brew.[24] At the same time as the food value declined, consumption increased. Annual sorghum beer production increased from less than 96 million hectoliters in 1953 to over 1,000 million hectoliters in 1976, increasing tenfold again by 1981.[25] While this increase reflected the large-scale migration of blacks to the cities, it also illustrated that in some instances, individuals were drinking more.

The practice of using beer as a reward for labor during plowing and harvesting was well established in rural communities. Communal beer drinking after work helped connect different households and foster mutual support.[26] The idea that beer was an appropriate reward for physical labor accompanied men to the cities.[27] Hundreds of hostel dwellers spent their leisure time drinking large quantities of grain beer in compound bars to reward themselves after long hours of physical labor.[28] In a typical hostel of 3,600 residents, 500 men could be found drinking in the compound bar between shifts.[29] But there was a darker side to drinking on the mines. Prevented from living with their families and deprived of the status of household head, migrant workers in bachelor quarters saw themselves as having little option but to while away their leisure hours at the bar. As one hostel dweller put it, "This [sitting at the bar] is part of my job."[30] The fusion of heavy drinking with the meaning of mine work presents a picture of the mining environment as alienating, a colonial economic system that was dysfunctional for black masculinities.[31] Compound bars were places where men blotted out stress and alienation. The bars justified drunkenness instead of facilitating the social reciprocity workers had known in their home communities and so undermined the idea of sociability as a reward for labor.[32] Yet in providing an escape, compound bars may be likened to the tot system on wine farms. As Pamela Scully put it, even rationed wine could envelop workers in "a social moment in which farmers could not share."[33]

There were other similarities in the circumstances of Coloured farm workers and black mine workers. The rough acidic wine given to farm workers exacerbated health problems and encouraged addiction; the poor quality of state-brewed grain beer also contributed to alcohol-related health problems. Heavy drinkers of grain beer suffered from chronic iron poisoning and skin disorders. The cast-iron pots used to produce both the home brewed and the Native Affairs Department (NAD) beverages were the source of poisoning characterized by cirrhosis of the liver, damage to the pancreas, scurvy, and bone thinning.[34] The NAD ignored these health hazards and rebuffed calls from Dr. Seftel of the University of the Witwatersrand's Medical School to improve the vitamin content of the grain beer.[35]

Addiction to grain beer was not confined to the urban areas. Unemployed migrants in search of cheap alcohol gravitated to beer halls in the homelands. As money became scarce, toxic concoctions provided the cheapest kick. Over time, one social worker observed, the habit of uncontrolled drinking propelled some men into a pattern of drinking "anywhere, anything and at any time."[36]

Men living with their families in the townships were said to abuse alcohol less than migrant laborers. But even these men succumbed to heavy drinking.[37] By the late 1960s, researchers found, 22 percent of urban black men and nearly 10 percent of urban black women were drinking at least twenty-five drinks per week.[38] Urban drinking cultures did little to curb excess. *Drum* journalists wrote of sophisticated men and women gulping spirits and quaffing beer "by the case-lot in a spirit of careless abandon."[39] For these male writers, excessive drinking was smart, subversive, and loaded with masculine bravado. Women were props that enhanced the men's scene.[40] As Jon Qwelane put it, "The real excitement of drinking in shebeens was the thrill of breaking 'the white man's law' and getting away with it—there is nothing quite as pleasing as beating the system."[41] Shebeens grew rapidly in popularity and operated more brazenly, "in spite of the law and not because of it."[42]

Despite these romanticized accounts, the urban drinking culture did not always make for sociability. As Windsor Shuenyane put it, the more usual scenario was one where "you get into a shebeen and slug as much as you can so that when the police get in, at least you've got it in your tummy."[43] Illegal drinking obscured the dangers of overindulgence, and the macho drinking culture that it spawned often led to a denial of the domestic violence, individual pain, desperation, shame, guilt, and loneliness suffered by families of abusers, as one social worker noted.[44]

A white physician at a Johannesburg hospital that treated malnutrition, pellagra, beriberi, heart disease, and cancer of the gullet—common diseases of poor urban drinkers—believed that they were signs of a deeper social malady.[45] The lifestyles imposed on black people placed them at enormous risk of alcohol abuse, the physician said. It was easy for men and women without adequate fuel and cooking facilities to subsist on readily available white bread, white maize, and white sugar, "pure muck concocted by the technological genius" of a modern food industry.[46] "European liquor" and junk food were rational choices for men whose tedious laboring lives encouraged drinking for "merriment or intoxication because tomorrow will also be a hard day."[47] On Monday mornings, those who had overindulged over the weekend "took themselves to work."[48] Heavy drinking, he implied, was a rational response to miserable circumstances, echoing the idea that all of the maladies blacks encountered were the result of social disintegration caused by colonial rule.[49] This perspective affirmed the contemporary anthropological argument that while "socialised drinking to intoxication" had served a positive purpose in precolonial society, habitual inebriation was a colonial phenomenon.[50] It echoed the perceptions of nineteenth-century missionaries, colonial administrators, and chiefs that habitual inebriation was a colonial problem.[51]

This sympathetic view of the alienation of blacks contrasts sharply with the hostile attitude of medical professionals at a Pretoria hospital in 1972. White doctors reported that 50 percent of African patients at Weskoppies were suffering from alcohol poisoning or toxic psychosis. However, they said, "medical science" could achieve little for them because "knowledge of the disease in the Bantu was inadequate." The "knowledge" the hospital compiled reflected a social Darwinist discourse. Physically, "the Bantu" appeared "to require less alcohol than his white counterpart before organic changes in the brain were manifest," declared one Pretoria psychiatrist, adding that "the Bantu supplements his alcohol by taking toxic concoctions" for cultural reasons.[52] There was little hope for rehabilitation, since "the average Bantu rejected the alcoholic" and few "Bantu nursing staff" accepted alcoholism as a disease.[53] The message was that if black people were unwilling to take responsibility for alcoholics, there was no reason why whites should do so.

In a similar vein, a government expert on deviance told those who attended a SANCA conference that "alcoholism and the abuse of liquor is part of a pattern of deviate [*sic*] behaviour of Bantu who already display criminal behaviour, are workshy, [and] smoke cannabis."[54] Deviant behavior among blacks did not warrant state investment in specialized rehabilitation centers, the expert claimed. A pilot rehabilitation center for blacks had received only 20 percent of its cases as court referrals. Individuals who committed themselves voluntarily could just as easily present themselves to conventional medical clinics in the townships where they lived.[55] This racialized discourse of black character during apartheid ran counter to the call of the World Health Assembly for governments to curb alcohol-related problems in developing countries.[56] Instead, the apartheid state increased arrests for drunkenness, further criminalizing the alcohol practices of blacks.[57]

Medical professionals and social workers soon found that compulsive drinking was a problem in the homelands. A massive increase in the disposable income of homeland bureaucrats in the 1970s and the investment of elites in bottle stores encouraged new drinking patterns among the well-to-do. A district nurse in northern Hammanskraal reported that "Bantu homeland development" had changed drinking patterns as more people began to drink as a sign of status.[58] In a bid to stop his employees from becoming inebriated during working hours, Chief Kaiser Matanzima introduced breath-testing in government buildings.[59]

The Bantustan elite turned their backs on communal drinking.[60] Many avoided sociable drinking altogether. "The drinking by our high class people is done alone or with their own social class," a district nurse observed.[61] The Bantustan elite, said one social worker, suffered from a "big shot complex" and had become the victims of a destructive lifestyle.[62] The chief medical officer of St Lucy's hospital at Tsolo in the Transkei described a similar pattern among "the professional and higher clerical grade men." The incidence of alcohol abuse was so high in this social stratum that alcoholism became known as "teachers' syndrome."[63]

Women also drank to excess. One social worker reported that the consequences of female drinking were "generally more insidious, more devastating than in their masculine counterparts."[64] Because many women drank at home, often in the presence of children, the effects of women's alcoholism were "doubly felt" by their families.[65] The social worker warned that alcohol abuse would affect the next generation of adults as children growing up in its shadow lost out on the healthy development of trust and confidence.[66]

But workers who were not part of the elite also drank heavily. Shebeens thrived in the homelands. A year after a series of strikes in Durban led to wage increases, Kwazulu homeland leader Gatsha Buthulezi claimed that improved incomes had led to excessive drinking. Higher wages were benefiting purveyors of alcohol rather than the families of workers.[67] Black intellectuals had a different explanation for the problem: there were no places of entertainment or recreation where black people with a little bit of money might enjoy themselves. "We've got no posh clubs, no concerts, no restaurants, no dances. This is why we have shebeens; some shebeens are posh. What would the white man do in this position?" asked a clerk in Natal. "There are no cinemas for Africans in places like Ladysmith, Eshowe, Umlazi or KwaMashu. The Indian owned cinemas in Durban are too far from African townships and few people have cars, and in any case many films are banned for the African."[68] More poignantly, a religious leader added, "People drink heavily because they are hurt deep inside, not because they live just above the breadline."[69]

Elite and working-class blacks desired and yet were ambivalent about alcohol. Colonial regimes repeatedly cast alcohol as a privilege, a reward for education and status.[70] At the same time, tight regulation of alcohol criminalized black consumers and traders, generating stress for both elite and working-class blacks.[71] The elite itself was divided between an older mission-educated generation that was sympathetic to the ideas of temperance—the Independent Order of True Templars still attracted a small following in the 1970s—and those with a more worldly outlook.[72] In the 1970s, ambivalence was amplified by the messages of commercial advertising that encoded brands with status.[73]

Towards the end of the 1970s, black consumption of clear beer surpassed that of sorghum beer.[74] Even on the mines, bottled beer consumption increased while grain beer declined in popularity.[75] This change was not simply a consequence of increasing urbanization and sophistication.[76] In the view of SAB, the corporate beneficiary of the new trend, the state's brewers, "had it coming." Comparing South African beer halls with Russian canteens, an SAB man said that both "served up beer like slops" in a way that suggested contempt for their customers.[77] Few would disagree. In a typical beer hall, hoses suspended over a bar filled large stainless-steel drinking vessels while men stood around concrete tables in a great crush of bodies and noise. While the state exhibited disdain, commercial alcohol producers made it their business to understand black sociability. "On the great plane of being black under apartheid, detached, marginal men went back several nights a week to touch sides and talk about the forces of life with their fellow men," said SAB marketing manager Bruce Starke. "You didn't belong to your job, you were separated from your family, you didn't own a house or run a town. The shebeen and quality drink filled this gap."[78]

While the trend toward bottled beer was discernible as early as 1969, it was given a boost in 1976 by the turmoil that followed the student uprisings against government plans to make Afrikaans the language of instruction in black schools.[79] Business was not disrupted for long; canny shebeeners offered donations to the students' cause and free drinks to students and their friends.[80] When schooling resumed, some of those who dropped out of school entered the shebeens as newly inducted drinkers.[81] This generation constructed new cultures of drinking born not of fear of arrests but of their own sense of power. The new set consumed alcohol "for days on end," said Lydia Mosala, a nursing sister in Guguletu. "Once they start drinking, they must finish the bottles of brandy or whiskey. They cannot put them away for tomorrow." These young drinkers invented customs like *Ukusul' inyembezi,* or "after tears"—a drinking ritual held after a funeral. Bereaved families soon found themselves under pressure to supply alcohol for this ritual.[82] Young people were taking control of tradition and using their political power to fuse present meanings with those from the past. Their drinking styles displayed a stronger desire for change than for continuity and drew rather more on what they knew about irreverent shebeen drinking than on respect for generational hierarchy.[83] Shebeen demands and SAB's willingness to meet those demands led to beer sales that surged forward "like a steam train."[84]

Desperate to turn the tide, the Western Cape Temperance Union campaigned to have beer halls replaced by milk bars, but these plans fell flat. One newspaper columnist quipped that the "heady details" of "granadilla delight, made with twenty five granadillas and twenty eight grams of Epsom salts" were unlikely to wean shebeen-goers off the bottle.[85] Anti-alcohol lobbyists campaigned against alcohol advertising.[86] Images of sociability in alcohol advertisements, they claimed, fostered values that relinquished cherished relations and desires in real life; by portraying drinking as a path to acceptance and belonging, advertisements encouraged the use of a harmful substance to fulfill human wants.[87] Liquor advertisements were dangerous because they excluded all anti-social associations with alcohol, said one SANCA official.[88] SANCA provided evidence that as drinkers in television commercials raised their glasses, so did the viewers.[89] The Medical Association of South Africa called for a ban on alcohol advertising and asked that it be replaced with counteradvertising.[90] But these efforts failed because local alcohol advertisements worked. Liquor producers, particularly SAB, sponsored events that linked alcohol with reward, status, and pleasure; the black press regularly published photographs of smiling and successful people having fun while they held glasses filled with alcohol.[91]

This did not mean that the black press was uncritical of excessive alcohol consumption. The *Sowetan*'s cartoon character Jo-Jo regularly satirized greedy shebeen queens and male drunkards. The cartoonist represented "Aunt Sel," the shebeen queen, as a large, ruthless, money-grabber whose dream was to sell huge volumes of alcohol. She is shown pouring booze down the throat of a shebeen drunk, reviving those who have passed out in order to ply them with more drink, and fussing over favorite customers, the "very big spenders."[92] The Jo-Jo cartoon sometimes "addressed" the pain of the dependents of alcoholics. In one scene, as a mother and child put a drunken husband/father to bed, the mother advises, "Wait till your dad sobers up . . . then see if he's got any money for your school books." Jo-Jo comments ruefully, "Kids today are definitely not as patient as their parents were." In another more serious cartoon, a tearful wife observes her drunken man lying in the bathtub: "Although he's being destroyed by booze, Alfred's basically a very decent, sensitive person. . . . I mean, who else would bath with his hat on just so that he can greet visitors politely," she says, and Jo-Jo observes that "Alcoholic Anonymous could probably save his dear life!"[93] More directly, the *Sowetan*'s advice columnist, Dudu, advises a "worried mother" to get in touch with AA for advice on her husband's drinking problem.[94]

Alcohol-related problems also appeared as news items. One reporter for the *Sowetan* decried the degeneration of *stokvel* "food and booze" parties. *Stokvel* associations were credit rings or savings clubs run by members who pooled funds that were paid out in rotation as a lump sum.[95] The recipient of the lump sum customarily threw a party to celebrate, augmenting her gains by selling food and home-brewed beer at the party. New-style *stokvel* associations to which men were invited in the 1980s sported names with a shebeen-like ring—"Ebony, Ladies Night, A-team, Progress, Ho Lukile, New Born Baby, Sunday Morning"—and introduced a powerful new drinking culture into township life.[96] The *Sowetan* lamented that these *stokvel* parties were becoming popular among "shebeen kings" and "playboys," encouraging promiscuity and causing domestic conflict.[97]

Concerned that alcohol abuse among blacks was reaching serious proportions, SANCA began to make stronger interventions by employing a black fieldworker and embarking on a program of prevention.[98] Mabiki Mtshali targeted young people in the greater Soweto region through peer counseling at schools. She wanted to prevent young people from following in the footsteps of parents or teachers who were heavy drinkers.[99] In some areas, concerned township residents approached SANCA for help. In response, SANCA conducted a survey in New Brighton near Port Elizabeth that asked residents to identify chronic abusers by their ill health and violent and antisocial behavior.[100] Convinced that intervention was needed, SANCA asked SAB for financial backing for a clinic. When the clinic opened, working-class drinkers readily sought help, but the elite remained aloof, as they had done in Soweto, where SANCA had established a clinic a decade earlier.[101] SANCA struggled to understand this reticence on the part of the elite, but its research yielded contradictory findings. On the one hand, SANCA found that one-fifth of black men and one-quarter of women in the metropolitan areas admitted that they needed advice about alcohol abuse.[102] On the other, they found that nearly 73 percent of black men and almost 39 percent of black women approved of weekend drinking to the point of intoxication.[103] SANCA, an overwhelmingly white organization dependent on government funding, was puzzled by black attitudes toward alcohol, and its scope of insight was limited by its social distance from black communities.[104]

Alcoholics Anonymous (AA) was not strongly promoted in black communities. However, an apocryphal story that circulated as early as the 1940s featured the salvation of a destitute black alcoholic named Solomon who lived on the streets of an East Rand township. Solomon was reputedly "the first South African" to achieve rehabilitation through AA. As he was rummaging in a litter bin for discarded alcohol bottles, Solomon pulled out a tattered copy of *Reader's Digest* magazine. He read about the founding of Alcoholics Anonymous and wrote to its New York office. AA sent Solomon its twelve-step program by return post. He followed their instructions to the letter and gained his sobriety.[105] The story of "Solomon" has become an AA legend. His character may be derived from Solomon ka Dinizulu, the Zulu paramount who achieved notoriety for his exemption from prohibition on the grounds of alcoholic dependence in 1933.[106] His character may be invented, but for our purposes, it is immaterial.

The narrative of Solomon's recovery is structured within the AA discourse of three stages—abuse, "hitting rock bottom," and recovery.[107] This modernist notion of alcoholic recovery is derived from American notions of self-improvement coupled with the idea of Christian rebirth.[108] It sets up the prospect of recovery as never beyond imaginative possibilities of the self. The recovered alcoholics are individuals who have "made a decision to turn our will and our lives over to the care of God as we understand him."[109] They are individuals who have "made a searching and fearless moral inventory of ourselves," who have "made a list of all persons we had harmed and [have become] willing to make amends to them all." They "were entirely ready to have God remove all these defects of character."[110]

The Christianity at the center of this discourse overlapped with the ideologies of individual effort and Christian nationalism that the ruling class in South Africa promoted.

While AA remained a respected option for those in need of help, in the South African context, the ideology of the organization did not reach out to women. In the late 1980s, as the number of white women seeking help increased, a SANCA counselor established a women's group and recast AA's twelve steps in a way that was more friendly to women. The feminist rhetoric of Women for Sobriety's thirteen steps spelled out how becoming sober could lead to women's empowerment. "Negative emotions destroy only myself. Happiness is a habit I will develop. Problems bother me only to the degree I permit them to. I am what I think. I am a competent woman and have much to give others. I am responsible for myself and my sisters." Women for Sobriety established a group for recovering female alcoholics at SANCA's Lulama Treatment Centre in Durban.[111] Whether by design or default, their program of building women's self-esteem did not include black women, and black women's empowerment seems to have remained beyond their understanding of sisterhood in the 1980s.

In theory, outpatient counseling centers were "open to all races presumably because government believes that whites can take a limited amount of non-racial contact," noted one Member of Parliament.[112] But because whites had access to a wide range of well-funded state and medical institutions and a choice of voluntary organizations and therapies, they generally avoided mixing with other races. Alcoholism had been associated with "poor whites" in the 1930s, but it was declining as a problem among the white population in the late 1970s. The ratio of estimated alcoholics to the total white population declined from 6 percent in the 1970s to 4 percent in the mid-1980s.[113] Afrikaner members of parliament continued to debate why whites were differently positioned in relation to alcohol and culture. One Nationalist politician expressed the view that "the responsible use of liquor is part of a larger pattern of life, of a way of life, of civilisation, of a culture."[114] He was opposed by an Afrikaner politician from a poorer constituency. Restraint was not a matter of culture but a matter of concern to all people, he said, pleading for government protection against "the dangers of liquor."[115] In this discourse, class mediated the possibility of therapeutic intervention.

The structurally deeper poverty of blacks had an even more devastating impact. In the late 1980s, the confluence of black poverty and alcohol abuse escalated when informal shack settlements sprang up in urban areas as an ailing apartheid regime relaxed its control over the movement of blacks. Millions of black people left the impoverished homelands, setting up informal settlements on the outskirts of the cities. Alcohol consumption became a major pastime as these drinkers spent more on spirits and clear beer than their more settled township counterparts.[116] One study found that one-third of men in informal settlements were engaging in risky behavior and another third admitted that they needed help. A quarter of the women in these settlements were at risk of alcohol dependency.[117]

By the 1990s, urbanization was taking place on an unprecedented scale. In Cape Town alone some 5,000 people arrived from rural areas every week. Liquor dealing was rife in the informal settlements.[118] Researchers reported that drinking in informal settlements was often accompanied by the sexual exploitation of women.[119] "Maybe there is a girl there that I love but I cannot tell her, or maybe she does not love me. I take alcohol and give it to her. It's easy to get her that way. She drinks my alcohol and afterwards I will take her to my shack. She will be shocked in the morning that she slept in my shack because she did not know what she was doing last night."[120]

Alcohol abusers demonstrated ambivalence toward their own behavior. "When we talk about alcohol we make as if it is something very important," said one, acknowledging that "alcohol is not good. It changes one. When you are not drunk, you speak properly, but when drunk you speak the other way. Alcohol misleads people. When we speak about it we tend to praise it. We do things that we never thought of doing and tomorrow we deny them. Alcohol works on our brains."[121] Alcohol was blamed for the high incidence of domestic violence in these poor communities, which was often silently acknowledged in the battered faces of abused women.

By the mid-1990s, it was widely acknowledged that the consequences of alcohol abuse exacerbated the stress of living in poor communities and could be devastating. Women and children suffered the most from the effects of alcohol abuse in these communities. Babies were born with fetal alcohol syndrome, children were kept out of school, and home violence was often related to alcohol. Researchers with the National Trauma Research Programme of the Medical Research Council pointed out that nearly all trauma cases, including domestic violence and motor vehicle accidents, were related to alcohol. They found that more than half the victims were women and children.[122] Probing the significance of the link between alcohol abuse and aggressive behavior, other researchers found that most blacks believed that drunkenness was no excuse for violence. The belief that individuals were responsible for their actions even if they were drunk apparently differed from views held in other African countries.[123] The idea that drunkenness did not excuse destructive behavior tied in with the view that alcoholism was largely a social problem; it also linked to the belief that alcohol abusers needed to take responsibility for themselves if they were to be rehabilitated.[124]

In sum, these experiences reflected particular standpoints in a society ordered and organized along racial lines; they showed how meanings of alcoholic dependence and alcohol abuse were tied to ideas about racial difference. They demonstrate how the apartheid regime determined not only who was to drink what type of alcohol but also who was eligible for what form of rehabilitation. In constructing blacks as "naturally heavy drinkers," the apartheid regime excluded those in need of help from the social services provided to white and Coloured alcoholics. Accounts of drunkenness and dependency also demonstrated the links between alcohol abuse and irresponsible antisocial behavior; both encouraged, at least in part, the social distortions of apartheid. But only a small group of anti-alcohol lobbyists condemned all forms of drinking. Most blacks drew a clear distinction between abuse and responsible sociable drinking. Place and gender were critical elements. As one drinker explained, "A man cannot drink at home. He prefers to drink with other people because he wants that noise."[125] However, even sociable drinkers slipped into dependency and found themselves unable to escape this noise.

five

Remaking the Old Order: Beer, Power, and Politics

Beer and politics were never far apart in South Africa. Efforts by the apartheid regime to reform labor relations and rejig the political system opened up new spaces for social engagement. Beer producers, liquor retailers, brewery workers, and consumers were among those who entered these new spaces. Fired up by the political moment, these groups engaged in confrontations over power, resources, and identities. Shebeeners pressed for legalization, black activists tackled SAB's efforts to break the ban on South African participation in international sports, brewery workers demanded trade union recognition, and university students pressed for more moderate drinking behavior.

In the late 1970s, under pressure from antiapartheid activists inside and outside the country, the Nationalist government began to cast about for reform measures that might incorporate people of color as junior partners.[1] They borrowed from reform models under way in other parts of the region, in Ian Smith's Rhodesia and in Southwest Africa/Namibia, where settler regimes were engaging in last-ditch efforts to control the inevitable process of change. The South African government's reform of apartheid also took into account codes of conduct drawn up by multinational corporations and recommendations for a new labor dispensation set out in two government commissions.[2] Blacks were to be allowed to form trade unions, albeit on a segregated basis. The homelands, erstwhile reserves, now ethnically purified bantustans, were to be expanded so that they might become self-governing and ultimately "independent."[3] Coloureds and Indians would be incorporated into national politics in an advisory capacity through a tricameral parliamentary system. While the majority of South Africans scoffed at this tinkering with apartheid, restructuring created new spaces through which people of color might advance their interests. Intense political activity permeated all aspects of South African life. In this context, the multiple sites of the production, distribution, and consumption of alcohol provided spaces for contestation and social change.

"Better than the Butcher, the Grocer and the Fish and Ships [*sic*] Man"

Shebeening took a hard knock in the political turmoil of the 1976 student uprising. Angry Sowetan students heaped scorn and derision on drunkenness, ransacked and torched shebeen premises, and poured shebeeners' liquor supplies into the streets. Their actions protested the destruction brought on black families by men who patronized illicit drinking houses. Black masculinity, in their view, needed to be purged of self-destructive behavior. School students called for a boycott of all Bantu Affairs Administration Board liquor outlets and shebeens until "after Christmas" of 1976. "We are not interested in any tradition that keeps our people down and drunk right through their lives," they said.[4] Shebeeners closed the doors to their front rooms and retreated to their back rooms. Even Soweto's popular Aunt Peggy's appeared "as quiet as the grave" as business was conducted surreptitiously. Patrons were invited to "enter if you are not a cop or a school child or a school teacher."[5] Government beer halls went up in flames.

But the youngsters did not gain control of beer drinking quite so easily. Migrant men responded with vehement indignation. How could boys tell men when and where to drink? This breach of the age hierarchy was an affront to conservative black masculinity. "*Ndiyi ndoda, utywala ndabolukela*" (I am a man, I am entitled to drink, I know how to drink), complained one patriarch.[6] Sophisticated urbanites too, were distressed at this attack on their status. "I run a car and I have a decent family. The shebeens have never reduced me to the level the students make out. I know how to drink," said another.[7] *Drum* magazine's booze columnist Casey Motsisi was dubious about the black consciousness ideology in whose name young men opposed beer halls and shebeens. "Black power! All very well. If kept within reason. Without reason it all adds up to black plunder. . . . Yes, this black blunder must come to an immediate stop. Black sense must prevail lest we find ourselves wallowing in the mud of our own making."[8]

Angry and bitterly disappointed, the students condemned the men of their fathers' generation. "Our fathers spend their weekends at the shebeens. When they finish work on Fridays they go straight to the shebeens. They spend all their wages there. We see them for the first time on Monday morning when they come home to ask our mothers for money to go to work," said one. "We believe shebeens have got to be stopped now and for good because they are undermining the black man and destroying his soul," explained another. "We are not interested in any tradition that keeps our people down and drunk through their lives," said a third.[9] "We cannot achieve our aims when half the nation is drunk. We are not fighting amongst ourselves. We are disciplining those who won't listen."[10]

If black students were united in their opposition to beer halls, they were divided in their criticism of shebeens. With few opportunities for self-employment open to blacks, their business activity was confined to small shops and illicit dealing in liquor. In the aftermath of the uprising, shebeening provided a viable living for those who had lost jobs or were unable to find one. As unemployment increased, more and more men were drawn into the trade. By 1979, Soweto's population of approximately 1.5 million (officially 1.2 million) was served by an estimated 2,000 shebeens and 2,250 bootleggers.[11]

Confronted by the youth and harassed by the police, shebeeners were anxious to recast the image of their activities and gain respectability. Toward the end of 1979, leading Soweto shebeeners formed an organization to fight for the decriminalization of the black liquor trade. Sponsored by sympathetic liquor producers, the Soweto Taverners' Association began lobbying the West Rand Administration Board (WRAB), the Department of Cooperation and Development (formerly the Bantu Affairs Department), and the local councilors appointed by government as part of apartheid reform. The Soweto Taverners' Association set about building a national organization and began touring the country to encourage local shebeeners to organize and affiliate with a National Taverners Association (NTA). At its launch in 1980, the NTA claimed a membership of 2,000; two years later the organization had 6,000 members.[12] eSpotini, the NTA's trade magazine, lobbied for legalization, kept its members apprised of developments, and promoted liquor products. It also publicized a Bursary Fund chaired by Professor G. R. Bozzoli, former vice-chancellor of the University of the Witwatersrand.[13] Shebeeners were on their way to respectability.

Rocks Machaba was chosen to serve on the organizing committee of the NTA, along with bootleggers Ray Mollison and Bra Boysie and shebeeners Lucky Michaels and Peggy Bel-Air Senne. Lucky Michaels, proprietor of the Pelican nightclub in Diepkloof, Soweto's elite area, was the NTA's first chairman, chosen for his leadership talents. His colleagues said that he "[is] a better talker than most of us, thinks faster on his feet, is charming and has the ability to cajole and persuade."[14] Michaels was young, dashing, and flying high. For many Sowetans, he was the epitome of success. At the height of his career as a nightclub owner, he drove a flashy 733i metallic blue BMW, dressed in the latest styles, and was surrounded by fashionable women; he was a smooth talker with a "cosmopolitan" accent acquired while roving in Mozambique and Zimbabwe in the 1960s. Once an amateur boxer, Michaels was adept at bullying as well as lobbying. Even his detractors conceded that the 43-year-old was a good choice for chair of the NTA.[15] The NTA's first president, Peggy "Bel-Air" (after the 1955 car of the year) Senne, was a second-generation shebeener with a friendly and vital image; he was perceived as the "elder statesman of shebeeners, a wily grizzled old racketeer."[16] In a discourse that tracked between more conventional codes of black masculinity and the streetwise talents required of a township entrepreneur, Michaels explained the choice of Bel-Air: "Mr Senne befits the portfolio because his age is ripe for such a position of high honour and responsibility. He has the necessary morality and charismatic and rational qualities to lend dignity to the executive and the whole association."[17]

These men fought for shebeeners to be recognized as respectable entrepreneurs. "We are authentic business people," Michaels declared as he traveled the country organizing branches of the NTA, "better than the butcher, the grocer and the fish and ships [sic] man. If any man can run a business under the strains we have been able to operate under and make it, he can only be the best." He urged shebeeners to move out of the margins and into the center, to stand tall and believe in themselves. "You must know you are the best business person before you can be one," he said. Distancing shebeening from criminality, he declared, "I am proud to be a shebeener. I kill no-one. I steal from no-one. I am a businessman serving a community."[18] Significantly, Michaels, like most others in the NTA, referred to himself as a shebeener rather than a nightclub owner or taverner. "Shebeen" evoked both defiance and commensality. Liquor traders of varying means tied their identities to a heroic past as they fought for a future that recognized their worth. In so doing, they made use of what Bob Connell calls the cultural resources of subordinated masculinities to rework their identities.[19]

Colin Hall, an SAB executive, affirmed shebeeners as "the greatest entrepreneurs in the world. They've survived—without training, without normal infrastructure, despite the problems that go hand-in-hand with illegality."[20] But township administrators were less welcoming of the idea of legality for shebeens. If shebeens were allowed to compete with Bantu Affairs Administration Board outlets, the township Administration Boards would lose revenue. In 1980, WRAB liquor sales, which represented about 40 percent of the national total, amounted to R40 million (R3.5 million of which was net profit). Even the less wealthy Eastern Cape Administration Board reported a net profit of R1.88 million for 1983.[21] Allowing black businesses in urban areas was taking reform too far, township administrators believed. It was not part of the vision of apartheid for blacks to become entrepreneurs outside their designated homelands. Some administrators argued that if blacks wished to sell liquor they should relocate to the homelands, where bottle stores were highly popular businesses.[22] Any softening of this principle meant that the apartheid government would have to commit itself to further reform.[23] But the illicit liquor trade was beyond control and change could not be staved off. On 29 May 1980, Minister of Justice Alwyn Schlebusch announced that licenses would be granted to shebeeners and bottle stores in the townships.[24] The NTA was euphoric. But the celebration was short lived.

More than a year later, there was still no clarity about the requirements for a license. In response, the NTA mounted a boycott of WRAB outlets.[25] Sis Cooksie, wife of boycott leader Peggy "Bel-Air," and her friend, shebeen queen Shelley Morolong, went around Soweto to "pick up shebeeners from their houses and station them at bottle stores to ensure that everyone boycotted."[26] For over a week, the NTA enforced the boycott. When one shebeener emerged from a WRAB bottle store with eight cases of beer, boycotters kicked the bottom box and the other boxes came crashing down.[27] Soweto's Administration Board was adamant that it would not sell its liquor outlets to the Soweto Taverners' Association and summoned the police to raid the shebeens.[28] The Department of Co-operation and Development maintained that if shebeeners wanted licenses they would have to apply for their homes to be rezoned as business premises.[29] To qualify, they would have to make alterations in compliance with strict building regulations. Only then would they be eligible to apply to the Soweto Community Council for licenses.[30] At the same time, the administration boards wanted to transfer township bottle stores to the community councils, which were advised to sell them to obtain revenue. The move was controversial.[31] The black community councilors were notoriously untrustworthy and many of them opposed the sale of the board's liquor outlets on the grounds that the community councils had no credibility in African communities.[32] Adding its voice, Soweto's Committee of Ten, a highly respected, self-selected group of professionals and businessmen, insisted that liquor licenses for blacks and whites should not be issued by separate bodies.[33]

In the first rush of applications, almost 4,000 shebeeners applied to the National Liquor Board (established by the Liquor Act of 1977) for licenses under the auspices of the NTA. By the end of 1983, only three applications had been granted, all of them to men outside of the shebeening business. Pat Mbatha, a Soweto businessman, owned a business site that the National Liquor Board declared acceptable for a tavern. Soweto tycoon Ephraim Tshabalala quickly converted his application for a dry-cleaning business to one for a bottle store.[34] When the WRAB began to sell off its liquor outlets, it awarded some bottle-store licenses to black businessmen involved in consortiums that included white partners.[35] Licenses for bottle stores were also granted to new generation entrepreneurs. Chris Mhlongo, a university graduate, gave up a job with an international technology giant, bonded his house, took out a bank loan, and bought a liquor store.[36] Some bottle-store owners began to protest that "too many" licenses were being granted to shebeens; bottle stores did not make money from shebeeners since the more successful players bought in bulk directly from distributors.[37] In these township "shebeen wars," a new hierarchy of elite businessmen came to dominate liquor retailing.

The politics of licensing and the power play within the NTA created a significant shift in the gender politics of shebeening. Men dominated the leadership and ran the meetings. Strategizing, lobbying, cutting deals, and confronting political opponents became the preserve of men. Even well-established women stepped aside, holding back from the new public arena of political negotiation and commerce. Those women who served on the executive of the NTA took up the administrative positions of secretary or treasurer, leaving the key decision-making roles to men. Shebeen queens were phlegmatic. Men might maneuver themselves into positions of power, but women were more successful shebeeners. Said Sis Dolly Malunga:

> Men fail as shebeeners because they go for girlfriends; they go
> for any beautiful woman and they give materially without re-
> ceiving. Women shebeeners are more consistent. We can give a
> boyfriend a plate of food, but he must buy his own liquor.[38]

Indeed, organizational power was not synonymous with commercial success. For Lucky Michaels, the political limelight meant that he "took his eye off the ball." By the time he was granted a license in 1985, registration was of little use to him. "By 1985 I was bankrupt," he said, "I got too caught up in charity [NTA] work."[39]

By this time, shebeen licensing had been overtaken by larger political forces. By the mid-1980s, black nationalist organizations had launched the final push against the apartheid regime. The government responded by declaring a state of emergency and sending the military into Soweto and other townships. As residents came into direct confrontation with the army and police, shebeeners were called on to provide material support and shelter for activists.[40] They also had to cope with the increased lawlessness that accompanied the "boiling violence" and interfered with business. Wandie Ndala, proprietor of Wandie's Restaurant, which was located next to a Soweto school, explained that it was only by "involving yourself with comrades and political activists on the ground that you survived."[41] Lawless elements also took advantage of the turmoil. For Sis Dolly Malunga, coping with increased criminal activity was a tough challenge.

> We had to cope with *itsotsi,* the gangs that harass people in the shebeens, take money, drink and girls from under your nose. Anything can happen any time. They jive naked on top of the table and they carry guns. They are influenced by Tupac, Nino Brown, and Ice-T, American gangsters. One has to remain calm and talk nicely.[42]

Sis Cooksie Senne added:

> We were once robbed in 1986. They took R500,000, our takings for the weekend. My nephew was shot, but he survived. The driver of the getaway car was caught, but the witnesses didn't want to stand in court, so we left it.[43]

Yet in other respects, antiapartheid resistance was good for business.[44] With Bantu Affairs Administration Board bottle stores closed, beer halls destroyed, and white towns "off-limits," shebeens were the only places for blacks to go. Between 1979 and 1989, the number of shebeens in Soweto doubled, reaching 4,000. Shebeen culture became more deeply embedded in township life. Almost every household was drawn in through proximity to a shebeen or through family members who were shebeen regulars.

Journalists continued to promote shebeen sociability as urban African culture. The *Sowetan*'s columnist Elliott Makhaya identified with drinkers who participated in the fast, hard-drinking male group culture of the townships. "The boys are knocking back *ispinza* [drinks] at the speed of thought so much that after an hour, the stock in the *phuza* cabin is now hot. Members of my *phuza*-congregation [drinking-congregation] out-classed [depleted] the freezer. We decide to move to Danny Talane's Tavern in Emalahleni."[45] Men constituted a collective, a *"phuza*-congregation," whose pastime was harassing female patrons ("molls" or "bitter halves") and plying them with "grog." These women typically "pout[ed] their glossy lips as they sip[ped] the grape and survey[ed] the room" before disap-pearing into the 'molls boardroom' (toilet) or a back room with one or other *majita* (wise boy). If they failed to catch a man, they simply became "sozzled to their doeks" (headscarves). As atomized creatures eyeing the *phuza*-congregation, women in this discourse were the denigrated "other" of macho male drinkers.

Makhaya's column constructed masculinity as homosocial, hard drink-ing, heterosexual, and promiscuous. This masculinity celebrated self-in-dulgence and rendered male responsibility inappropriate, at least over the weekend. Proponents of this model of masculinity relegated duty to women, whom they derisively referred to as "domestic." Such men portrayed women as failing to understand male behavior. "You are not the only one who suf-fers the domestic as the booze blues," Makhaya wrote, exonerating male self-indulgence.[46] Makhaya's journalism negotiated different tensions than those of the earlier *Drum* journalists who, as Dorothy Driver observed, rep-resented "modern" black men and women in ways that were "both imposed on and negotiated in the magazine."[47] For Makhaya, the metro swinger of 1980s Soweto drove a smart car, dated multiple women, and drank in she-beens as often as possible. He liked to be seen at *stokvels* and at extravagant parties on weekends. Only occasionally did he talk politics.[48] Conspicuous consumption appeared to generate little ambivalence for this new man.

Shebeeners themselves had become more sophisticated. Competitive entrepreneurs dressed in suits and elegant women were often featured in *Beer Business*, SAB's newsletter to the trade. Chris Senamela, Daveyton's first licensed taverner, was a graduate of SAB's "partners in profit" train-ing program and obtained a loan to renovate his premises to comply with the new licensing requirements. He employed a security guard to screen customers using a metal detector as they entered his upmarket tavern.[49] Men with experience in bootlegging moved into the distribution trade. They built warehouses, stored stocks in bulk, and supplied shebeeners with bottled beer around the clock. Bulk supplier Bra Boysie, onetime NTA trea-surer, bought the house next door, joined it to his home, and converted the double property into a warehouse. Overseeing the four men who packed boxes, Boysie spent his life among the crates, seldom visiting his family, whom he had moved elsewhere.[50] Operating on an even larger scale, Bra Bys had a warehouse in Soweto that was "almost the size of the SAB Baragwanath depot." Thirty-eight truckloads of supplies were delivered to him every weekend by the early 1990s. Bys's turnover reputedly reached R2 million every Friday to Monday in the mid-1990s. But he did not flaunt his wealth. The slightly built man said little, drove a nondescript car, and told nobody where he lived.[51]

These township suppliers and the bigger shebeens relied on huge discounts for bulk purchases from SAB. Passing on this discount to their clients, they operated on tight margins. However, large discounts also caused big headaches. When shebeener Fanny Mokoena was unable to pay the SAB Baragwanath depot, her property was confiscated to pay her debts and she had to start all over again. As a woman in a male-dominated industry, Sis Fanny found it difficult to ask the questions that might have prevented her failure. To prevent others from falling into debt, she established an organization to support new female entrants to the shebeen business.[52] As more and more shebeeners found themselves in financial difficulties, SAB cut down on discounts for bulk purchases and insisted on collateral for credit. But some shebeeners were not impressed. The NTA objected to taking out an SAB insurance policy as collateral. SAB exercised too much control, they complained. Since shebeen sales amounted to R579.5 million per year, NTA members believed they should be represented on the SAB board. When SAB balked, the NTA called a boycott of SAB products at the end of November 1992. But the strike was bad for business, and within a few days SAB and the NTA agreed to set up a task force to facilitate ongoing dialogue.[53]

By the mid-1990s, the attraction of legality had faded for many shebeeners. Complying with licensing requirements was too expensive. It also meant paying taxes. Most shebeeners gave up on the idea. The NTA soon became the voice of licensed bottle store owners and taverners and transformed itself into the Liquor Traders Association, later the national South African Liquor Traders Association (SALTA). Since 1979, the NTA had provided a discursive space for shebeeners to redefine themselves as entrepreneurs running respectable businesses and providing recreational services in their communities. Organized action had brought men to the fore. As SALTA, the discourse of entrepreneurship became even more male centered and women were further sidelined. Learning from the NTA's experience, SALTA developed a keener understanding of the difficulties of complying with licensing regulations. They also accepted that legal recognition had created divisions between shebeeners that were likely to persist. "Those who expect an overnight transformation in the status of township liquor distribution should be cautioned," said a SALTA leader, who warned that "there's still lots of wait-and-see on the cards."[54] Of the estimated 120,000 shebeens across the country in 1991, only 2,445 had obtained licenses.[55] Nat Nakasa's prediction that "the shebeens will be with us for a long time to come" was amply borne out.[56]

"An Injury to One Is an Injury to ALL": Brewery Workers Organize

Brewery workers were affected by the unsettled politics of the 1980s, particularly by the massive increase in trade union activity across the country. Relatively more skilled and better paid than many other workers in manufacturing, SAB employees were initially slow to show an interest in trade unionism. Technology rather than politics dominated their working lives.

SAB's "supertanker" breweries were capital intensive and designed to operate with a high degree of automation.[57] Labor was replaced by technology at each stage of the brewing process. The traditional circular hand-beaten copper kettles gave way to rectangular stainless-steel vessels with a central control panel from which the entire brew was controlled. Brewers achieved scientific control of the beer recipe through conveyors that enabled the brewer to select and preset a recipe on an electronic panel and have the ingredients poured into the mix at the press of a button. Metering pumps ensured that measurements of additives such as flaked maize were standardized and delivered automatically. Advancements in the filtering of chemical waste and technology for monitoring and controlling effluent reduced the need for human labor.[58] Bottling, canning, and packaging were also automated. Bottling lines operated at high speed, producing 1,600 bottles per minute. At Alrode, a plant that produced 1,000 cans per minute, the processes of unloading, conveying, washing, filling, seaming the can, pasteurizing the beer, checking the fill level, coding, and packing for dispatch were all operated by a single worker from one control panel. Where before eight laborers per shift had loaded the palletizers (conveyers carrying crates of beer to the final dispatch point) manually, two men operated six automated lines in the early 1980s. Conveyers running on tracks reduced the need for forklift trucks and their drivers.[59]

But the skilled labor needed for these sophisticated operations was scarce, and SAB's training center in Durban could not make up the shortfall. Brewers and specialist technicians were brought in, mainly from the British brewing industry, at considerable cost. Like other manufacturers,

SAB was eager for educational reforms that might lead to the development of a more skilled labor force. SAB also welcomed the apartheid regime's reforms in labor relations and established in-house workers' committees.[60]

Employees of SAB were awakened to the benefits of independent labor organization in 1981 when their colleagues at the Isando plant joined the Sweet Food and Allied Workers Union (SFAWU). After support from the union had strengthened the Islando workers in their wage negotiations, word spread to other SAB plants. Cape Town's Pinelands depot, where several young men who had participated in the 1976 student uprising were employed, invited SFAWU's Chris Dlamini to meet with them.[61] Inspired, they took up the challenge of organizing their more conservative migrant colleagues at the Newlands Brewery. Within two years, each brewing plant and distribution depot across the country had elected shop stewards. These men set out to recruit 51 percent of the work force at each SAB plant. Once it had achieved this goal, the union began to press for recognition. In 1984, Pinelands depot and Newlands Brewery workers engaged in joint wage negotiations with SAB for the first time.

More broadly, the labor movement consolidated its forces by forming the Congress of Trade Unions (COSATU), which introduced a policy of industrial unionism. On Republic Day, 31 May 1986, SFAWU amalgamated with the Food and Canning Workers Union to form the Food and Allied Workers Union (FAWU). SAB workers began to organize on a national level, and by the end of the year they formed the National SAB Shop Stewards Council, comprising eighty-four representatives. While full-time shop stewards who were given time off for trade union activity that did not involve SAB matters would be a new experience for the company, SAB appeared to welcome the new dispensation.[62] In 1987, FAWU and SAB signed a national recognition agreement that provided for wage negotiations at a national level, giving impetus to the National SAB Shop Stewards Council.[63] For the shop stewards, striving for a better life was primarily about an improved standard of living for workers, but the struggle also involved a quest for dignity, power, and self-assertion. Worker action became an aspect of subjectivity, leading to a redefinition of self.[64]

The first test for SAB shop stewards came in the midst of the 1987 national wage negotiations. Shop stewards demanded that workers and their representatives be included in consultations about changes in working conditions; representation and consultation were critical issues in reforming labor relations. At this point, shop stewards and workers wanted to engage in consultation about overtime. SAB wanted to increase its beer volume by 210 million liters a year; the brewer could do this by keeping packaging and transport lines working around the clock in tandem with the continuous brewing process.[65] In mid-1987, the Rosslyn plant introduced a system of "continuous production" with dramatic changes to the shift system. Work routines and the lifestyles of workers were disrupted as the shift system ate into nights and weekends. When more than 300 workers at the plant refused to accept the new conditions, they were dismissed.[66]

On 11 September, 1987, nearly 1,600 workers at SAB's Isando, Alrode, Denver, and Wadeville plants in the Transvaal refused to work overtime. Withdrawal of this labor was a powerful blow, costing SAB an estimated R150,000 per day.[67] For nine long weeks, no overtime was worked. SAB claimed that it was "at a loss to understand what precipitated the strike," since the continuous shift system was not new to South African manufacturing. But, as FAWU general secretary Jan Theron explained, workers would not accept "unilaterally imposed" changes to working conditions.[68] Such changes required "joint study" between workers and management. Accustomed to driving the labor process, SAB management chafed at the slowdown brought about by conflict with labor. In a desperate bid to put an end to the industrial action, SAB applied for a conciliation board hearing and appealed to the courts to declare the overtime ban an illegal strike.[69] But the court ruled in favor of the workers. Both local and appeal courts held that voluntary overtime was not contractual; employees were not obliged to do overtime work.[70] If the definition of work were to encompass voluntary overtime, workers would be deprived of their right to "withhold labor they are not contractually obliged to perform." The court pointed out that this right was widely recognized as "an important weapon" of workers "in the bargaining process that underlies the theory of modern labor law."[71] Legislative reform and trade union recognition meant that following appropriate procedures was critical for harmony in the workplace. SAB agreed to reinstate all workers who had been locked out in the course of industrial action. Both the strike and the court's verdict brought workers into the public eye, removing them from structural invisibility.[72]

Industrial action highlighted the vulnerability of SAB's distribution depots to union activity. The depots were staffed by crews of men who loaded and unloaded trucks and drivers who distributed crates of beer to shebeens and bottle stores. They were the link between the brewery and the retailer. The opportunity for political agitation and disruption was stronger here than in the more controlled environment of the brewery. SAB was at pains to find a way around this vulnerability. First, the brewer declared transport a noncore activity and looked for ways to outsource its truck fleet. In 1987, the Western Cape region, SAB instituted a pilot scheme for "owner-drivers." Drivers in the employ of the SAB were offered loans to purchase their vehicles and contracts to transport SAB products. Self-employed operators contracted to SAB would be responsible for their own distribution crews and reduce the need for SAB to maintain its own distribution depots. With this deft move, SAB exorcised a particularly militant sector from its workforce. Also, owner-drivers would be responsible for their vehicles, which would be less vulnerable than SAB trucks in times of political turmoil. Carefully trained and tightly controlled by legal contracts, owner-drivers promised a safe, cost-effective, and politically acceptable way of distributing large volumes of beer to predominantly black consumers living in townships. Early in 1988, SAB reported that eleven drivers had independent contracts and an option to purchase their vehicles from SAB.[73] In 1991, SAB's Newlands branch also offered SAB drivers the opportunity to participate in the owner-driver scheme, promoting it as a great chance for a worker to become one's own man.

Concerned that they were about to lose their jobs, shop stewards at the Pinelands distribution depot asked the union to look into the implications of the scheme. In the meantime, the workers acted on their own initiative, securing a written guarantee from Newlands management that none of the crew would be retrenched when the depot closed down. Their comrades at other depots were less fortunate and faced redundancy as SAB introduced the owner-driver scheme across its operating regions. For their part, the owner-drivers fell between two stools. As "self-employed" men, they were not protected by the Labour Relations Act; they could not join a trade union or embark on strike action. But they were tied to their former employers by tight contracts that restricted the use of the trucks to SAB business.[74] Although this outsourcing was in line with the international trends, the context for the initiative was shaped by local political changes in the era of the reform of apartheid.[75]

By mid-1989, F. W. de Klerk had taken over as president of the country and youth organizations sympathetic to the exiled ANC had adopted a strategy of making the country ungovernable. Rumors of the imminent downfall of the apartheid regime were rife. In this climate, FAWU and SAB embarked on their annual wage negotiations. As antiapartheid activity drew in more and more workers and spilled over into trade union politics, some SAB shop stewards developed an acute sense of their own power. Claiming that unless they "asserted themselves" they would be "trampled on," leading shop stewards pushed the union to demand substantial wage increases (38 percent) and paternity leave. As the FAWU general secretary observed, these demands were driven by a desire to achieve a new social order.[76] For its part, SAB sought to set limits to this muscle-flexing and argued that as a "progressive employer," the company was at risk of being "milked."[77] Encouraged by the union's determination to push ahead with their demands, 6,000 members of FAWU at seven breweries, two malting plants, and thirteen distribution depots embarked on a strike that was to last nine weeks.[78] However, as some workers began to question the wisdom of the decision to strike, the union struggled to keep its members disciplined. Incidents of workers lashing out at political rivals, strikebreakers, and scab workers were reported across the country. A nonstriking worker in Kimberley was stabbed by a shop steward, and the child of a nonstriker in Pietersburg was injured when his home was firebombed. SAB delivery trucks were stoned; one SAB driver averted an attempted hijacking. There were also deaths: one SAB driver was shot at the wheel near the Prospecton plant outside Durban, and at the Newlands plant, the teenage son of a scab worker died from detergent fumes after lowering himself into a beer tank to retrieve a fallen spanner.[79]

Beyond the workplace, shop stewards called for a boycott of beer. Youths "inspected" shebeens, spilled their beer, and routed the patrons. "Don't sell beer or we will burn your house down," they threatened.[80] The boycott was supported by the NTA and the National Stokvels Association but not the more conservative Ukhamba Association.[81] Zanosi Kunene, vice-president of Ukhamba, reported that bottle-store owners were being intimidated. "We have had a mixture of types walk into our stores and demand to know why we are selling beer. Without giving traders an opportunity to explain, unemployed looters and hooligans have smashed or taken beer. FAWU members (and high school pupils, believing the boycott is 'for the struggle') have also been enforcing the action," Kunene said.[82] SAB struggled to counter media reports of a widespread beer boycott and an impending dry Christmas. Describing this story as "so much junk," SAB's marketing director claimed, "We are brewing, bottling and selling appreciably more beer than we were this time last year."[83] Nor was SAB's marketing man to be unsettled by the fact that the members of the NTA had purchased Windhoek Lager from Namibian breweries. His demeanor became a little more subdued, however, when he pointed out how a boycott would affect shebeen workers. "There are 1,400 licensed black liquor outlets and no one knows how many shebeens. Each of these probably employs six people, which means that just the licensees employ 8,400 people. What the union is saying is that all these people must starve."[84]

When the strike finally ended six weeks after it had begun, FAWU was weakened. Hundreds of workers had been dismissed and those who remained were disenchanted with the union. The leadership admitted that they had not focused clearly enough on the immediate needs of the workers. Instead, they had allowed their demands to be clouded by the general grievances of black people under apartheid. The fault did not lie entirely with the union. A labor analyst pointed out that SAB had "forced the "power route" by declaring a dispute on the third day of negotiations. The union was not the only loser. SAB's "power" strategy had damaged its relations with the union so seriously that both agreed to embark on a process of mediation.[85] In the course of mediation, SAB and FAWU agreed to establish a national forum for negotiating issues such as canteens, ablutions, and housing subsidies that were not considered to be substantive labor issues. Although the forum skirted core issues, it allowed both the union and SAB to save face.

"A Purely Political Thriller": SAB's Sponsorship of the Rebel Soccer Tour

SAB began sponsoring soccer in the early 1960s after prohibition was lifted. But the company's appetite for multiracialism in sport developed more slowly. Its support for the nonracial South African Soccer League did not extend beyond the odd case of beer for fund-raising events. SAB's official sponsorship went to the more conservative National Football League (NFL), which had been established by members of the Johannesburg City Council and the white English-speaking United Party.[86] SAB's sports sponsorship increased in the 1970s when it began sponsoring the white Castle Cup and the black Castle League.[87] Like all major beer producers, SAB looked for opportunities to manipulate sports audiences through advertising that linked its brands to the risk and reward of deep masculine play.

SAB had little patience with the International Olympic Committee's decision to expel South Africa from the Olympic Games in 1970 and the encouragement this gave to anti-apartheid calls for an international sports boycott against South Africa.[88] The brewer chafed at the loss of the big matches that "put a real head on spectators' thirsts."[89] By the end of the 1970s, SAB was funding several successful international rugby and cricket tours that South Africans described as "multinational" and that frustrated attempts to isolate South Africa.[90] By 1979, as SAB took on more sponsorships in a bid to create advertising opportunities, the cost of sponsoring the rebel tours was double what it had been in the previous year and the boycott was cutting deep into SAB's profits.[91] Most white sports enthusiasts supported the tours and lauded SAB for its initiative, rewarding the brewers with increasing demand. The very act of cocking a snook at the

IOC heightened the intensity of the experience and gave white sporting masculinity a sharper edge. The political risk of flouting the ban rendered play more dangerous. Players, spectators, and sponsors were drawn more closely together, and beer drinking affirmed these bonds.[92]

After successfully hosting rebel cricket and rugby tours, SAB began making plans to bring international soccer players to South Africa. Its purpose in hosting a rebel soccer tour was to demonstrate that there was space in a reforming South Africa for multiracialism in sport. With its own attempts to halt the international sports boycott floundering hopelessly, the apartheid regime gave SAB the go-ahead.[93] Soon after the 1982 Soccer World Cup, SAB approached international players who had made headlines and invited them to join an SAB-sponsored team to play against South African teams. The white South African press was enthusiastic. Sy Lerman, who had recently won SAB's Journalist of the Year Award, spelled out the brewing company's vision of the tour.[94] The SAB International XI was a "long awaited breakthrough tour" that would "pierce the effects of South Africa's FIFA [Fédération Internationale de Football Association] imposed international isolation." It would afford black players an opportunity to overcome their "limitations" and test their "nerve and composure" against international competitors.[95] More crassly commercial objectives also informed this initiative. As Varda Burstyn has pointed out, sponsors favored star-studded teams for their capacity to organize and exploit their audiences.[96] From this perspective, SAB's modus operandi in cobbling together a team of well-known players was an old trick.

Lerman celebrated SAB's defiance of the antiapartheid sports lobby and welcomed the international stars in a racialized discourse. Argentine World Cup players Osvaldo Ardiles and Mario Kempes, he predicted, would contribute "aura, glamour and grandeur" to the team while "Third World player" Tscheu La Ling of Indonesia and "Black British player Calvin Plummer" would add a "strong element of curiosity."[97] The tour was announced in full-page newspaper advertisements that celebrated Lion Lager—"Now, the Lion's share of World Cup soccer comes to South Africa." The players were introduced to the public through teaser advertisements that paired the brand with the physical attributes and skills of the foreign stars. Under the Lion Lager logo, each player was identified by a single feature of his sporting prowess as the bylines asked rhetorically, "Can anyone match the skillful striker Tscheu la Ling?" or "Can anyone outperform skilled defender Ivan Golac?" or "Can anyone outreach ace defender Dave Watson?" A few days later, a leading Johannesburg newspaper announced that "due to an error in the *Rand Daily Mail* advertisement department[,] 'teaser' ads were placed on 14 July announcing that Hans van Breukelen, Tscheu la Ling and Justin Fasham would be taking part in the tour—in fact they will not be taking part."[98] The tour was in trouble.

Even as SAB paraded the international players who came to South Africa in public and Osvaldo Ardiles, the Argentine World Cup player, and his teammate Mario Kempes were fêted at a launch party, the press headlines read: "Ardiles Warned: Don't Play, as Row Hots Up." Tottenham Hotspur, Ardiles's club, had apparently told him that "his career would be in jeopardy if he went ahead with the six-match rebel soccer tour of South Africa."[99] Six Southampton players failed to show up; British football clubs had been encouraged to recall their players by Labour MP Denis Howell. South Africa was undermining international sporting authorities and "didn't care a tinker's cuss" about the Commonwealth games, he said.[100] The British Parliament condemned the tour as "phoney," and the English Football Association launched an inquiry into what action should be taken against those who chose to participate.[101] The day before the tour kicked off, the Argentines and Brazilian Jose Dirceu withdrew, leaving the SAB XI with only twelve players to draw on. The opening match was a damp squib—a goalless draw with "amateurish" refereeing that was watched by a mere 8,000 spectators.[102]

There was more to come. On 17 July, Soweto's glamour clubs, Orlando Pirates, Moroka Swallows, and Kaizer Chiefs, also pulled out of the tour. SAB scurried about looking for a black team to play against its SAB XI team. On 18 July, they got hold of Amazulu, who had played a National Professional Soccer League (NPSL) match in the morning and asked them to stand in for Pirates in the afternoon. As anti-apartheid crowds outside the stadium chanted "mercenaries," Amazulu lost 1 to 0 to the SAB XI in front of a paltry crowd of 5,000.[103] Sy Lerman was furious with the teams that withdrew. "Brutus, immortalised as the back-stabber who headed the queue to plunge a dagger into Julius Caesar's back[,] must have moved over in his grave yesterday and reserved room for Orlando Pirates, Iwisa Kaizer Chiefs and Moroka Swallows," he wrote. Unable to stop himself from thrusting the racist knife, he added: "Their withdrawal has not helped the antiapartheid cause at all and has harmed SA soccer mortally. No outsider can help but wonder what madness, immaturity and irresponsibility now grips black-controlled South African football. ... And don't put the blame on pressure from political organisations. They did their job as they had to! But they have pressurised soccer before and been rebuffed."[104]

While Lerman continued to look for soccer officials who might save the tour, SAB, embarrassed by the "squabbling, opposition and outcry, both locally and overseas," wanted to end the venture as quickly as possible.[105] The SAB XI played one final game against a Transvaal team before the tour collapsed. George Thabe, president of the NPSL and erstwhile supporter of the tour, announced its demise, citing "feelings against the tour" by some blacks.[106] SAB marketing director Peter Savory admitted that "the level of support for the tour among players and football followers alike was nowhere near that which had been anticipated."[107] The men at SAB and their most-favored journalist had got it wrong. Members of the soccer clubs had mixed feelings. Abe Machele of Moroka Swallows said, "It would have been suicidal to go through with the tour." The club had underestimated the opposition to the tour, and their fans would have stayed away. But John Mabaso of Orlando Pirates expressed unhappiness at the cancellation of the tour and the way sport had become embroiled in politics.[108]

The cancellation of the tour was clearly a victory for the antiapartheid movement. Lekgau Mathabane, a director of National Food Distributors and a member of Soweto's Committee of Ten, which was comprised of influential black businessmen, said:

> The black community—who account for about 70% of SAB's sales—feel that the company should be brought to book for its involvement in the tour. SAB either disregarded black views on buying SA into international sport or did not take the time to even find out. It should have known all along that the South African Council of Sports (SACOS) has been opposed to it.[109]

Kehla Mthemba, chairman of the Azanian African Peoples Organisation, explained that ten mostly black political organizations had been opposed to the rebel tour. Mthemba was quoted as saying that "most of the black community" was "well aware that the tour was an attempt to lull them into believing the situation in South Africa was being normalised. But," he added, "our opposition has proved to ourselves and the world that we still have our pride and dignity." Moreover, he denied that organizations opposed to the tour used condescension or threats. "The clubs were appealed to as black people living in South Africa."[110] Mthemba's appeal to soccer organizers for black dignity and pride had been highly successful. The men who heard his call did not necessarily subscribe to black consciousness ideology; that they had not been consulted about the tour was sufficient evidence of a callous disregard of black views. For Mthemba, complicity and resistance were elements of a discourse that stemmed from subjectivities as well as from politics.

Opposition also came from organizations aligned with nonracial ideology. These organizations decried the manipulation of black sportsmen for the purposes of window-dressing apartheid. The South African Non-Racial Olympic Committee (SANROC), an antiapartheid group based in London, celebrated the stand of the South African teams that refused to participate in the SAB tour. "The time has come to take stock and realise that black footballers are no longer pawns in a game played to make apartheid look respectable," SANROC members felt. They urged South Africans to look toward the African Football Confederation for leadership rather than to "a made-up team of European has-beens" coming in through the "back-door."[111] SAB's commitment to paying the international players the full contracted sum of R50,000 must have provided little comfort to the troubled players.

Black newspaper readers were incensed at the arrogance of journalist Sy Lerman, whom they lambasted for "ramming his views down our throats"; they decried rebel tours as serving the interests of "that multi-million rand organisation SAB which makes its money out of the black man's sweat and his thirst."[112] They called on SAB to get its priorities right and spend money on humanitarian causes or on workers' wages rather than squandering millions on rebel tours.[113] With somewhat different priorities, white readers expressed fear that the price of beer would increase to cover the one million rand SAB had to pay out for the disastrous tour.[114] SAB went out of its way to nip such fears in the bud and rebuild its public image. The SAB Community Trust, which supported health, welfare, and education projects, was "far ahead of the field in South Africa," the company claimed.[115] Moreover, SAB reassured the sporting fraternity that its sponsorship policy would not change, despite the fiasco of the tour. "The community helps us and we wish to help the community," SAB's top marketing executive said, relying on an abstract notion of community as market. The company developed a set of guidelines that it hoped might remind its managers of the need to talk to black men rather than acting on their behalf. It declared that SAB would support only sports that appealed to spectators and tours that contributed to the development of the sport. SAB would require sporting bodies to consult players and supporters to ensure that events were "in the total interest of the total community," and in the future sponsorship would be "totally integrated in every sense."[116] While black women remained silent throughout this conversation, they formed a significant component of the SAB community—the number of women drinkers in Soweto alone exceeded the number of white male drinkers in South Africa as a whole.[117]

Negative press continued to dog SAB after the tour. A leading business journal distanced itself from SAB's high-handed approach. "It might be appropriate to grant a course in market research for SA Breweries executives who totally misread black attitudes to the disastrous tour of the SAB international soccer team," jeered the *Financial Mail*.[118] SAB's Gary May fingered the media as partly responsible for the fiasco.[119] The *Rand Daily Mail* offered up a little self-criticism, acknowledging that SAB's rebel tour had exposed "deep divisions in feeling and outlook" and that the basic lesson to be learned was that "whether through arrogance or ignorance, it is dangerous to take black views for granted." The editor concluded, "The lesson goes well beyond the soccer field."[120]

SAB had hoped that sponsorship of the rebel soccer tour would promote multiracial sport. Instead, its efforts demonstrated the vulnerability of economically powerful white men in the process of reconfiguring the nation. SAB retreated from the politics of sport, confining reform to its own organizational and production processes. But antiapartheid resistance forged ahead. By the mid-1980s, South Africa was in the grips of a low-intensity civil war. Successive states of emergency were declared, giving the apartheid regime the right to use the armed forces and police against the people. While the militarization of society made a sham of reform, the reality that apartheid was collapsing created the possibility of institutional defiance of racist regulations such as university segregation. Liberal institutions such as the University of Cape Town began to admit a few black students, changing the demography of the campus and the character of protest.

Hypermasculinity and Beer Culture among White University Students

Through beer drinking and mass spectator sport, masculinity was charged with a particular intensity, or hypermasculinity, which Varda Burstyn defines as a master narrative of "erotic, heroic, masculine idealisations."[121] Competitive student sports, particularly intervarsity contests, provide a window on the making of a hypermasculine culture. At annual contests between the rugby teams of rival English and Afrikaans universities, players and spectators were infused with deep competitiveness and youthful exuberance, lubricated by massive beer sponsorship. In the mid-1980s, in the context of heightened political awareness, antiapartheid resistance, and apartheid reform, the institution of intervarsity sport and the hypermasculine culture that it fostered came under attack.

With its emphasis on the "rough masculinist traits of stamina, strength, speed and courage," rugby had for almost a century provided a suitable site for a contest over racial virility, cultural superiority, and power between Boer and Brit.[122] Since its inception in 1911, the annual intervarsity clash between the University of Cape Town (UCT) and Stellenbosch University was a highly charged, intensely racist masculinist moment in the university sporting and social calendar, an event with national reverberations.[123] Fueled by heavy beer drinking, intervarsity activity dominated much of campus life for six weeks in the run-up to the rugby match. It was a ritual that included sing-song, drinking contests, beer fests, and a final "groot brag" party in the week before the game built "a whole supporting network for the team up to the day, to the event, to the occasion."[124] UCT cheerleader Joey Burke explained:

> You know, to get a seat on the sing-song stand for intervarsity you had to make sure that you attended so many practices. Songs like "Virgins of Varsity—Come friends, There'll always be Immorality here, Sexuality here, Men of the sex-starved clan are we, Standing on the sides of Fuller Hall, Virgins of Varsity, Here's an invitation, To win your admiration, To hell with masturbation, Come friends"—these kind of songs were fantastic. And we had a band playing the music and there was a vibe— everybody was wearing scarves—everybody got a package with the scarves and a hat—these were sponsored by SA Breweries— Ohlsson's would be UCT and Stellenbosch would be Lion Lager. It was a contrast of colours: blue and white against maroon. I have never seen a whole university come together and support a crowd like that with such uniformity. Whether it was the alcohol that did it or not the fact of the matter is that the spirit of UCT was unbelievable. It was a seriously crazy culture. It was a culture within a culture—that rough macho stuff and alcohol.[125]

Men's residences where house committees ran initiation practices were the principal sites for hypermasculine, beer-swilling, erotic male behavior:

> When I was initiated onto house com, I had to drink down-downs and then they tied me to the revolving doors of [women's residence].[126] And then Campus Control came, and they untied me and said "Run for your life, Campus Control's here." And then I was running back to my room with Campus Control behind me. I spun round the revolving door, went upstairs into somebody's room that I didn't even know. He said, "What are you doing?" You can imagine, this naked guy, barging into one of the rooms. Cos not everybody participated you know. There were quite a few, a lot of people were appalled you know. And we

also had to sing to the girls with candles in our underpants, you know, for this whole committee thing.

Handling the entertainment portfolio on house committee also meant organizing the annual beer race.

> It was a running race. They used to start from one point, one drinking spot on campus, then move to the next spot, down your beer, move to the next stop then take off your clothes and move to the next one and down your beer and get more and more and more drunk around the campus. By the time you finished, you were absolutely plastered. Gone. It was quite a scene.[127]

After the race, the crowd converged on the residence pubs.

> I mean, it was, when we did the entertainment, if you didn't drink, you were not part of the whole entertainment. It was compulsory basically to drink, no matter what. Drinking was initiation as a student. You had to drink up. When I was entertainment chairman for the first year, everything was related around drinking. There were always down-down competitions, always in the res pubs. We all had our own pubs. There was serious sexism that went on in the pubs. Only certain chicks were allowed to come into the pub. It was very much a macho, a kind of male macho scene. The chicks allowed were only chicks from next door, and they had to be, like, the girlfriends of House Committee members.[128]

The presence of women at interresidence "down-down" parties provided a key element of hypermasculine entertainment. Writing in the student newspaper, one young reporter captured the spirit of the moment:

> Individuals were losing themselves fast and furiously. Women were doing their best to become appendages of men and the men couldn't wait. What a dog show, what a dog show. Boys chanted, "On your back! On your back! On your back! Baxter girls are virgins!" followed by, "Come friends, there'll always be immorality here" and "Waltzing Matilda, Waltzing Matilda, Waltzing Matilda!" Down, down, down!

A bottle of Tassies (cheap Tassenberg wine) was offered to the first woman to identify herself as a virgin; this challenge had "male participants unable to contain themselves, chanting challenges to the blushing winner to end her predicament."[129]

Some female students were apparently "willing" participants in this misogynistic play, perhaps as Bourdieu suggests, because they had internalized the powerful effects of male domination and were acting out of a desire for acceptance, in the same way that sociologists have observed of students at fraternity houses in the United States.[130] Other women students objected strongly, pointing out that the "beer swilling macho culture" of intervarsity projected women as "objects available to satisfy men's lust." They wanted, instead, a culture "that doesn't degrade women and in which women and men feel equally comfortable to participate."[131] This demand was supported by SATISCO, a black student organization dedicated to transformation in sport that saw the drinking culture at white universities as neither inclusive nor able to build nonracial student unity. In 1989, the newly constituted women's movement confronted the Intervarsity Committee. Cheerleader Joey Burke recalls:

> Women's Movement summoned Intervarsity and said: "This is highly macho and what are you going to do to change the sexism of intervarsity? How are you going to accommodate the women of UCT?" And I said, "Well, first of all, we've started having female cheerleaders," and they said, "Yes, so what about it?" So I said, "Can you tell me what the issues are?" And they said, "Waltzing Matilda, f___ little Hilda" and there were others. And I said, "OK, no problem, we'll stop it." And they said, "How are you going to stop it?" And I said, "I can't stop the students from singing that song but I can put a ban in place. I can say that the Women's Movement has requested that we don't sing this song and it's no longer in the sing-song books." So we took it out. But the minute a student went on stage, they started singing it. It wasn't the cheerleader, it was the other students. I used to say, "Sorry, I can't be cheerleader," and I would try another song and they used to drown me out. But we were summonsed. The Women's Movement summonsed us.[132]

The rugby fraternity was unrepentant. That they acted in the interests of male domination explains little. Rather, as Bourdieu argues, we need to understand that men are under great pressure to take up the challenge of "pursuing glory and distinction in the public sphere" while demonstrating prowess in the sexual and reproductive sphere. This "exaltation of masculine values," Bourdieu points out, is constantly threatened by the "fear and anxiety aroused by femininity," generating a vulnerability that "leads to sometimes frantic investment in all the masculine games of violence, such as sports in modern societies, and most especially those which most tend to produce the visible signs of masculinity."[133] Since manliness "must be validated by other men," individual men may behave in ways that spring from "the fear of losing the respect or admiration of the group."[134] Men become trapped in this exalted masculinity.

Certainly the men at the helm of the two universities allowed space for a hypermasculine culture to flourish, defending its practices and protecting those who, on occasion, fell afoul of university regulations. But they also had to answer to concerned parents and take note of the rapidly changing political and social sentiments sweeping the country. Both institutions recognized that the future of intervarsity, at least in the short term, rested on the ability of the male students to contain their drunken and unruly behavior. As sponsor of intervarsity at the two universities, SAB took its share of responsibility by promoting the "buddy system," which encouraged designated drivers to stay sober to drive their buddies home.[135] Warned not to overstep the line, students at the 1989 match concentrated less on beer and more on the cheerleader, whose "wild antics" had him "skidding across the floor on his chin."[136] Burke's leadership inspired great singing and chanting. Spirits were high. Delighted that calls from a minority of students to boycott intervarsity sports had not led to a poor turnout, one wise guy called out, "UCT spirit beats the shift to the left," and the crowd responded, "Shift to the right!"[137] Beyond the rugby stadium, student politics continued to shift to the left as student action against conscription and political repression escalated.[138] The year of the 1989 match, even the Moderate Student Movement passed a resolution calling for an end to the state of emergency and the repeal of apartheid legislation. Finding himself in disagreement, one student announced that he would leave the room and "go and fetch a beer."[139]

Match day, fueled by the intense emotion of deep play, fired the spirit of hypermasculinism. Like the Balinese cockfighting contests described by anthropologist Clifford Geertz, intervarsity rugby provided a moment for men to come together and imagine, perform, and celebrate masculinity. It was an intense moment of risk and competition, generating a language of sexual innuendo, male prowess, and aggression. Both on and off the field, men who participated tested and affirmed their masculine esteem.[140] In 1990, the intervarsity teams were unusually evenly matched. At half-time a score of 12 to 13 added to the intensity. UCT appeared to have won, and seconds before the final whistle, cheerleader Joey Burke raised his arms to signal victory. Hundreds of students rushed onto the pitch in wild ecstasy. As UCT's captain yelled, "Get these students off the f_____ pitch!" Burke spun into action. "In thirty seconds, I had the students back behind the touchline," he recalled.[141] Moments later the final whistle blew and UCT celebrated a glorious game.

The winning players became symbols of a victorious masculinity. "Varsity's success was built on flair, imagination, innovation and on-the-field organisation," raved Michael Owen Smith of the *Cape Times*. They "did everything at top speed and this, really, was their key to victory." Intervarsity rugby was a "great place for stars to be born."[142] "How lovely to see UCT heroes Michael Kirsten and Lance Sherrell being hoisted shoulder high by deliriously happy Ikey students. Sherrell in particular savoured the moment, punching the air in delight and staying on the field with his supporters long after the final whistle had sounded," rhapsodized a letter to the editor.[143] "They should erect a monument to fifteen brave men at the UCT rugby club," wrote Willem van de Putte on the sports page. He reported how spectators too had engaged in deep play at the match, singing "We will, we will, rock you!" as the stadium resounded with their voices. Brushing aside behavioral excess, van de Putte added, "And who can blame the ecstatic supporters who streamed on to the pitch with two minutes remaining if they woke up with thudding headaches yesterday morning."[144]

Burke, the leader of intervarsity's deep play, had "wowed out."[145] But the moment was poignant. "I knew that when I left, that was the end. The end of that singing culture. And it was, basically. It was the end of that big, huge era. . . . All that whiteness."[146] Intervarsity rugby contests stopped with the advent of democracy in 1994. When competitive sporting arrangements between universities resumed, they did so under an entirely different regime.[147]

However, rugby remained a key marker of manliness and status among white students. In February 2008, a talented young Afrikaner musician, the son of a philosophy lecturer, took part in an international piano competition in the Z. K. Matthews Hall at Pretoria University. He won the contest. When adjudicators announced his name, "everybody jumped up" and cheered. "It was like a rugby match," the winner said with a grin.[148] The auditorium's symbolic transformation into a sports stadium affirmed a potent masculinity.

Like most other aspects of social life, the story of bottled beer in the 1980s is bound up with wider political conflicts. Mobilized in shebeens, breweries, and sports stadiums and on university campuses, activists confronted the authority of those in power. At the same time, they challenged the behavior of dominant men and criticized their ideas about appropriate masculine behavior. By putting forward alternative visions of what it meant to be a man, they claimed a new authority for themselves. Shebeeners lobbied for licenses and called for recognition as legitimate businessmen. Brewery workers confronted their employers and asserted the authority and power that came with trade union solidarity. Activists opposed to breaking the sport boycott claimed pride and dignity for black men as they blocked the SAB rebel soccer tour. Progressive students opposed to the hypermasculine drinking culture at a liberal white university insisted that alternative understandings of masculinity would enhance sociability among men and between men and women. Framed by a sense of impending political change, these political engagements provided opportunities to enunciate visions of a future, transformed beer culture.

six

Heritage and Beer Tourism: Reimagining Beer after Apartheid

In the politically fragile moment of negotiations during the transition toward democracy, the meaning of beer, like the meaning of nation, was unstable. Democratic elections brought apartheid to an end and ushered in a majority African government, but they did not automatically bring forth a new South African nation. There was no ready-made narrative that might provide a guiding fiction for a nonracial, multicultural nationalism.[1] While postapartheid South Africa had yet to imagine itself as a community, national identity remained in flux, the subject of constant rhetorical struggle.[2] Many interested groups, some more organized and powerful than others, jostled to promote their own understandings of the past. Defining heritage became a critical activity as vested interests inside and outside the state sought to translate their own meanings into land claims, marketable products, public monuments, or places of entertainment.[3] The moment provided an opportunity for beer producers to extend the use of heritage beyond the branding of single products.

Commercial uses of heritage, Patrick Wright argues, lift aspects of history out of their contexts and restage and display them as events, images, or ideas.[4] From this perspective, the power of heritage is not so much its association with the past as its "immediacy and givenness."[5] As J. E. Tunbridge and E. J. Ashworth put it, heritage in commercial usage is "a contemporary commodity purposefully created to satisfy contemporary consumption";

the past is imagined as a "variety of possibilities, each shaped for the requirements of specific consumer groups."[6] A utilitarian view of history as commercial heritage is widely accepted in the drinks industry. As a Coca-Cola archivist put it, "The only utility for history lies in its pragmatic business applications."[7]

Establishing the commercial meaning of beer entailed more than the celebration of beer as an example of capitalist success. It entailed, at least in part, negotiating competing narratives of the place of beer in society. In the early 1990s, the narrative of beer as a source of colonial revenue and exploitation dominated public culture in South Africa. This story of state-run beer halls and opposition to them was captured as heritage in the Kwa Muhle Museum in Durban, the city that had pioneered municipal control of sorghum beer brewing for the purposes of revenue collection in 1908.[8] The museum's objectives were spelled out in its mission statement: "This is a museum about power and powerlessness and the struggle for dignity by ordinary people. Let this never be forgotten. Let us be mindful of the abuses of the past and celebrate the human capacity, in all its diversity and richness, to overcome."[9]

SAB, the nation's producer of clear beer, sought to construct a rather different narrative of the meaning of beer for the people. For SAB, municipal beer halls and police raids in search of illegal liquor constituted a folk narrative, a prehistory to its own story of clear beer as heritage. The corporation used the opportunity of its centenary in 1995 to establish a monument to bottled beer as the nation's longest-standing popular drink and so claim a place close to the heart of the new nation. SAB constructed two heritage landscapes: a visitors' center in Johannesburg and a national monument in Cape Town. Their purpose was to create "something highly visible and long lasting that would encapsulate SAB heritage and carry it forward" and so celebrate the nation's people as an embodied market.[10] This initiative was part of a move toward constructing a corporate brand identity as SAB concentrated increasingly on the core business of beer brewing. The corporate brand would project a past about beer that had meaning for the present.

For SAB, this meant celebrating itself as a capitalist enterprise. In 1990, SAB's in-house magazine, *Beer Business,* reprinted an article from the press for the benefit of the black retail trade. "Three cheers for capitalism," read the original headline. "SA Breweries, our only sizeable brewer, is the archetypal private sector monopoly. . . . White socialists in Pretoria impose discriminatory taxes on it; black socialists cite it as the sort of company that must be nationalized 'in the public interest.'"[11] In fact, the article continued, SAB was a great economic asset, providing jobs and substantial sums in income taxes, excise duties, general sales taxes, and utility levies to the national coffers. "Any guesses on how much it would cost the State if it were nationalised?" asked the journalist.[12] These statements spelled out how SAB saw itself. Deftly worked by those skilled in representing commerce as public culture, such ideas would be woven into SAB's tale of beer brewing as a national heritage.

Black purveyors of alcohol—shebeeners, taverners, bottle-store owners, and distributors—also took up the opportunity to define and market a heritage associated with bottled beer and its consumption. Shebeens were becoming popular tourist destinations for visitors in search of authentic black experiences. Black businessmen responded by establishing shebeen routes through which they linked township drinking spots to a past of protest and a new nation of entrepreneurial initiative. Shebeens became lived heritage landscapes—socioscapes[13]—where visitors might spend time drinking (and eating) with African people in a township. Shebeen routes offered an indigenous experience, an alternative to the colonial wine routes of the Western Cape. They hooked into mythical accounts of shebeen queens that highlighted African resilience and feisty female initiative.[14] Thus, in the commercial beer industry, heritage signified emotion, the "intangible ideas and feelings" of sociability, nostalgia, and camaraderie. It was less about the poignancy of black working-class suffering than it was about the romance of sociable drinking under apartheid.

The SAB World of Beer: The Market as Heritage

As the year of the centenary of the SAB, 1995 was an auspicious moment for the making of heritage. For senior marketing manager Bruce Starke, it was an opportunity to celebrate 100 years of SAB and give something back to the people. Casting about for an appropriate way of bringing a narrative and its audience together, Starke led a group of employees on a tour of brewery museums and visitors' centers in Japan, Ireland, the United States, and Netherlands. These corporate museums were places of commerce, edification, and pleasure. In them, distinctions between mercantile display and public exhibition were blurred and Disney-style "imagineering" created opportunities for visitors to experience carefully presented aspects of the themes of the museums.[15] The SAB group observed that Ireland's Guinness museum was housed in a historical building. At the Heineken museum, they saw Louis Pasteur as a hologram welcoming visitors and went on a simulated bone-rattling conveyer belt, their bodies becoming bottles as they sped to the corking point.

On its return, the study group faced the challenge of selecting a place. While Cape Town's Victoria and Albert Waterfront was the country's busiest tourist spot with over six million visitors annually, the place had no particular association with beer or with SAB.[16] A historic malt house at the Newlands Brewery site in Cape Town reverberated with corporate history, but the Cape was cut off from the African market, secluded behind a mythical curtain of seaweed. It was not home to SAB's most popular brand, and its own Ohlsson's Lager was in deep trouble in the mid-1990s.[17] Castle Lager and Charles Glass, SAB's largest brand and its original brewer, were associated with the Witwatersrand near Johannesburg, locus of the corporation's major market. Greater Johannesburg, a city of seven million people, was South Africa's gateway to the African continent, and SAB decided to locate its Centenary Centre in the center of an imagined post-apartheid future city. SAB secured a 99-year lease in Newtown, Johannesburg, site of a new cultural precinct and urban renewal initiative, and selected an internationally acclaimed company to design the space.

On a business trip to the United States, Starke pushed a letter under the door at the offices of the creators of architectural firm Staples and Charles, which had designed The World of Coca-Cola. Staples and Charles agreed to construct a heritage landscape for SAB in Newtown, Johannesburg. Choosing this prestigious design team did not imply that SAB wanted to mimic The World of Coca-Cola, the soft drink giant's museum in Atlanta, Georgia. Rather, SAB's museum would explain the brewing process in detail.[18] SAB wanted its Centenary Centre to convey a message that combined production, branding, and consumption. The Centenary Centre would show that beer brewing had a long and progressive history and future, that beer was brewed with skill and care, and that consumers could judge its quality and identify the characteristics of their preferred brands. SAB executives believed that the heritage landscape should be a place of fun that engaged its visitors; it should not be a "read-only" space.[19] In response to these goals, the architects created a plan that experimented with exhibition furniture, props, and interactive moments to create a place of entertainment and spectacle as well as provide information. They combined scientific detail with historical re-creations and imitations. Their images, models, and dioramas constructed synergies between beer commerce, natural landscapes, and local cultures. The men at SAB's Beer Division were so impressed with the plans that they doubled the budget after the architects presented their concept.[20]

Let us take a walk through the Centenary Centre (now The SAB World of Beer) in the mid-1990s. A banner that says "Making beer, making friends" greets those who enter the center, dwarfing Harry Moyaga's bust of Nelson Mandela at the entrance. Like a fairy tale, the story begins at the beginning; Hathor's Hall, the first exhibition space, sets out a myth of origin; "Ancient Egypt" is the cradle of African brewing. A puppet show, both parody and promotion of the meanings associated with beer consumption, tells a tale of an Egyptian goddess who prevented death and war. Defying instructions to kill her people's enemy, Hathor danced, sang, and drank herself into oblivion. Her temple in Mesopotamia, land of pharaohs and enchanting goddesses, became a place of beer and friendship. Enter an explorer, Dr. Sompisi, a short black sub-Saharan figure dressed as a colonial archeologist in pith helmet, khaki shorts, and long socks. He comes upon the temple that bears the inscription "Let he who enters here be eternally refreshed" and meets Hathor, temptress of the Nile, represented as a large irresistible bovine with a feminine human body to appeal to a stereotyped fantasy of African men: wealth in cattle and a nubile beer brewer. The horns on the goddess's head contract sensuously as her flirtation with Sompisi becomes more risqué. "Holy cow! My mother warned me about women like this," he exclaims. The words play on European drinking songs while the goddess disappears to "slip into something more comfortable" and returns without her bovine head. "Oh! Inkosi yam! She sure has stood the test of time," groans Sompisi in punning mock ecstasy. "Your Castle or mine?" The puppet show is a sophisticated piece of design engineering and creativity, but its public reception has been "mixed," often provoking strong reactions. "People either love it or hate it," said the manager of the center.[21]

The bright light of the Egyptian room dims as we move into sub-Saharan Africa, represented by the Ukhamba Chamber ("*ukhamba*" means "clay drinking vessel"). Chairs are laid out in front of a screen that fills with tropical greenery, domed grass huts, and bare-breasted women at the press of a button. This fecund naturescape of home-brewed sorghum is presented as authentic "African tradition." Nobantu (a name that means "of the people"), a buxom African woman, prepares clay pots and explains that beer is an African woman's power. Since men ranked their wives and mistresses by the quality of their brew, beer making was competitive. "You can judge the hospitality of a woman by the size of her sorghum granary," Nobantu tells us. Beer maintains gender order; it signals women's desire to please men and their submission to male control. This view, narrated by a distinctly un-African voice, ignores the use of beer to regulate male hierarchies of power and avoids the significance of beer as libation for the ancestors.[22] Like the tale of Egyptian brewing, it rests on the idea of an adult male heterosexual fantasy. It conveys a key assumption of commercial beer producers: good brewers make beer that tastes good and pleases men. A gourd of sorghum beer at the foot of the screen offers a taste of traditional brew.

Lured by melodies of European tavern tunes expunged of lyrics (which have the potential to be divisive in their cultural specificity and disruptive of the notion of beer as a universal drink), visitors enter the European gallery. Replicas of beer tankards and other items showcase fine European handicraft and portray beer as the drink of Belgian kings. The chronological tale of European brewing begins in medieval monasteries, mixing sacred and profane in one tun.[23] It culminates in the invention of modern brewing science by Louis Pasteur, "researcher of fermentation and diseases of beer, discoverer of microbes that cause some beer to spoil," a narrator tells us. Emerging from the cavernous gloom of old Europe, we enter the Green House, where hops and barley grow toward the sun. This naturescape, complete with a waterfall and a fish pond, creates a naturalized utopian zone. Inviting visitors to taste and smell the hops and barley, it engages the senses and affirms the narrative of beer as a wholesome beverage.

Heritage Hall is the place where prehistory ends and SAB's corporate heritage begins. Under a banner that reads "When gold is found, breweries follow," the narrative of Heritage Hall quickly dispenses with Cape colonial brewing to focus on the Witwatersrand. Charles Glass, purveyor of Castle Lager among mine workers, is singled out as the original brewmaster. His portrait adorns the wall of an elegant nineteenth-century office, and the brewer himself comes to the window in hologram form. Annoyed by the interruption of a visitor, the irascible brewer abruptly pulls down the blind. Outside his office, handcrafted beer barrels, corking machines, brass hydrometers, and copper beer-sampling flasks combine historical artifacts with objects replicated for the exhibit.[24] As we move further into this room, the passage of time is conveyed through a 1920s-era delivery van parked outside a pub. A replicated colonial bar completes a streetscape and invites contemplation of what lured British miners from the coal pits of Wales and Cornwall to the dusty gold mines of the reef. In an image on the barroom wall, Russian strongman George Hackenschmidt lifts a barrel of Castle Stout on a visit to South Africa before World War I. We are encouraged to interact with the exhibit with an invitation to lift similar beer barrels at the pub door. This pairing of beer and macho masculinity assumes a homosocial beer culture and implies a natural link between masculine sociability and macho men.

The sound of metal chafing on metal lures us toward the dim light of a replicated underground mineshaft where almost-life-sized miners who are effaced of racial characteristics shovel gravel, load trolleys, and heave ore in a diorama of a relentlessly repetitive and thirst-generating labor process. Props are positioned to link mine work, beer drinking and sociability. Opposite the diorama of the mineshaft a sign reads "Warning: This road passes through proclaimed Bantu locations," and beyond it is a replica of a 1960s shebeen, the drinking hole of African workers in apartheid townships.[25] "In the sometimes harsh politics of South Africa, 'spots' like this offered their customers special oases of hospitality and community," reads the publicity brochure. A plaque attests to the social service rendered by the shebeen queen: "In her house, despite periodic police harassment, life had a sense of normalcy—a place where friends could meet, share views, discuss politics, and relax with a beer and some good music." This sympathetic view of she-beens reflects popular understandings of shebeening as economic survival, sociability, and defiance. It contrasts sharply with the colonial association of shebeening with criminality and with the vulnerability of shebeeners described by a supporter of the campaign for their legalization as "people with not much status in their community."[26]

The image of the successful shebeen located in the front room of a respectable family living in a substandard township house is a contrived but nonetheless iconic image of the past.[27] Photographs on the walls of the shebeen at The World of Beer depict several generations of Western education and gender order in the family—a bespectacled couple poses formally for a studio photograph and a young bride wears a white dress. Shiny ceramic ornaments are displayed on a gleaming sideboard, and empty chairs arranged against the walls, coffee tables littered with empty quart bottles, and ashtrays jammed with cigarette butts suggest an evening of "loading the table" with quarts of lager. The kitchen, where drinkers who are less well-to-do imbibe, is littered with empty sorghum cartons. There is no loading of the table here: the kitchen offered a less convivial ambience for sorghum drinkers, who were often newly urbanized and poor. Social demarcations within and between shebeens indicate the extent to which drinkers adhered to ideas about social stratification, defying apartheid's leveling of black people into a uniform working class. They demonstrated that even in the city, beer drinking was encoded by social rules, albeit newly invented.[28]

There are no physical bodies in the shebeen, but voices can be heard. The languid drone of men's drawling is set against combative female voices. The women talk about troublesome men—both lovers and husbands—and the hopefulness of a young couple about to marry. Their chatter is interrupted by quarrelsome customers. "I said to him, 'This is my place, I built it' . . . I am so angry." Then suddenly, "OK, OK, guys. Please! Come on, come on!" followed by more talk of the upcoming wedding. It is clear that gender relations are conflictual. Gone is the playful harmony of the utopian gender order set out in the Ukhamba chamber. The shebeeners' voices allow for the possibility of engagement with the display and convey a sense of polyphonic chatter. Produced by the advertising agency HerdBouys, these shebeen conversations invite visitors to ponder the complex ways that industrialization, migrant labor, and dealing in alcohol shaped men's and women's lives. In their contempt for their customers and (by implication) their own line of business, the agitated shebeeners momentarily disrupt the capitalist discourse of supply and demand that runs through the SAB metanarrative. These powerfully authentic sound bites reconstruct scenes that convey social relations and so allow visitors to engage with the representations of the past. But they do so without undermining the commercial objectives of the heritage landscape; the narrative remains compatible with corporate discourse.

On the second floor of the building, the visitor is taken through SAB's rendition of "the modern art and science of brewing" that was prefigured downstairs by earlier generations of European brewers and scientists. The brewing process is demonstrated using kettles of burnished copper once used for commercial brewing. A sensation of scale is generated by the size of the giant copper vessels—a mash tun (where maize and malt are mixed), a lauter tun (which acts as a sieve), and a wort kettle (in which malt and hops are combined). Windows cut through the copper invite visitors to peer into the fermenting, mixing, mashing, and boiling of ingredients in the giant cauldrons. Nearby, a cross-section of finely magnified barley grains heightens the contrasts in scale. Brewing is rendered playful by the grinning faces of Bongani the biochemist and Bert the brewer, who perform a contrived duet on a small television screen mounted against a mash tun. Bongani talks the language of science and Bert presents the art of brewing. "Stealing the Castle recipe? Over a century's experience is a blooming difficult thing to steal," quips one. The duet culminates in the recitation of the elements of a good-quality lager: "Good head, clarity, aroma, classic lager taste." At this point in the tour, the visitor may experience a sense that artificial dialogue, gadgetry, and gimmickry have created a "pastiched and collaged" scenario of corporate self-promotion.[29]

SAB beer brands are introduced as personalities in a simulated gaming area set up on a mezzanine floor. Video terminals in carrels screen recent television advertisements of each brand. In the mid-1990s, the message across all brands was one of multiracial sociability and national pride.[30] Brand advertisements were simple, feel-good messages of sociability, offering easy access to a new national identity. There was no neat fit between this message and the lived past, however. While The World of Beer constructs an inclusive narrative featuring African people, women, and members of the working class, it stops short of mapping the complexities of social relations in beer history. Framed by the commercial objectives of the center, the installations, displays, and storyboards leave little space for engaging a genuinely critical history.[31]

A corporate film is the grand finale of the tour. As at The World of Coca-Cola, the theatre doors close automatically and the lights go out. The opening sequence achieves a shock effect. Roaring wind, deafening thunder, and electrifying lightning burst into the darkened room. In the calm that follows, a virgin landscape yields the natural ingredients of beer—water, hops, and barley. "We who know this land understand the soul of Africa," the narrator booms. "We are a vital force, an energy indivisible from the essence of this land. That force may blow beyond our borders, but we will always remain the brewers of Africa." This all-powerful conquest of the African landscape is the central thread in the film's narrative. It is presented through the subnarratives of black magic and white technology that cast SAB as brewers for (rather than of) Africa. The film melds landscape and corporation into a single national symbol of power, creating a sense of "the irreversible historical time of progress."[32] The corporate voice is the voice of god. It signals that "SAB has gone where Rhodes failed to go," eliding imperialism and progress.[33]

The film cuts to the chief executive of SAB, who declares, "At SAB we're fiercely proud of the role we play and the success we've achieved in the tapestry of African life." Juxtaposed with the godlike voice that precedes it, business parlance is anticlimatic; it is a reminder that the film is a mythical representation of corporate power. As the fantasy world of the corporate imaginary recedes, one is reminded that real power is in the hands of SAB's hard-driving executives, crushing competitive strategies, relentless acquisition of assets, and expanding markets across the country, the continent, and the globe. Finally, a pub overlooking Newtown's cultural precinct offers a free beer and a chance to shake off museum fatigue.

Nelson Mandela, first president of democratic South Africa and icon of the antiapartheid struggle, addressed the opening of the SAB Centenary Centre on 15 May 1995. Mandela identified the history of beer as a pathway to national understanding and endorsed the SAB narrative of nation-building. Decrying the liquor industry's exploitation of mine workers and the colonial prohibition of "certain types of liquor," he celebrated shebeens as places of creativity. He praised SAB as a progressive corporation and an economic powerhouse whose employment practices ran counter to apartheid prejudice.[34] The SAB Centenary Centre, like the corporation of which it was the brainchild, was a national economic asset, Mandela said. Its establishment in Johannesburg's inner city created a flagship of urban renewal and a boost to tourism. (Edited out of the printed versions of Mandela's address was the president's admission that he was not a beer drinker himself.)

The Centenary Centre's fortunes were tied up with those of its surroundings. Several years after it opened, the view from its windows brought a dilapidated and unsafe inner city environment into focus. The rundown precinct marked the decline of Johannesburg's urban renewal initiative and served as a reminder of the vulnerability of even the most powerful of corporations to the vicissitudes of politics. Not surprisingly, the corporation's vision of heritage seekers flocking to the center did not immediately materialize.[35] Making the most of its assets, SAB promoted the conference facility at the center. Company groups, predominantly white sports teams and college students, toured the exhibits. Few visitors were black, despite the corporation's initial belief that visitors to the center would be primarily black men between the ages of eighteen and thirty-five.[36] "It's difficult to promote the museum concept in black culture," explained SAB's Windsor Shuenyane, whose task it was to draw blacks to the Centenary Centre. "People in Soweto don't bundle their kids into a taxi and say, 'Today we are going to see the Africa museum or the artists that South Africa has produced.' It is a problem getting blackie to visit a museum." In his view, the absence of a museum culture was a consequence of South Africa's political history. "Up to now, we have resisted getting into museums as museums display the culture of the oppressor. And we don't have a coherent national identity as black South Africans." Nevertheless, Shuenyane believed that much was to be learned about science and industry at the brewing corporation's "museum" sites.[37] Over the next decade, as the Newtown precinct and the city's urban renewal drive picked up, The World of Beer saw itself increasingly as a place of hospitality and began to attract substantial numbers of visitors.

SAB Ohlsson's Heritage Centre:
Heritage as Physical Resource

The motivation for SAB's Ohlsson's Heritage Centre was not the centenary of SAB but the expansion of the Newlands plant. In 1995, the Newlands plant, known as Ohlsson's Brewery, embarked on a massive overhaul. When building commenced, residents in the neighborhood began questioning the anomaly of an industrial plant in a residential area. Negative publicity challenged SAB to define its understanding of responsible corporate citizenship. John Eastwood, the manager of Ohlsson's Brewery, proposed restoring the malt house, Mariendahl Brewery, and the old distillery and opening them to the public. The project would enable the corporation to effect a "huge aesthetic facelift" and demonstrate its concern for people, place, and environment. It would also promote beer culture beyond branding and provide an alternative to the Cape wine route. Opening the site to the public and obtaining national monument status would secure SAB's ownership in perpetuity.[38] The Newlands project would not compete with the Centenary Centre; rather, it would add refinement to the image of SAB as "big, brash and brassy" and establish a "robust beer culture" at the Cape.[39]

In contrast to the purpose-built Centenary Centre, the SAB Heritage Centre in Cape Town was sited in a restored malt house originally built in 1821, a brewery built in 1859, and a distillery now used as a center for environmental education. Inspired by the corporation's centenary and his own impending retirement, John Eastwood wanted to bring built and natural environments into harmony with the locality of the Liesbeeck River, the nineteenth-century Josephine (flour) Mill, and, a stone's throw away, Newlands forest and Herbert Baker's memorial to Cecil John Rhodes. Ohlsson's Brewery's built environment would now be celebrated along with "the Newlands springs, bursting from the side of Table Mountain chosen so long ago by Rutgert Mensing," as its natural heritage, an SAB pamphlet proclaimed.[40] Recent landmarks added new definition to the area. The Newlands sports stadium, rugby and cricket museums, and a Sports Science Institute superimposed a twentieth-century sporting ethos on the locale of the historical brewery.

SAB Heritage Centre on the Ohlsson's Brewery site was opened to the public in 1995 and received national monument status in 1996.[41] The site achieves its power through infusing geographic space with historical time. Restored buildings contrast with an adjacent modern and technologically sophisticated brewing plant. As artifacts of "active preservation,"[42] the buildings provide a vehicle for the SAB heritage tour, which begins in the restored malt house, its floor laid out for the drying of barley. Storyboards explain the process and set out a narrative. A covered walkway leads from the malt house, past a burnished copper kettle, and along a linear water sculpture. A sense of process in—and passage through—time is conveyed in the nostalgia of riveted brass plates and in the quiet movement of water along an abstract brewing process.[43] Beyond the water feature, an excavated kiln and underground canal reveal nineteenth-century bricks weathered by time and the elements offset by green ferns protruding from loamy "mortar." A glass elevator, the signature of the preservation architects, protrudes on the outside of Mariendahl Brewery, rising up along the slopes of Devil's Peak, enhancing interaction between built and natural environments. Stopping abruptly, the elevator deposits its passengers in a low-ceilinged room. Whitewashed walls, solid wooden floors, and heavy beams, markers of the Cape Dutch architectural tradition, testify to a colonial heritage. Oiled wood conveys the meaning of craft in a working environment—hand-worked, solid, organic. Uncluttered by exhibition furniture, the space evokes deep nostalgia.

Storyboards suspended from the beams guide visitors along the controlled, narrativized passage, encoding the place to convey a corporate message that celebrates Jan van Riebeeck as bringer of "clear beer" to the southern tip of Africa and extols the virtues of Scandinavian entrepreneurs Jacob Letterstedt and Anders Ohlsson, who implanted the brewing tradition at the Cape.[44] These founding fathers are the icons of the SAB center; their images are interspersed in the narrative and a commissioned collage affirms their status in the boardroom.[45] They are described as men of vision, ambition, and drive. Their life histories testify to enormous appetites for wealth and power. Jacob Letterstedt's redistribution of wealth to his home country earned him a Swedish knighthood. His successor, Anders Ohlsson, supported the arts in his Nordic homeland with the profits from six breweries in the Newlands area.[46] The storyboard refrain "great brewers make great public benefactors" attests to their contribution to "the culture of western man" in southern Africa.[47] Highest praise is reserved for their entrepreneurial acumen. Anders Ohlsson's ability to effect mergers, "weaving together the disparate threads of a charmingly parochial industry" is much lauded.[48] Ironically (or inevitably), the same drive toward cartelization led to SAB's takeover of Ohlsson's itself in 1955.[49] History slips into corporate heritage as progress and the SAB merge into one. Relations between the beer magnates and their workers and the local community are edited out. Strife, difficulties, and industrial conflict appear not to exist despite the possibilities that such narratives might provide a more inclusive conception of Ohlsson's heritage.

Tucked at the end of the history of European beer barons, the Africa room is adorned with colonial images of black people and a small collection of sickles, hoes, stamping blocks, calabashes, and clay pots. A banner contrasts an unchanging Africa with imperial progress: "From Cape to Cairo, the beer tradition has remained unchanged for centuries." The display confirms the notion that meanings are changed when objects are exhibited in a museum.[50] Juxtaposing African brewing objects with modern scientific technology and entrepreneurial initiative highlights the achievements of modernization and colonialism, implying a lack of progress in African brewing. There is no hint of conflict between indigenous and colonial brewing and consumer traditions. Nor is there any reference to colonial restrictions on African brewing.[51] The result is that African brewing and consumption are rendered the colonized other. The heritage monument is unable to escape its racialized past.

When she was asked whether black people had not played a part in the brewery's history, preservationist Gwendoline Fagan retorted, "So what is African about it? You can't make a brewery African when the brewery was built by Swedes. Any attempt to do so would be false. The history of breweries can't be Africanised."[52] She continued, "It was Germans, not so much slaves who were lent by the Dutch East India Company to the farmers. There was no reason to bring out the slave story."[53] The architects also struggled to conceptualize which public the heritage center might serve, Gabriel Fagan noted: "If you design you must be acutely aware of the user. This is not easy in the case of a museum because you don't know who the user is. It is like shadow boxing."[54] For the preservationists, the brewery remained a place of production. They clearly worked with a concept of heritage as physical resource, a perspective endorsed by the brewery's general manager with whom they "lived and ate the whole exercise" and who confessed that he "hadn't really thought about" constructing an inclusive history of the place.[55]

As a preserved landscape associated exclusively with white male founders, the center was ultimately a place without a public. It missed the point, as Doreen Massey puts it, that the specificity of a place is not derived from "some internalised history." Rather, it is constructed through a set of social relationships, "articulated together at a particular locus."[56] Cast as overwhelmingly white, male, and entrepreneurial, these relationships could not convey an open-minded tolerance of difference. Rather, progressive white heritage was contrasted with static black brewing history, disabling black South Africans as interlocutors and agents. This configuration was discordant with the utopian message of multiracial nationalism in contemporary SAB brand advertisements.[57] In neglecting to break up the colonial corporate monologue and allow for dissonant interpretations of the past, the heritage center fell short of its bid to become a center of public culture.[58] Without the reflection afforded by the ending of apartheid, sociability remained an unselfconsciously white affair.

Shebeen Tours as a Heritage Experience

Critical engagement with SAB's sense of heritage came from black liquor dealers in Johannesburg and reflected a relationship that was simultaneously dependent and competitive. Aspiring businessmen in the liquor industry were particularly concerned that they should not be excluded from the commercial possibilities of heritage marketing. They were anxious that by incorporating the shebeen into the Centenary Centre's exhibition, SAB was usurping a history that black entrepreneurs might profit from. These entrepreneurs sought to "take back the shebeen" and market "the real thing" to international tourists in the townships, its authentic home. For over half a century, shebeening provided a living for some Sowetans. Shebeeners also sheltered those who dodged the law, paid protection money to gangs, offered solace to the weary and a place of laughter, relaxation, and escape for their patrons. The idea of a Soweto shebeen route as a means of experiencing black South Africans' "proud history" was mooted by the minister of economic affairs for Gauteng Province. SALSA's chairman promoted the idea; SALSA's goal was to attract 5 percent of Johannesburg's international tourists.[59]

Soweto (South Western Townships) heritage was not the exclusive preserve of shebeeners. Township tours encompassing memorial spots and other landmarks were already running in Soweto, and a shebeen tour would overlap with these to some extent.[60] Originating in the 1930s with the construction of Orlando, the township expanded as new areas were added. Tens of thousands of people were forcibly relocated into such townships under apartheid legislation and hundreds of thousands of others moved in from the impoverished countryside. The population swelled to over three million in the early 1990s. Soweto's reputation as a place of style, trendsetting, and radical politics grew. Each area in the sprawling township acquired a local identity derived from its residents and proximity to migrant hostels or railway lines, the type of housing, and the size of the yards.

Localities were known for the ambience of their shebeens and the "queens" and "kings" who ran them. Naledi, Tladi, and White City in the west were known for hard drinking, fighting, and no-nonsense shebeen queens, while Orlando and Meadowlands in the east boasted superior dwellings and stylish upmarket shebeens. Some shebeeners provided shelter for *lala-vuka* drinkers—those who drank till they passed out and then started drinking again when they woke up. While the majority of patrons "hot-footed" it down to the local shebeen, there were some who cruised along in their motor cars. The trip was not always smooth. Wide enough for military vehicles to pass, township roads exposed cracked, dry surfaces to the elements. Dust took the sheen off spanking new vehicles and scuffed the shoes of trendy young women who promenaded its sidewalks. It hung like a shroud over the squat tin-roofed houses and coated the scraggly trees in a reddish-brown filament of sand. Beyond the sprawling township, white Johannesburg's skyline boasted high-rise buildings, gleaming highways, and monumental mine dumps. This "romance" of Soweto was what the black economic empowerment businessmen sought to evoke in a shebeen route.[61]

The idea of a shebeen route through Soweto was not easily implemented. By the mid-1990s, the once-booming black liquor trade had fallen on hard times. Sales were down and the market was shrinking. A new world of opportunity that included the possibilities of changed lifestyles and entertainment lured middle-class blacks out of the townships. People with money were moving into the suburbs and frequenting city night spots and casinos. At the same time, the working class struggled with escalating unemployment.[62] More resources went into coping with the burdens of HIV/AIDS, and scores of people put their hopes and their cash into lottery tickets. "Tata ma chance, tata ma millions!" lottery advertisements sang out, and shebeens lost custom.[63]

A new generation of educated and upwardly mobile men in the black retail liquor industry initiated talks about a Soweto shebeen route. The South African Liquor Traders Association (SALTA) met with SALSA representatives and then invited the Federated Hospitality Association of South Africa, an established white-run organization, to join them to discuss ideas for a shebeen route. This gathering of aspiring and mainstream food and beverage traders wanted to bring Soweto into the tourism mainstream. They saw a shebeen route as a good business opportunity for established shebeeners and newcomers to the liquor industry. It would incorporate the SAB Centenary Centre rather than operate in opposition.

Packaging shebeen history for tourism presented enormous challenges. In the museum precinct, time could be both synchronically and diachronically arranged. The Centenary Centre defined "shebeen" as occurring during a specific moment—the ending of prohibition in the 1960s—and thereby created a monument. It was more complex to market people and their daily lives as heritage. Shebeeners were not museum exhibits. They were men and women who had recently confronted debt and bankruptcy and for decades in the past had run the gauntlet of police raids, liquor boycotts, and political uncertainties. No less than the new entrepreneurs, they were committed to a future that was very different from the past. And they were under pressure to license their premises or face closure. Meanwhile, shebeeners continued to serve customers in whatever space was available. Once again, they were on the wrong side of the law.

Shebeeners were suspicious of young, upwardly mobile businessmen who told them what to do. As SALSA leader Chris Mhlongo admitted, "We are telling some of our people to maintain their shebeens as a monument but it's not very easy because a shebeen is always a home, a dwelling, so you cannot tell somebody to keep your house like this whilst I am making mine bigger."[64] According to black economic empowerment analyst Okechukwu Iheduru, this sensitivity was rare among South Africa's new business elite, whose thirst to become "filthy rich" eliminated old loyalties.[65] Such insensitivity was not viable for those whose business depended on support from the black community. Certainly the SALSA man attempted to straddle the disjuncture between self-interested profiteering and commitment to community; he also believed that shebeeners would see the benefits of progress. "The shebeen era is at a moment of professionalisation and internationalization [i.e., in their bid to attract foreign tourists]. Shebeens are no longer survivalist but a viable business option," Mhlongo said.[66]

Marketing townships as socioscapes with shebeens as installations placed patrons and shebeeners as objects for tourist consumption. Asked if shebeen goers might not resent becoming the exotic others of a tourist gaze, Mhlongo replied with confidence. "I would disagree directly. *Ubuntu* [understood as African generosity and tolerance] does exist. Shebeen goers would see it as being recognized as people to have foreigners coming in. There would be an exchange of ideas. We would have interpreters on shebeen tours." In the black economic empowerment vision, a multiplier effect would occur. Residents who did not sell liquor would enter the tourist economy to trade in curios; they would draw on the township's "ethnicised past" to market Soweto as a place of many cultures. "A shebeen route is the trump card for Gauteng tourism," Mhlongo confidently said.[67] It was a sure route to the tourist dollar and euro.

However, the imagined Soweto shebeen route struggled to get off the ground. At the same time, shebeeners in areas less encumbered by competing interests among liquor retailers established tours more quickly. While tours got under way in Mamelodi (near Pretoria) and Kwazakhele (near Port Elizabeth), many Soweto shebeeners remained skeptical of subjecting themselves and their patrons to the tourist gaze.[68]

In seeking to make the idea of sociable beer drinking part of an inclusive national identity, SAB's visitors' centers and the township shebeen tours shared a common vision. However, unlike the multiracial nationalism of SAB's beer advertisements, the company's visitors' centers did not succeed in constructing a vision for beer as lubricant for the entire new nation. As monuments to free enterprise, proclaiming the power of consumption to build a strong economy, SAB's tourist centers ruled out the possibility of multiple perspectives on the past and closed off the opportunity to create a new critically engaged tourism.[69] While some black entrepreneurs imagined shebeen routes as socioscapes of apartheid history that could provide an authentic African experience, it was not clear how the presence of tourists would affect the sociability shebeen goers relied on. Shebeeners feared that their patrons would stop coming if they were confronted with the disjuncture between lived environments and heritage landscapes. Beer tourism in the first decade after apartheid remained a discordant set of spaces.

seven

Global Competition, World Class Manufacturing, and National Economic Restructuring

For SAB, maintaining market dominance was not simply a matter of fending off competitors. Critically, dominance was tied to the brewer's ability to meet the demand for quality mainstream beer at an affordable price. This meant that SAB needed to keep abreast of international developments in technology and workplace organization. In the context of massive changes in brewing technologies and the opening up of South African markets to global competition in the 1990s, it also meant becoming globally competitive. Following the advent of democracy in South Africa, any changes that SAB made in the interests of becoming internationally competitive had to comply with the regulations laid down by the country's new institutions. In the early 1990s, it was not clear how government would balance the needs of labor with those of the national economy; it was also not clear what limits labor might set on management strategies.[1]

By 1995, it was evident that the most significant of the new state's restructuring initiatives was the Labour Relations Act (1995). Institutions established by the act, including the Labour Court and the Commission for Conciliation, Mediation and Arbitration, a council for alternate dispute resolution, upheld the right of workers to a fair hearing. In recognizing workers' rights to collective bargaining and strike action, the new labor dispensation represented a powerful weapon; trade unions that negotiated recognition agreements with their employers were in a powerful position to protect their members. Management efforts to introduce new workplace dispensations would have to follow prescribed procedures involving contin-uous discussion through workplace forums and cooperation with manage-ment.[2] The aim of the Labour Relations Act was not to hobble management but to prevent the rise of adversarial relations. The law was a hurdle rather than an obstacle for companies seeking to introduce workplace changes.

A second significant aspect of government policy was Black Economic Empowerment (BEE), a strategy for ensuring that blacks acquired a stake in the free-market system. BEE was initially a catchall term that "encompassed among other things, black entry into business as owners and as managers, advancement in the workplace through the erosion of the industrial colour bar, unionisation, acquisition of equity, redistribution of existing wealth, and the rise of the black consumer."[3] The idea became more tightly defined over time to mean increasing black ownership and power in the formal sector of the economy.[4] Its precise legal meaning unfolded slowly. In 1997, on the initiative of the Black Management Forum,[5] a nonstatutory Black Economic Empowerment Commission began exploring different models for facilitating the entry of blacks into the economy through the acquisition of businesses; the commission's report was presented to President Thabo Mbeki in 2001.[6] The Black Economic Empowerment Act (2003) was fol-lowed by the Department of Trade and Industry's "code of good practice," a guide for businesses embarking on change. Later, BEE charters were drawn up for particular economic sectors. As a major manufacturer, SAB was required to follow the state's prescriptions. But the brewer approached BEE with caution, arguing that to be sustainable, empowerment initiatives should not be confined to business deals that transferred ownership of economic resources on paper. If the deals were to be sustainable, new own-ers should demonstrate their ability to manage and run their businesses efficiently in a competitive market. Moreover, in SAB's view, small business development and equity should be recognized as significant elements of the empowerment process.[7]

A third state initiative was driven by the new competition authorities. Soon after the advent of democracy, South Africa's Competition Board ex-pressed concern about the absence of competition in the liquor industry.[8] Overlapping ownership of manufacturing facilities, wholesale outlets, retail outlets, and "special events" blocked competition. The board wanted to see this overlap removed and SAB's monopolistic structure dismantled. SAB objected. In its view, disallowing such overlap would disrupt beer distribu-tion. The company also argued that increased government intervention in business was not the way to build the postapartheid economy. If there was anything to be learned from the apartheid era, it was that "government and the state should not interfere unduly in the wealth creation process which is properly the business of business," SAB told the Truth and Reconciliation Commission in 1997.[9] But the competition authorities were not easily put off.

At the same time, the international alcoholic beverage industry was becoming more consolidated. "The big brewers are circling each other," Graham Mackay, CEO of SAB, wrote in 1998.[10] SAB believed that survival depended on expanding its global footprint. Management moved in this direction in the mid-1990s. The first step was to access international capital markets. To this end, SAB formed a new company, SAB plc, and constituted SAB Ltd as a wholly owned subsidiary of SAB plc. In March 1999, SAB plc listed on the London and Johannesburg stock exchanges.[11] The second step for SAB was to embrace "world class manufacturing," the ideology of leading global manufacturers on the new frontier of business.[12] "Frontier" implied the juxtaposition of two distinct cultures and the possibility of conquering or accommodating differences. Either way, it represented a borderline that businesses would have to cross if they were to survive in the international economy.[13] Positioning oneself at the business frontier was not simply a matter of engaging market forces.[14] It required a global outlook and a managerial mindset that was strategically and structurally flexible and that understood technological innovation as "a necessary part of normal commercial life."[15] This commitment entailed endless internal restructuring to reduce costs, improve efficiencies, utilize new skills on the shop floor, and create new systems for managerial hierarchies to follow in corporate structures.[16] Appropriating Mohamed Ali's advice to boxers, idealogues of the new business ideology advised those seeking to implement it to "float like a butterfly and sting [competitors] like a bee."[17] SAB set off in this direction in the early 1990s. In the meantime, pressures in the marketplace began to mount as outside competitors began eyeing the South African beer market.

Purity and Nationalism:
Competition in the Premium Lager Market

SAB had achieved dominance in the local market through its mainstream brands; it expended relatively little energy on the premium beer market.[18] But the market for premium beer was growing. The demise of apartheid heralded new lifestyles and aspirations for many South Africans, and growing consumer appetites led to a rapid expansion of demand at the top end.

In turn, changes in consumer tastes and demands opened new opportunities for competitors. Namibian Breweries Ltd (NBL) began to make inroads in the premium lager market in the early 1990s. NBL was the first serious threat to SAB's market dominance since the 1970s.

NBL's desire to compete with SAB had deep roots. The Namibian brewer had produced limited quantities of German-style lager for the small Namibian market in the 1980s, a time when SAB "profited handsomely" from its sales to the South African Defence Force, then involved in a low-intensity war on the northern border of Namibia. NBL believed that SAB gained over 10 percent of its local market through "intimidating" northern Namibians to buy Castle, Lion, and Amstel, known disparagingly as "boerebier."[19] Following Namibian independence in 1990, SAB sought to establish a brewery at Oshakati in the north, close to the Angolan border, and announced that Aaron Mushimba, President Sam Nujoma's brother-in-law, would own 51 percent of the shares. Trade and Industry Minister Hidipo Hamutenya rejected SAB's scheme. "We are not going to allow this. NBL plays a significant role in our economy in which it is one of the largest taxpayers and employers," he said.[20] The Namibian government would not be taken in by SAB's request for Export Processing Zone status either; this was a ploy to avoid paying taxes, the government realized. Nor would the government allow SAB to persuade it that a "South African type black empowerment strategy" offered an appropriate path to development.[21] NBL looked for allies among other African brewers perceived to be under threat from SAB to discuss strategies for warding off the South African brewer. Kenya Breweries, which was extremely vulnerable in 1997 following SAB's takeover of Tanzania Breweries and investment in Ugandan Nile Breweries, offered advice.[22] Its executives felt that neither the Namibian nor the Kenyan market was large enough to cope with another brewery.[23]

NBL defended its dominance in the Namibian market as fiercely as SAB defended its market share in South Africa. Complaining that SAB had introduced 750-milliliter nonrefundable bottles in a deliberate attempt to "damage" the market, NBL said it was impossible to sort its own bottles from those of its competitor, a process that was labor intensive and time consuming. SAB scoffed, pointing out that its bottles were embossed with the company logo. To fend off SAB's "bullying tactics," NBL called for tighter competition legislation in Namibia and in the Southern African Development Community more generally. In a bid to improve its image by demonstrating its commitment to the Namibian people, SAB made its Castle Lager the official sponsor of the national soccer team, the Brave Warriors. Almost ten years later, in 2006, encouraged by support from

Namibian trade unions for a new brewery, SAB once again sought approval from Nujoma's government for a brewery in northern Namibia.[24] Namibians, including trade unions, would own 51 percent of the shares in the new venture and SAB would provide managerial and technical skills. Far from creating unemployment, SAB claimed, the plant would stimulate maize production and create as many as 2,000 jobs.[25] Again the Namibian government turned down SAB's proposal.

In South Africa, the battle between NBL's Windhoek Lager and SAB's Castle Lager was intensifying. In 1997, NBL's exports to South Africa amounted to a quarter of its output of 750,000 million liters. Windhoek Lager, which was becoming increasingly popular among urban professionals, began making significant inroads in the premium market. Windhoek Lager's key selling point was its claim that it was produced in a process that followed Reinheitsgebot, a sixteenth-century German law that prohibited the use of ingredients other than malt, hops, water, and yeast in the brewing of beer. Introduced as means of ensuring that there was sufficient grain for bread in 1516 in Germany, the term "Reinheitsgebot" had become synonymous with purity.[26] To counter this marketing ploy, SAB cut prices and launched a massive "Project Natural" campaign. Castle Lager advertising images showed only those ingredients approved by the Reinheitsgebot. NBL complained to the South African Advertising Standards Authority (ASA) that the advertisements were misleading. SAB in turn complained that NBL's advertisements set up images in which an unnamed lager was associated with a laboratory beaker, implying the use of harmful additives. The ASA ruled against both companies. An NBL campaign whose slogan was "No secrets, no additives, no hurry" continued to build brand loyalty while NBL loyalists and others opposed to SAB's dominance labeled all its brands "mega-brewery fizz."[27] At the same time, international forecasts predicted that discerning consumers would be looking for new values such as environmental friendliness as signs of the quality of a product.[28]

In mid-2000, the advertising authorities forbade SAB from claiming that Castle Lager was voted the best beer in the world. SAB could say only that Castle Lager had been voted the champion beer in the bottle and can section at a contest in Burton-on-Trent in England. Furthermore, SAB had to submit all Castle Lager advertisements to the ASA for clearance before publication.[29] At the same time, the Namibian Advertising Board ordered SAB's Castle Brewing Namibia to take down its billboards claiming that Castle Lager was "Windhoek's lager" since the slogan was "likely to deceive or cause confusion in the minds of the public"; it was an infringement on

NBL's trademark.[30] Castle was not brewed in Windhoek, did not qualify to be termed Windhoek's lager, and, foulest of all, consumers might be hoodwinked into "believing that Castle is also brewed in the same tradition as Windhoek Lager and tastes the same as Windhoek Lager."[31]

Back on SAB's home turf, the South African premium market continued to come under pressure, and SAB got up to its old tricks. In 1997, SAB sought to head off Felsenkeller Hofbräu, NBL's new premium brand, with its own Hofbräu München, licensed to SAB by Staatliches Hofbräuhaus. In a strategy that mimicked the Stallion/Colt battle of the 1970s, SAB obtained a court interdict to prevent NBL from launching its Hofbräu brand for five weeks. NBL teamed up with Bavaria Bräu, a microbrewery producing German-style lager in South Africa, to complain that SAB was abusing its position as monopoly producer by offering to pay retailers to upgrade their stores on condition that they did not stock any other producer's products.[32] NBL could withstand such tactics, but Bavaria Bräu could not; it went into liquidation.[33] Keeping the momentum going, NBL set up the Pure Beer Society in April 1999, one day short of the passing of the Reinheitsgebot some 483 years earlier. The move may well have been intended to counter SAB's Charles Glass Society, which had been formed in 1994.

NBL's ability to withstand SAB's competition in Namibia and to "claw away a 33% share" of the premium beer market in South Africa in 1999 was not due simply to consumer preference for taste or advertising campaigns.[34] Anthropologist Robert Gordon believes that for Namibians, beer was not simply a beverage. Beer provided postcolonial Namibians with a "capacity for personalization," a means of creating a national identity and of distinguishing their nation from its dominating neighbour.[35] Postindependence Namibians were driven by the powerful emotions of heritage and nationalism, which were constructed as mutually reinforcing. NBL strategically deployed nationalism and purity in the local and South African markets to differentiate itself from its competitor and draw consumers into its orbit. Its efforts were aided in part by the power of rumor to upset brand identities. Rumors that SAB used chemical additives in its brands spread like wildfire, took on a pseudo-scientific "truth," and proved difficult to deflect.[36]

In 1999, SAB plc acquired Ceske, a brewery at Plzen in the Czech Republic, and with it, the world's original pilsner lager, which dated back to 1842. Undeterred by the weakness of the rand at the time, SAB imported Pilsner Urquell, an international premium brand with heritage, culture, and purity that was unrivaled in the South African market.[37] SAB had acquired a brand that might provide a riposte to Reinheitsgebot.[38]

Becoming World Class:
Organizational Redesign of the Shop Floor

Maintaining SAB's competitive edge—its ability to keep prices low and quality high—required it to keep abreast of technological developments. Internationally, production techniques were changing rapidly. In the new global context, competitiveness centered on the ability to manage people and technology and the relationship between them in a rapidly changing environment. Machinery was becoming increasingly complex, and the range of interconnections between technology, information, and skill was changing the nature of work. As one SAB manager put it, the latest machines did not simply run by themselves, "they also fix themselves [and] diagnose their own errors. . . . Decision-making logic has been programmed into the technology."[39] Operators no longer simply monitored mechanical activity; they had to respond to information, maintain equipment, and implement quality checks. The key was to "keep structures flat and maximise the responsibilities within the line organisation."[40] This meant that there was no place for unskilled and semiskilled workers on the shop floor. SAB managers felt that the next step toward international competitiveness was to embrace the new business ideology of post-Fordism, or the concept of "world class manufacturing," which centered on the notion of a flexible production process based on flexible systems and machinery and a flexible workforce.[41] In this model, production was organized along the lines of the Japanese-inspired methods of total quality control (implying no wastage in the production process) and "just in time" (a strategy for keeping inventory stocks to a minimum).[42] Embracing flexibility entailed overcoming the skills and education deficits of the workforce so that workers could cope with information processing. Managers also wanted to recast the character and composition of the workforce without violating the new Labour Relations Act (Act 66 of 1995) or provoking organized labor.

The context in which SAB operated posed enormous challenges. In 1992, SAB set up a manufacturing development team to work on a model for redesigning workplace organization in line with the Japanese approach. The development team initiated an experiment in "best operating practice" (later termed BOP 1); operators and artisans moved away from narrow definitions of operating tasks into horizontal team structures that could approach "core processes" in a more integrated way. The aim was to establish whether team structures would improve performance, increase responsibility, and achieve flexibility in the work process. The end goal was improved worker performance and enhanced factory efficiencies. Success would be measured by the amount of beer actually produced as a percentage of "what could possibly be produced."[43]

First, SAB introduced voluntary part-time adult education in all its operational regions. Since many of its members had not completed more than a year or two at secondary school, the Food and Allied Workers Union welcomed SAB's encouragement of workers to attend the weekly two-hour classes (one hour of which was on company time). But progress was slow. Operators were not acquiring the proficiencies needed to develop multiple skills. In response, SAB introduced full-time adult education courses (fast-track classes known as Adult Basic Education and Training [ABET]). SAB was encouraged in this initiative by national moves to find ways of measuring the value of prior learning and work experience. The South African Qualifications Act (1995) made it possible for informal learning to be measured against formal learning and for adult education courses to become officially recognized. SAB hoped that its "competency acquisition process" would align with the education and training levels set out by the National Qualifications Framework that would be implemented under the act.[44]

After three years, SAB's BOP 1 experiment proved only moderately successful. SAB's training had not yielded the anticipated results. Line managers were concerned that problems were still not solved on the same day, on the same shift, "in real time." While workers were able to operate three machines, their skills were limited to a specific set of tasks. Operators, artisans, and quality controllers were still not "interfacing information" effectively enough to improve efficiencies.[45] The experiment had led to some improvements, but it had achieved only limited multiskilling and flexibility in performance. Management concluded that operators needed higher levels of education if they were to handle information more efficiently and communicate more effectively. Precisely how this was to be achieved would be guided by a deeper application of the principles of world class manufacturing.[46] What this meant in SAB's case was that workers needed to become conversant with a range of machines and operations and interact with information across these functions. They would need to work as teams and communicate across them and so engage in a process of continuous learning. In this model, communication meant less dependency on external technicians and created the possibility of greater initiative by workers on site. This daunting challenge was made more so by the protection afforded workers by the Labour Relations Act. But SAB had the right man; newly appointed managing director Norman Adami would lead restructuring at SAB from the front.[47] Adami was tough, determined, and ambitious. The challenge for him and SAB was how to "remake" the workers through education and training so that they would behave in fundamentally different ways.

The support of organized labor was critical to this process. In February 1995, SAB managers invited FAWU representatives to join them on "a visit to the future."[48] Together, management and workers' representatives would embark on an international study tour of leading manufacturers. En route, the members of the joint study group would discuss how they might adapt what they observed to local conditions.[49] SAB, an unthreatening brewer from a developing nation, was warmly received by leading breweries in Germany and by Miller Brewing Company in Trenton, Ohio, in the United States. The observations of members of the study group suggested that German breweries, where the number of workers on the shop floor had been reduced to a mere handful, represented the high road of capital-intensive automation. Some of these advanced breweries employed as few as three operators on a bottling line that processed 50,000 bottles an hour. SAB managers were excited by what they saw at Miller: the Trenton brewery combined state-of-the-art technology with an approach to operating that was team based and process oriented and featured operators with multiple skills. They were keen that the union should see the Trenton "combination" route as the way forward.[50]

Soon after the tour, SAB arranged a conference where trade unionists and members of the new business elite with trade union backgrounds debated the implications of the world class manufacturing strategy for the new nation and its workers. FAWU leaders struggled with the competing pressures of nationalism—that is, the desire of the government to encourage economic growth and the need of workers for job security. "We are going to be scared of WCM," said Ernest Buthelezi, national organizer of FAWU. "It is a new concept for workers and management, but we have to grapple with it and make sure we understand. Our shop stewards must become world class manufacturing."[51] A few months later, FAWU and SAB management established a joint "world class manufacturing task force" to look into job grading and how many jobs would be lost through the implementation of the WCM model. But the union would not turn its back on its workers. In December 1995, FAWU announced that it would continue to participate in discussions about world class manufacturing on condition that SAB called a moratorium on retrenchment.[52] Management turned to the International Labour Organization for backup, sending a delegation of shop stewards, FAWU officials, and SAB's industrial relations staff to Geneva.[53] The ILO's "enterprise forum" was hosting a workshop on the global problem of economic growth accompanied by increasing unemployment.

Leading manufacturers across the globe, said the ILO, were moving toward more automated technology and restructuring their workplaces. These processes inevitably entailed retrenchment. But, the ILO insisted, trade unions had developed expertise in working with management to facilitate restructuring. "The example of SAB shows that labour-management relations are an extremely powerful factor contributing to both economic and social success in restructuring," eulogized the ILO.[54]

In 1997, following the Geneva workshop, SAB and FAWU set up Project Noah, a social security net for retrenched workers. Project Noah provided the traditional services of financial and emotional counseling for retrenched workers, but it also trained interested former employees to become entrepreneurs.[55] Some retrenched SAB workers established small businesses, including a company that made traditional games such as *morabaraba* (played by moving pebbles from one pocket to another until all but one of the pockets were empty), bakeries, panel-beating shops, and sign-writing companies, some of which contracted with SAB. While the ILO hailed the project as a model of what might be done to soften the blow of retrenchment, two shop stewards on the project's committee resigned. Distancing themselves from a strategy that they believed divided workers into past and future, they declared that "Project Noah was giving SAB a green card to retrench."[56]

Meanwhile, an opportunity for further experimentation with workplace changes presented itself when the Alrode Brewery at Alberton on the East Rand needed to augment its packaging facilities. This expansion was a moment for much excitement at the brewery. As a "green-field site," the pilot project at Alrode Brewery enabled SAB to develop a deeper approach to "best operating practice" (BOP 2) in line with world class manufacturing strategies. It was an opportunity to apply the "learnings" from the Miller Brewery in Trenton. Starting from a zero base, SAB was able to install the latest technology without having to adapt outdated equipment. Once the best available high-speed technology was installed, production managers could experiment with innovative work processes.[57] Four full-time FAWU shop stewards worked alongside management to design the work process, establishing job titles and skills criteria to use in the company's recruitment of appropriately competent workers. Since the level at which the recruitment bar was set had implications for the prospects of employees, it became critical to establish the levels of literacy and numeracy required of new recruits. Once again, SAB used the National Qualifications Framework and its guidelines for Adult Basic Education and Training as a guide. After compiling the information about what data the new process operators would need to manage, the project team compared these operating tasks with the literacy and numeracy outcomes listed for the different levels of ABET. They then set the entry specifications for each position in the team. The new structure was "more than the sum of its parts"; it would generate new synergies that "freed up value," said one SAB manager.[58] SAB finally had a blueprint for a world class manufacturing strategy.

World class manufacturing, or flexibility, changed the meaning of what it meant to be a worker. With fewer workers taking responsibility for a wider range of tasks, individual progress rather than collective action characterized the workplace. The new design held out the prospect of career advancement: a "best operating practice" operator with the required higher education levels could take a trade test and become an artisan, then move up the ladder to "process operator." With further training, he (most employees in the manufacturing plants of the SAB were men) might become a team leader. The path to becoming a new man in the employ of SAB was to acquire the "necessary literacy and numeracy skills to operate in the changing world of work" and to adapt to new situations in a flexible manner.[59] At the same time, it meant living with continuous workplace restructuring and job insecurity. Career rather than union was the watchword of the future.

In the view of one of its designers, restructuring achieved its goal of increased productivity "by a mile."[60] But BOP 2 was not a cost-saving exercise; the wage bill for fifteen new positions exceeded that of twenty-one redundancies on a packaging line.[61] Even so, satisfied that the pilot had moved the labor process a step closer to flexibility, the SAB board adopted a business plan for implementing the new processes across all its plants. But shop stewards objected. Applying their own learning from the international study tour, they insisted on a moratorium on retrenchments as a condition of further cooperation. Drawing on the "Heineken concept," FAWU reiterated that the union would not support the rollout of BOP 2 unless there was a three-year moratorium on retrenchments.[62] It also objected to the outsourcing of noncore activities (such as laundry work) at Newlands. FAWU refused to be part of a joint agreement about workplace change. But management was adamant; their march toward world class manufacturing was not to be halted. Workers who were not included in the new vision were disposable. As Jacobus Joubert Burger, SAB's industrial relations manager, put it, "Some of those guys were not ever going to be able to be trained up to do that job. . . . There's no ways [sic] you're going to be able to train up all those people, they just won't be able to make it." SAB did not want to wait for natural attrition nor did it have the patience for a protracted voluntary retrenchment process. "We had the details, we knew what needed to be done, it was time that we got a bit more traction on the whole thing," said Burger.[63] If BOP 2 could not be achieved in one stroke at the national level, the company would negotiate its implementation brewery by brewery, line by line, across the country. To this end, management began "rolling out" the process at the first brownfields sites, where the new process would have to be retrofitted into existing plants and buildings. Progress was uneven; some breweries, such as Prospecton in KwaZulu-Natal, moved ahead rapidly, while others, such as Newlands, took several months to prepare for the changes. In the case of the Polokwane brewery, changes were postponed on the advice of the brewery's general manager.[64]

At the end of August 1998, SAB's Newlands Brewery conducted a "readiness assessment." One year later, Newlands management presented a business plan for organizational redesign at the plant to the Western Cape region of FAWU. As SAB's principal export brewery, Newlands handled an extraordinary "proliferation of brands and packs" and bottle types, each with a different height and diameter.[65] Every time a bottle or pack was changed, multiple adjustments had to be made on many machines throughout the packaging line. Quality control was a challenge. If labels needed straightening, machines had to be adjusted, time was lost, production costs were raised, and ability to meet demand was threatened. Because the nearest SAB plant was hundreds of kilometers away, Newlands did not have the option of limiting the range of its products. For SAB, accelerating the pace toward the new workplace design was a matter of urgency. Existing training was not delivering fast enough; the new shop floor needed a more flexible workforce with sophisticated competencies.[66]

SAB's rollout of BOP 2 at Newlands began cautiously in 1999 with line 1 in the packaging department. Once line 1 was up and running, Newlands management readied themselves for the final drive. Human resources manager Khaya Ngcwembe advised workers to participate in SAB's ABET classes in order to "help prepare . . . [themselves] . . . for the future requirements by the company."[67] In November 2000, management conducted a workshop in preparation for rolling out BOP 2 on all manufacturing lines at the brewery. All positions in the old structure were to be declared redundant, new entry-level specifications were to be drawn up, and employees who did not meet the minimum entry requirements were to be redeployed or retrenched.[68] Critically, ABET levels of literacy and numeracy were deemed to be a necessary but not sufficient qualification for the job; employees needed to demonstrate competence as a result of further training in order to secure a position. On 1 December 2000, Pieter Keyter, the SAB manager who had implemented BOP 2 at SAB's Prospecton Brewery, was transferred to Newlands. On 18 January 2001, management presented its business plan to shop stewards and FAWU officials. Again, management explained that all the posts on lines 2, 3, and 4 would be made redundant and workers would have to apply for new positions. Alarmed by the imminent retrenchment of a large number of its members, FAWU requested that consultation be held off for a month while it studied the business plan. Management balked at the delay and insisted that consultation take place on a weekly basis, but the union went off to study the document, leaving management to hold its consultation meetings alone.

In the meantime, SAB gave letters to employees informing them that they needed to reapply for the new positions, which were advertised internally. The company screened applicants to assess their ABET levels. Those deemed to have the requisite ABET levels passed on to the next stage—psychometric testing. Unsuccessful candidates were handed "regret" letters. Two deaf-mute men, who had been employed over a decade earlier for their ability to cope with a noisy environment without adverse effect, were now "unable to operate effectively in the new system."[69] Eleven other positions were removed as the tasks were outsourced as noncore activities. When he was asked what these retrenchments had to do with world class manufacturing, the general manager of the brewery replied candidly, "Arguably, not a lot."[70] By 31 August 2001, 164 positions had been declared redundant; 26 workers were redeployed and 138 were retrenched. Nearly all those who lost their jobs were black men. Ironically, a substantial number of those who were retrenched subsequently registered with a labor broker and were regularly sent to the Newlands plant, where they worked as temporary employees on lines that were not operating on the principles of flexibility. These men performed "precisely the same work as before their retrenchment" with substantially reduced pay and none of the benefits of their full-time colleagues.[71]

FAWU sought legal redress in the Labour Court.[72] In his arguments, Colin Kahanovitz, counsel for the union, slammed the ideology of world class manufacturing. "Everything under the sun, so it would seem, is a component part of this pliable and elastic business philosophy," he railed, arguing that the dismissals were unfair on substantive grounds.[73] He claimed that SAB had not demonstrated that new skills were needed on technological or production grounds and that the retrenched workers had been unfairly dismissed. The court declared that inappropriate educational tests had set the workers up as unable to be trained. In his ruling, the judge held that dismissal on the basis of inadequate ABET scores was tantamount to blaming workers who had been disadvantaged by apartheid for their lack of formal education. To add insult to injury, he said, the brewer had ignored the principle of last in, first out set out in the National Recognition Agreement (1987) with the union. In the terms of this agreement, SAB recognized FAWU as the representative of its employees across all its facilities nationally, and SAB and FAWU agreed to negotiate each year over wage increases and to follow a process of negotiation in the case of labor disputes. Many of these men had given a lifetime of service to SAB; it was callous to exclude them from the future, said the judge as he declared that the dismissals were unfair on procedural grounds. The judge appeared to concur with Advocate Kahanovitz that SAB's consultation was a sham; the decision to implement BOP 2 had been taken by the SAB board in 1998; and by the time consultation began at the Newlands plant, the path to restructuring had been determined. SAB, the unions' counsel argued, was not interested in any ideas that might emerge through consultation.[74] The corporation had been in such a great hurry to implement the latest fad in business ideology that it had refused to wait for the workforce to be reduced by natural attrition; its aim was to arrive ahead of others at the new frontier of competitive capitalism come what may. Such thinking was inimical to the FAWU tradition of worker solidarity and to the National Recognition Agreement SAB had signed with the union.[75]

In its ruling, the Labour Court declared that in a market-driven economy, there was no objection to a company restructuring in order to increase profitability. The judge added that world class manufacturing was a valid rationale for retrenchment. The court also rejected FAWU's contention that "incapacity" that was attributable to the Bantu education system was the true reason for the dismissal of 25 percent of the Newlands Brewery's workforce. From the judge's perspective, the flaws in SAB's approach to adult education, particularly its use of ABET as an instrument for measuring workplace competencies, were the real weaknesses in SAB's case. Acting Judge Gamble took his cue from the union's expert witness, Darryl McLean, who had told the court that generic ABET standards did not "necessarily accurately and adequately reflect workplace-specific language, literacy and numeracy requirements" and that they did not constitute valid instruments for testing these "contextually embedded" skills. Indeed, he suggested, workers provided with appropriate "contextual clues" might perform complex calculations. But they were unlikely to do well in a written test that was "disembedded" from the workplace.[76] Since SAB's ABET assessment was not conducted on real problems in a real or simulated work setting, it tested schooling competencies and failed to assess the "types of competencies required for multi-skilling" that SAB was looking for.[77] SAB's ABET tests, the court concluded, had no validity in predicting the ability of workers to be trained.

The court agreed with FAWU that SAB was not seriously interested either in ABET training or in consultation with workers. "The model of restructuring and the entry level specifications for the new jobs had been fixed nationally by the company in a unilateral fashion at a very early stage of the world class manufacturing exercise," the court said.[78] ABET was merely a mechanism for getting rid of unwanted workers. For some workers, dismissal had been substantively unfair. In all instances, dismissal had been procedurally unfair. ABET training at Newlands was sporadic, underfunded, and flawed in its content and implementation. Workers had not been informed in good time that their future in the company depended on specific ABET levels: the brewery manager had cited budgetary constraints when the program was suspended and workers affected by redundancy had been given a last-ditch opportunity to begin fast-track classes in the final stages of BOP 2 implementation. The court declared that Denise Smith, SAB's expert in organizational design, had demonstrated a "relatively superficial understanding of the use of ABET as an instrument of measurement."[79] The judge also concluded that SAB had chosen to ignore the comments of its external assessors, who had warned that ABET measured neither competency nor trainability.[80]

SAB could not lay claim to having pioneered a world class manufacturing model of ABET, the judge continued. The brewer had blotted its copybook by using a potentially valuable learning device as a mechanism for implementing an unfair labor practice. Further, SAB had acted unilaterally when it failed to win the union over to its business strategy, disregarding the spirit and letter of its agreements with the union. The ruling was a significant precedent. SAB would not be able to undertake an exercise of this kind and in the same way again.[81] The court instructed Newlands Brewery to reinstate sixty-one workers who had been unfairly dismissed on substantive grounds and to compensate fifty-four men whose dismissal had been procedurally unfair. It would have to compensate the families of five workers who had since died. SAB was also ordered to pay the costs of FAWU's counsel, a relatively unusual ruling in South African labor cases.[82]

The case was a landmark. It was heard in the new postapartheid Labour Court, which had the status of a supreme court and was presided over by a judge. Argument was framed in terms of the new labor legislation that accorded workers the rights and protections that had been hard won in the struggle against the racial capitalism of the apartheid era. Courtroom demeanor was expected to conform to the values of the South African Constitution and the Labour Relations Act. In this court, economic power was not accorded any privileges, said Acting Judge Gamble as he reminded senior counsel for SAB to restrain his aggressive manner. Litigants in the Labour Court were "to be dissuaded from flexing their financial muscle in attempts to embarrass their opponents."[83]

Despite the ruling that business did not simply have carte blanche to recast ABET to suit its own needs, Ingmar Boesenberg, general manager of Newlands Brewery, had no regrets. World class manufacturing had achieved a "sea-change in the structure of work," he said, claiming that productivity had improved and efficiency at the plant had risen from 53 percent to almost 70 percent.[84] Advocate Jeremy Gauntlet, the counsel for SAB, dismissed the view that his client's efforts to implement ABET did not stand up to scrutiny. The criticisms presented by the expert witness who testified on behalf of the workers amounted to little more than the rumblings of academics who were not in touch with the realities of the workplace, he said. SAB's efforts had achieved international recognition from none other than the ILO, he claimed.[85] His client would not take back workers whom the court had reinstated, he said. SAB would fight the court's ruling.

Outside the courtroom, economic power prevailed. SAB dragged its feet, avoided reinstating the dismissed workers, and prepared for another round of litigation. Anxious to avoid further legal costs, FAWU settled the dispute with SAB in October 2005. Retrenched workers were paid compensation of up to twenty-one months' pay and SAB covered the union's legal costs.[86] The settlement was a victory for SAB. The brewer's industrial relations manager called FAWU's legal officer to arrange a celebratory meeting. He praised the union for taking the pragmatic route.[87] Angered by the union's capitulation, a group of retrenched workers from the Prospecton plant in KwaZulu-Natal challenged the right of the union to settle on their behalf and took FAWU to court. In the Durban Labour Court, Judge Ngcamu dismissed the case, declaring that the union had not acted in bad faith when it opted to serve its members by negotiating compensation rather than insisting on reinstatement.[88] While many of these workers adhered to the ideal of the "new man" that had emerged in the 1980s antiapartheid struggle, they were confronted by the reality that in postapartheid South Africa, the working-class militant trade unionist had to make way for the skilled educated workers of the era of global competition.[89]

By the beginning of the new millennium, SAB had moved on to the next level of world-class manufacturing, closing down small, labor-intensive plants in the former homelands and opening up new sites in cities where capital-intensive production followed the principles of world class manufacturing. When SAB closed down its Butterworth brewery in the former Transkei, the company constructed a new megabrewery at Ibhayi near Port Elizabeth that was closer to supplies and to markets. As a new site, Ibhayi required no painful restructuring. Even so, the construction process was driven by global rather than national economic imperatives. SAB ignored the government policy of "preferential procurement" and shunned the slogan "Proudly South African," instead selecting its suppliers from among those who followed world class manufacturing principles such as just in time.[90] The Ibhayi plant's highly capital-intensive labor process could be managed from the Newlands plant, some 700 kilometers away. SAB's Ibhayi operation was one of the most sophisticated capital-intensive breweries in the world; 60,000 bottles and 38,000 cans of beer rolled off the production line every hour. Yet Ibhayi was run by only fifteen "superworkers" per shift.[91]

From Advancement to Black Economic Empowerment

SAB's efforts to promote black advancement at the management level were less dramatic than its efforts to restructure the shop floor. From the mid-1980s, the brewing giant had followed a path of affirmative action or equity for salaried staff.[92] In 1990, equity targets were set at 50 percent. In 1992, only 46 percent (1,900 people) of the salaried staff was black.[93] But two years later, this figure had risen to 53 percent.[94] Group Operating Executive Graham Mackay instructed his subordinates to monitor affirmative action as they did beer volumes. However, he realized that achieving equity in the management structure wouldn't be an easy task for white executives. Talking to Caroline White, he said, "You have to rank it [SAB's equity program] with those [fundamental policy] objectives because it is so much easier to employ whites. They are easier to find, easier to acclimatise, [it is] easier to get objectives out of [them] because you understand how their minds work."[95] But the difficulties went beyond numbers. SAB lamented that black managers identified more readily with black blue-collar workers than with white management.[96] In a bid to get black supervisors to think like managers, Mackay required them to participate in a series of "value sharing" workshops.[97] However, diversity training was not enough to convince three black men in SAB's training department that wage disparities with their white colleagues were not racially motivated. Since their white counterparts earned 15 to 17 percent more than they did, they laid a charge of "unequal pay for work of equal value."[98] SAB admitted the discrepancy in wages but argued that this was a consequence of incremental increases related to job performance, experience, seniority, length of service, and the upgrading of posts. Race was not the cause of the discrepancy, it claimed. The court upheld SAB's argument and ruled that "affirmative action was only a shield"; it could not be used as a weapon to bring action against an employer in terms of the Labour Relations Act (Act 66 of 1995).[99] What the court seemed to be saying was that while SAB was not technically at fault, it had not managed expectations or prevented the slow pace of change from leading to resentment.

SAB promoted only a handful of black professionals into senior positions. In 1998, Vincent Maphai was appointed corporate affairs director of the Beer Division alongside men such as Monwabisi Fandeso, who ran SAB's Rosslyn plant (in the 1990s the biggest brewery in the southern hemisphere), and Magapa Phaweni, brewing manager at the Rosslyn plant. Clifford Raphiri, manager of the Alrode plant, became SAB's first black director of manufacturing. These men were sophisticated professionals who occupied powerful positions in the "hard" areas of production and management.[100] They were the new leaders of world class manufacturing. When observers noted that corporate black men were beginning to replace white managers at SAB, one journalist quipped, "Move over Charles Glass!"[101]

Surveys conducted by employer organizations and business houses repeatedly found that SAB was a good place to work. In the first five years of the new millennium, SAB won a slew of awards, including "best company to work for," "most admired company," South Africa's "most ideal employer," and South Africa's "most caring company."[102] Explaining why SAB was so highly rated, Managing Director Norman Adami declared that the brewer's human resources strategy was a "key determinant of success." SAB, he said, had "always paid a disproportionate amount of attention to people practices. It's in our DNA." Regarded as "a business that invests in people development," SAB had become the "employer of choice" for professionals. Like so much of SAB's corporate culture, this feature too, was a legacy of apartheid. "Internationally, the industries who have similar reputations have been in the fields of institutional technology, financial services, and consulting. In South Africa, top people want to go into the brewing industry."[103] Significantly, the labor elite employed on the shop floor conceded that SAB was a desirable company to work for.[104] But a key issue in the new political dispensation was how far SAB would support black economic empowerment as ownership of corporate assets.

In the early 1990s, SAB observed at close range the fate of one of the first black economic empowerment initiatives when the state-owned National

Sorghum Breweries (NSB) was privatized. In mid-1991, NSB sold 40 million shares to its distributors and consumers and reserved 30 percent of the shares for its 3,500 employees. The remaining 4 million shares were taken up by the state's Industrial Development Corporation, which underwrote the deal. The new chief executive officer, Mohale Mahanyele, reported to a board that was 70 percent black and worked with a management team that was 83 percent black. In Mahanyele's view, NSB afforded blacks an opportunity to participate in black economic empowerment in a far more meaningful way than small businesses did. As "controllers, directors, distributors, managers, owners and shareholders," blacks had genuine power and substantial incomes.[105] NSB boasted fifteen breweries and control of 80 percent of the sorghum market; SAB's Traditional Beer Investments accounted for most of the remaining market share. NSB was afforded a protected honeymoon as its exclusive rights to brew and distribute sorghum beer outside the homelands, which it inherited from the apartheid state, continued until mid-1995.

Mahanyele, who was ambitious and energetic, immediately extended NSB's repertoire by acquiring Jabula Foods (producer of instant beer powder) from the Premier Group and launched the Vivo clear beer brand. These moves were bold, designed to protect NSB in a declining sorghum market that from 1991 was subject to excise duty.[106] But NSB overreached itself. It was not long before Vivo flopped. Then NSB formed a partnership with United Breweries of India, which acquired a 30 percent stake in the new company. In 1995, NSB acquired the license to brew United Breweries' Kingfisher Premium Lager, providing a second chance to take on SAB in the clear beer market. United Breweries' involvement signaled a major change: its insistence on bringing its own management expertise into NSB led to much speculation that the Indian company would soon be the senior partner.[107] Keen to get out of producing sorghum beer without losing brand control, SAB proposed that NSB take over TBI's operating assets so that SAB could divest itself of its sorghum brewing plants. In exchange, SAB wanted ownership of all NSB's trademarks. But the Competition Commission turned down the application because the deal would have given NSB a monopoly on sorghum beer production and SAB control of all sorghum brands.[108] NSB continued to struggle and finally, in 2004, ceded control to United Breweries of India, which formed United National Breweries (SA) (Pty) Ltd. Ironically, as the sorghum beer industry was finally freed from colonial control, it passed into the hands of foreign capital. The new owners streamlined their operations so that the largest sorghum brewer in Africa employed just 900 workers.[109] Ambitious and a little naïve, the NSB experiment had foundered on the rocks of a declining market in sorghum beer, formidable barriers to entering the clear beer market, and inexperienced management.

Meanwhile SAB's moves to divest itself of its noncore businesses, including heavy industry, matches, textiles, shoes, hotels and supermarkets, generated much anticipation in black economic empowerment circles.[110] The selling-off process was conducted so "fast and hard" that it caused a stir, and when price and speed rather than black empowerment imperatives determined the successful bidder, those in search of black economic empowerment deals were put out.[111] However, early in the new millennium, SAB was presented with an opportunity to embark on a major corporate black empowerment initiative that would enhance its core business. Rheem Crown Plant, a division of Highveld Steel and Vanadium Corporation Ltd, was collapsing; it was one of only two bottle-top manufacturers in South Africa. SAB was anxious to prevent its exit from the market. Bottle tops were a key component of the brewing industry because properly manufactured tops were essential to the quality and image of beer. SAB proposed that Coleus Packaging (Pty) Ltd, a wholly owned SAB subsidiary and the producer of 5.5 billion crown corks annually, acquire the ailing Rheem, turn the company around, and sell it to a black empowerment company. This two-stage move would achieve the twin objectives of saving a manufacturing concern and transferring ownership to black capital. But the plan generated consternation in the beverage industry.

The proposed deal was a vertical merger; SAB was buying one of its suppliers. It was contested by a competing crown cork manufacturer, Metal Closure Group Pty Ltd (MCG), and its customers Distell Limited and Guinness UDV. MCG had been established at the behest of Distell in 2001 in the wake of the collapse of Crown Cork SA a year earlier. Distell was concerned that its supply of bottle tops should not disappear with the collapse of Crown Cork. Black shareholders, including the empowerment consortium Wiphold, which was headed by four black executive women and held shares in Distell, acquired 44 percent of MCG's shares.[112] They argued that since SAB and its subsidiary Amalgamated Beverage Industries, the main bottlers of Coca-Cola, accounted for 78 percent of the crown cork market, the proposed merger might lead to their foreclosure as a supplier.[113] They also feared that as both owner and customer, SAB would seek preferential treatment over other customers. SAB's alternative to taking over Rheem was to set up an in-house plant; given the pace and volume of production at SAB plants, it needed delivery of corks with its brand insignia on deadline. With this fact in mind, the Competition Commission gave conditional support to the merger.[114] The Competition Tribunal made the final ruling and spelled out that SAB had to turn the company around and "sell at least 40% to a black empowerment partner" within two years.[115] SAB complained that the ruling "stampeded" it into a "fire sale to meet an arbitrarily imposed deadline."[116] SAB was given leave to apply to the tribunal should it believe an extension was necessary.

In 2003, the deal went through when SAB Coleus Packaging became the formal owner of Rheem Crown Plant. In September 2005, SAB advertised the sale of Coleus Packaging as a black empowerment deal. In April 2006, Nokusa Investments, one of 600 bidders, acquired a 40 percent stake in Coleus Packaging. Led by Moses Hadebe, Nokusa's bid was broad based, including Shandura, a professional women's group; Izindophi Community Project, a women's project in rural KwaZulu-Natal; and the Kapano Disabled Movement. Another 5 percent of Coleus Packaging's equity was taken over by 65 employees. Coleus Packaging's share of the crown cork market was now just under 100 percent. In June 2006, Coleus Packaging entered into a joint venture with Crown Corks of Uganda, and the new company became the sole supplier of some 750 million bottle tops for the Ugandan market.

Beyond the crown cork project, SAB's approach to black economic empowerment centered on small business. The brewing giant did not approve of ownership without responsibility or managers without expertise. If South Africa was to have a viable economy, businesses would need managers who operated on firm business lines and adopted a sustainable approach to transformation of the postapartheid business world. SAB executives were critical of the shortcomings of the "business deal" approach to black economic empowerment.[117] Simply transferring ownership to blacks was not achieving economic development, and the vision of an ever-expanding pool of black shareholders was not materializing.[118] For SAB, economic empowerment was at least partly about "bringing the country's 'second' economy into line with the formal 'first' economy" through the development of small businesses.[119] In SAB's view, small businesses were sustainable, they empowered blacks, they facilitated entrepreneurship, and they contributed to the economy. SAB believed that substantial empowerment would be achieved in the alcohol industry if the government were to license the 200,000 shebeens that were operating illegally after the end of apartheid; this group represented about 74 percent of all shebeens and taverns.[120] However, the new Liquor Act (Act 59 of 2003) failed to resolve the problem of the illicit industry. Rather, it devolved responsibility for alcohol licensing to provincial governments, generating much confusion and no agreement on the definition of a shebeen across the provinces. The

Gauteng regulations defined a shebeen as "any unlicensed operation whose main business is liquor and is selling less than ten (10) cases consisting of a dozen 750ml of beer bottles per week," but Gauteng liquor dealers declared that this definition made no sense at all.[121] Most shebeeners operated highly profitable businesses with substantial turnover, placing them well outside the province's definition. Frustrated alcohol associations approached the Constitutional Court for a redefinition. The court duly ruled that the number of cases of beer defining a shebeen in Gauteng province should be increased from ten to sixty.[122]

Meanwhile, SAB continued to train taverners, shebeeners, and bottle-store owners under the Mahlasedi Taverner Training scheme and to expand the owner-driver scheme. SAB's Mahlasedi Taverner Training scheme provided business training for licensed tavern owners in the townships. Licensing created a division between legal taverns and illegal shebeens. By 2004, SAB had contracted with 248 owner-drivers, each of whom employed crews of at least four people; these crews were responsible for the distribution of at least 50 percent of SAB's product.[123] SAB also outsourced some distribution centers through a system of "tandem-franchising."[124] As co-owner, SAB provided mentoring and financing for the franchisees when they took over distribution depots; most of the franchisees were former SAB employees. David Moloi, who had worked for SAB for some fifteen years, co-owned Westonaria Beer Distributors, the first distribution centre to be franchised. Another former SAB employee, Simphiwe Chiliza, took over the Madadeni distribution depot in Newcastle, Kwa-Zulu Natal.[125] SAB also sought to expand its procurement of supplies from black business in several ways. Among these efforts was the establishment of a project for emerging farmers to grow barley under irrigation in the Taung area in the northern Cape, augmenting supplies from white barley growers in the southern Cape.[126] While these efforts provided real support for small businesses, the uncertain economic climate in the first decade of the twenty-first century slowed the progress of such projects and other small businesses.

The final challenge of going global required SAB to manage its corporate brand. Anxious to offset rumblings that profits acquired in South Africa were funding SAB's expansion across the globe, the company sought to promote itself as a driver of national economic development. Television advertisements cast SAB as a brand that was at one with the South African nation, fostering progress and human development. SAB spokesmen told stories about local social investment that promoted SAB's commitment to entrepreneurship, the environment, health, and education. In these representations, SAB sought to characterize itself as powerfully, authentically, and deeply South African, a major player in the business of nation-building. Partly defensive, this corporate branding was also aggressive, a means for SAB to hold its own on the new business frontier.[127]

In sum, global competition rather than economic nationalism informed changes in the brewing industry from the mid-1990s. SAB's response to international competition was to move its domicile closer to the capital markets, expand its global footprint, and introduce internationally competitive production methods in all its breweries. While these strategies propelled SAB to the top of the global brewing hierarchy, they created new social divisions at home. SAB's redesigned workplace and ideology of world class manufacturing rendered poorly educated and relatively unskilled workers obsolete and directed new opportunities toward a small number of hand-picked, highly skilled technicians with effective communication skills and an ability to take responsibility. Older men with substantial years of service were cast aside and encouraged to take on the risks of self-employment. Some continued to service the outsourcing needs of local breweries, increasing their vulnerability and dependency on SAB. The meaning of work changed overnight, unsettling the identities of men whose status had become associated with stable employment.[128] While postapartheid labor legislation provided a space for challenging the new manufacturing trend, there was no stemming the tide of change.

The postapartheid state's guidelines had led to some black economic empowerment activity in the brewing industry, but the retail industry in the historically black areas continued to be characterized by a large number of small businesses that were mostly illegal and mostly dependent on SAB. Nor was the new Liquor Act (2003) able to provide a satisfactory solution to the problems of licensing. By handing over the task of regulation to the provinces and leaving the definition of shebeen so arbitrary that dealers petitioned the courts to have it changed, the act sowed confusion. Alcohol dealers were neither affirmed by the postapartheid administration nor buoyed by consumer demand. In the absence of effective policing, there were no barriers to entry, and the number of shebeens continued to increase.

The "new man" of postapartheid South Africa, then, was neither the collectively conscious trade unionist of the antiapartheid era nor the small business retailer or distributor fostered by the large firm. Rather, the future belonged to the problem-solving supertechnicians positioned at the new frontier of business.

Epilogue: Global and Local

SAB's ability to shape the South African beer market made it an enormous powerhouse that was hungry for acquisitions in other markets. By 1997, SAB had become the fourth largest brewer in the world by volume and had positioned itself in readiness for global competition. SAB plc's first moves followed its established path of buying up ailing breweries in developing markets in Africa, Eastern Europe, and China. But by 2000, the pace and character of competition had intensified. Survival meant playing the tough, often zero-sum game of "merger mania."[1] In 2002, SAB bought the ailing Miller Brewing Company from U.S. food and tobacco company Philip Morris.[2] Miller was not the first brewer that SAB had bought from tobacco merchants (it had acquired ICB from Rembrandt in the 1970s), but the acquisition was dramatic. It catapulted SAB from the emerging markets of Africa, Asia, Latin America, and Eastern Europe into the U.S. market. The move signaled that SAB was prepared to take on the top dogs in the global brewing industry rather than be swallowed up in the mergers and acquisitions game. SAB's chief executive officer Graham Mackay commented, "This is a transforming deal for us, for Miller, and for the global scene. It works in its own right and will lead to more industry consolidation."[3] SAB's South African operation, formally SAB (Pty) Ltd, became known internally as "Beer South Africa."

The SAB-Miller deal was, of course, a transforming moment for the people at Miller and for the U.S. brewing industry. Since Miller had been in decline for fifteen years, radical intervention was needed and the risk was high. Observers questioned whether SAB could turn Miller around in the face of competition from Anheuser-Busch, the number-one U.S. brewer. Others pointed to SAB's deal-making abilities, management expertise, and aggressive marketing strategies as indicators of potential success. The big question was whether SAB's corporate culture could rescue Miller. Industry analysts were skeptical, arguing that an American business needed an American perspective with "American executives at the helm."[4]

SAB tackled the task of implementing world class manufacturing priciples in characteristic style. Mackay fired Miller's CEO, replacing him with trusted South African lieutenant Norman Adami, renowned for his robust style of communication. Adami employed Denise Smith (who was redeployed from SAB's brewery in the Czech Republic) to head up human resources; Smith applied SAB's psychometric personnel rating system at the former Miller plants and Adami promptly fired 200 underperforming executives. Those who remained were subjected to tough reviews and performance-related pay; those seen to be "busting a gut" were rewarded.[5] Over the next two years, Adami brought ten more South African executives to Milwaukee, where they filled the positions of chief financial officer and head of corporate strategy, among others.[6] Miller underwent a cultural shift. "Stormin Norman: Adami Has Beaten Miller into Shape. Can He Build Market Share?" asked a leading South African finance magazine.[7]

In the first few months, the new team had to confront a host of inherited problems, not least of which was a disastrous advertising campaign known as "Catfight." The series of advertisements featured two buxom young women seated at an outdoor table arguing about how Miller Lite adds to their fun. The argument escalates into a muddy wrestling match. One late-night edition of this advertisement apparently included the invitation "Do you want to make out?" Sales declined in response to this ad. The series was awarded the grand prize for sexism by Advertising Women of New York.[8] While SABMiller's head office claimed that the Catfight campaign drew more on parody than critics had given it credit for,[9] they forgot, perhaps, that SAB had recently been chastised by the South African Constitutional Court for its failure to appreciate parody.[10]

Adami arrived too late to stop the Catfight ads but condemned their focus on "buzz" rather than on brand, quality, and taste.[11] His own strategy was to go directly after the competition. This he did in a series of advertisements announcing that Miller Lite had fewer carbohydrates and calories than Bud Light or Coors Light. Anheuser-Busch, brewers of Bud Light, responded with advertisements claiming that their brand was the king of beers. In a provocative but humorous vein, SABMiller launched a series of mock political commercials, declaring that Miller Lite and Miller Genuine Draft wanted to be the president of beers. "This is America!" one Miller ad announced, "We don't kowtow to a bunch of tiara-wearing crumpet eaters."[12] Miller Lite sales increased by some 18 percent.

In the meantime, Anheuser-Busch was given a boost by its very public trumping of SABMiller's bid for China's Harbin brewery.[13] Harbin's CEO, Peter Lo, announced in June 2004, after almost a year of intrigue, that SABMiller's offer had been "wholly unsolicited and not welcomed by the management and employees of Harbin" and that he was "delighted that Anheuser-Busch has stepped in as a white knight with a counterbid."[14] As SABMiller smarted, Anheuser-Busch continued to pack the punches. In their "Unleash the Dawgs" campaign, Anheuser-Busch targeted the heritage and manliness of Miller brands. For SAB, heritage and manliness were the pillars of beer brand identity. Budweiser's advertisements alleged that SABMiller was "South African owned" and ineligible to run for president; Miller Lite, Budweiser's advertisements cried, was nothing but the "queen of carbs." SABMiller immediately draped its brands in red, white, and blue and advertised itself as "American born since 1855."[15] But Anheuser-Busch continued to play on American xenophobia by promoting the idea that foreign investment was "bad," implying that SABMiller was gaining profits in the United States to send home to South Africa.[16] Adami appealed to the courts to stop Budweiser's negative imaging.[17] A federal court ruled that Anheuser-Busch was not to refer to SABMiller as "owned by South African Breweries" but said that it could use the phrases "South African owned" and "purchased by South African Breweries."[18] Anheuser-Busch's "queen of carbs" slur also sparked critical reaction. Tough-talking Norman Adami commented, "That's a very macho accusation against a brand that has been giving them a royal shellacking," while the Gay & Lesbian Alliance Against Defamation in New York pronounced the Anheuser-Busch slogan "pretty overtly sexist" and "one step away from being homophobic" since it used "queen" as a derogatory label for an effeminate man.[19] Uncomfortable with the rough edge of the beer wars, one advertising analyst commented, "This is getting dirty, into the gutter."[20]

The beer wars incurred heavy advertising expenditures on both sides, but SABMiller's efforts to take on its rival went beyond marketing to distribution. Unlike South Africa, distribution in the United States is channeled primarily through grocery stores and superstores, which together accounted for almost a quarter of market volume in 2004.[21] In 2004, Anheuser-Busch accounted for more than half the volume of beer drunk in the United States, while SABMiller accounted for 17.8 percent.[22] To boost sales, SABMiller believed that relations with distributors needed a fresh approach. With his eye on moving bigger beer volumes, Adami cut administrative jobs and, with the help of the indomitable Denise Smith, linked salaries to performance. At the same time, he created 100 new jobs in sales. Invigorated and keen, the augmented sales team was welcomed by distributors. One Miller wholesaler in southwest Florida enthused, "Adami brought a new discipline, a new desire to win."[23] By the end of February 2004, sales were up; Miller was turning around and Anheuser-Busch was on the back foot. In a few months, Miller Lite's market share had climbed to 8.2 percent from 6.9 percent while Bud Light, an Anheuser-Busch beer and the top-selling brand in the United States, had slipped to 15 percent from 15.2 percent. In November, SABMiller reported an increase in Miller's overall U.S. market share for the first time in years.[24] By late 2005, Bud stock was down 12 percent from its mid-2002 level and SABMiller's CEO reported "the stalling of the steamroller advance by Anheuser-Busch."[25] Even ardent U.S. nationalists conceded that SAB's "South African culture" had succeeded where Miller's former management had failed.[26]

In 2004, as a merger between Belgium's InterBrew and Brazil's Ambev (to create Inbev, brewer of 202 million hectoliters a year) was announced, Mackay sent a letter to SABMiller shareholders informing them that the global brewing industry was entering a new phase of consolidation, a time when giants would merge. Couplings could occur between SABMiller and Inbev or Heineken or between Anheuser-Busch and Inbev or Heineken, he forecast in an interview in 2005.[27] Archrivals competed in many parts of the globe as the big dogs circled each other. To gain a little leverage in its attempts to erode Anheuser-Busch's dominance, SABMiller formed a joint venture with Molson Coors, the third largest brewer in the United States.[28] The joint venture, MillerCoors, would help reduce costs and streamline distribution.

In July 2008, the merger that Mackay had anticipated occurred as InBev made a bid for Anheuser-Busch, which was struggling to cope with high grain prices and competition.[29] After holding out briefly, Anheuser-Busch capitulated.[30] Anheuser-Busch Inbev, producer of 460 million hectoliters per year, was easily the largest brewer in the world by volume. SABMiller, which produced approximately 150.8 million hectoliters a year, was second.[31] While the brewers absorbed the news with little fuss, the drinking public did not. That an American brewing icon since 1860 was now controlled by a Belgian-Brazilian brewer unleashed a barrage of angry nationalist sentiment. A call for comments put out by the New York Times online elicited passionate responses: "America is for sale at rock bottom prices. It will not be long and there will be nothing for Americans to own. It will all be in foreign hands," said one blogger. "52 million in debt. I don't think the whole country of Belgium is worth that amount. I guess that's why Carlos [Carlos Brito, Brazilian born CEO of InBev who led the deal] had to go to 7 banks around the world to get this amount. The next thing he will do is put Brazilian sugar cane in all the beer—much cheaper I understand," said another.[32] For some patriots, the takeover of Anheuser-Busch signified a destruction of heritage. Unable to identify with a brand that had lost its American identity, they threatened to switch to local brews.

In the meantime, there was trouble in South Africa. In April 2006, the International Football Federation announced that Anheuser-Busch would sponsor the 2010 World Cup (a major International Football Federation event) amid speculation that SABMiller's South African operations had been upstaged.[33] However, without a global brand, SABMiller saw little value in sponsoring international television coverage. Instead, SAB Ltd decided to sponsor the local team and distribute beer to football fans. But a painful blow was struck in March 2007 when Dutch brewer Heineken cancelled SAB's license to brew Amstel, for decades SAB's lucrative premium brand in the home market. Heineken's move was precipitated by concern over SABMiller's expanding global footprint—particularly its acquisition of Bavaria Brewery in Colombia, where Heineken had its own interests. As SAB hurriedly brought in several of its own premium brands, including Miller Draft, Heineken exported Dutch-brewed Amstel to South Africa and begun construction on a local brewery.[34]

SAB launched a slew of recently acquired premium brands into the South African market. Two key brands—Carling Black Label, the biggest seller, and Castle Lager, a longtime favorite—remained synonymous with sociability in the mainstream market. Castle Lager's core values were "re-affirmed" as "generous, outgoing, sincere, hospitable, optimistic, caring," with a touch of "uniquely South African 'can do/make a plan' resilience."[35] But the local market remained under pressure. State regulation of liquor retailing, external competition, and increasing consumer options suggested that there was no room for complacency for those in the deep play of competition. Norman Adami returned to South Africa, and after a break of several months, he was appointed CEO of SAB Ltd in October 2008. In Adami's view, SAB's international achievements were driven by its success at home; there was no tension between the local and the global. "We are not a global company with a history in South Africa," he said. "We are a South African company that has gone global. This is a critical component of the way we think."[36] It was in South Africa, after all, that SAB had honed its competitive strategy.

Appendix

Table 1. Production of Malt Beer and Unfortified Wine in the South African Beer Industry, Selected Years, 1951–1991[1] (in hectoliters)[2]

Date	Beer	Wine
1951	1,001,480	371,500
1953	1,023,120	462,060
1955	824,600	555,840
1957	757,950	490,920
1960	800,190	879,290
1963	1,137,360	709,900
1965	1,703,700	1,475,220
1967	1,673,340	1,557,640
1970	2,903,300	2,111,530
1973	3,972,760	2,761,980
1975	5,496,020	2,625,020
1977	5,607,740	1,990,070
1980	7,508,240	1,869,990
1983	11,586,270	2,048,740
1985	12,284,190	1,832,810
1987	16,721,820	1,609,540
1991	17,710,000	2,092,740

Notes
1. South Africa's Department of Statistics provides no figures for malt beer after 1991.
2. 1 hectoliter = 100 liters.

Source: Compiled from Government of South Africa, Department of Statistics, *Monthly Bulletin of Statistics* (Pretoria: Government Printer, December 1961); Government of South Africa, Department of Statistics, *Monthly Bulletin of Statistics* (Pretoria: Government Printer, December 1965); and Government of South Africa, Department of Statistics, *Monthly Bulletin of Statistics* (Pretoria: Government Printer, December 1968); Department of Statistics, *Quarterly Bulletin of Statistics* (Pretoria: Government Printer, 1970); Department of Statistics, *Census of Manufacturing: Manufacturing Statistics,* December 1972–December 1993 (Pretoria: Government Printer, 1972–1991).

Table 2. Average Percent Change in Beer Prices and Excise Duties in South Africa, 1958–1996

	1958–1962	1963–1967	1968–1972	1973–1977	1978–1982	1983–1987	1988–1992	1993–1996	Average
Nominal beer price[1]	1.7	2.4	2.4	2.8	3.3	3.2	4.8	4.1	3.1
Nominal excise duty	2.1	4.2	3.3	2.1	1.7	1.1	3.5	4.3	2.8
Consumer prices[1]	2.2	2.9	4.4	10.8	12.6	13.9	13.2	7.9	8.5
Real beer price[2,1]	1.7	2.7	1.1	-4.3	-5.1	-6.6	-2.2	1.5	-1.5
Real excise duty	2.6	6.8	3.3	-6.0	-8.8	-11.3	-5.2	1.9	-2.2
Pure beer price[3]	1.1	-0.6	-1.3	-2.5	-1.9	-3.9	-0.9	1.4	-2.2

Source: Loanne Sharp, "The South African Breweries Ltd: A Case Study in Monopoly Conditions, Conglomerate Diversification and Corporate Control in the South African Malt Beer Industry" (Master of Commerce thesis, University of Cape Town, 1997), 8.

Notes

1. Nominal beer price is the price SAB determined based on it costs.
2. Real beer price is the effective price paid to SAB after accounting for inflation.
3. Pure beer price is the price that accrued directly to SAB after accounting for the excise duty.

Notes

INTRODUCTION

1. Competition Tribunal of South Africa, "In the Large Merger between Distillers Corporation (SA) Limited (Primary Acquiring Firm) and Stellenbosch Farmers Winery Group Ltd (Primary Target Firm)," Case No. 08/LM/Feb02, Non-Confidential Version, obtained from Competition Tribunal, Johannesburg. Also available at http://www.comptrib.co.za/comptrib/comptribdocs/261/08LMFEb02.pdf.

2. Ibid. See also Michael Fridjhon and Caroline Pool, *Research Report on the Liquor Industry for Who Owns Whom: Essential Business Information* (Randburg: Who Owns Whom, 2004), 6. In the United States, concentration in the brewing industry was curtailed in the early 1950s by federal intervention. See A. M. McGahan, "The Emergence of the National Brewing Oligopoly: Competition in the American Market, 1933–1958," *Business History Review* 65 (Summer 1991): 229–284.

3. See Charles D. H. Parry and Anna L. Bennetts, *Alcohol Policy and Public Health in South Africa* (Cape Town: Oxford University Press, 1998); Charles D. H. Parry and Anna L. Bennetts, "Country Profile on Alcohol in South Africa," in *Alcohol and Public Health in Eight Developing Countries,* ed. L. Riley and M. Marshall (Geneva: World Health Organization, 1999), 135–175. Beer volumes increased from 1,001,480 hectoliters (26.4 million gallons) in 1951 to 17,710,000 hectoliters (467.8 million gallons) in 1991, while wine volumes increased from 371,500 hectoliters (9.8 million gallons) to 2,092,740 hectoliters (55.3 million gallons) in the same period. See Table 1 in the appendix.

4. Cape of Good Hope Liquor Laws Commission, *Report of the Liquor Laws Commission,* series no. G.1-90 (Cape Town: Government Printer, 1890), 30.

5. Ibid., 3. In the Cape of Good Hope Liquor Law Amendment Act (Act no. 28 of 1898), the term "native" encompassed male "Kaffirs, Fingoes, Basutos, Hottentots, Bushmen and the like; half-castes and all persons of mixed race living as members of any native community, tribe, kraal or location."

6. Editorial, "Indigenous Australians and Liquor Licensing Restrictions," *Addiction* 95, no. 10 (2000): 1469–1472.

7. See the minority report to Cape of Good Hope Liquor Laws Commission, *Report of the Liquor Laws Commission* (Appendix 1); see also Editorial, *Natal Mercury,* 6 April 1890.

8. The Cape of Good Hope Liquor Licensing Act (Act no. 28 of 1883) declared that no liquor was to be "sold, supplied or given to natives" in native locations without the permission of the governor.

9. After the formation of the Union of South Africa in 1910, legislation could be applied across all four provinces, as was the case with the Liquor Act (Act no. 30 of 1928).

10. Jonathan Crush and Charles Ambler, "Introduction," in *Liquor and Labor in Southern Africa,* ed. Jonathan Crush and Charles Ambler (Athens: Ohio University Press, 1992); Paul la Hause, "Drinking in a Cage: The Durban System and the 1929 Riots," *Africa Perspective* 20 (1982): 63–75.

11. For an exception to the preoccupation with liquor as either exploitation or survival, see Nigel Penn's account of Ruttgert Mensinck, brewer of Cape malt beer, in *Rogues, Rebels, and Runaways: Eighteenth-Century Cape Characters* (Cape Town: David Philip, 1999), 9–72.

12. For commercial liquor in the gold rush, see Charles van Onselen, "Randlords and Rotgut 1886–1903," *History Workshop* 2, no. 1 (1976): 33–38; for African liquor commerce, see Christian Rogerson, "The Survival of the Informal Sector: The Shebeens of Black Johannesburg," *GeoJournal* 12, no. 1 (1986): 153–166.

13. Emmanuel Akyeampong and Charles Ambler, "Leisure in African History: An Introduction," *International Journal of African Historical Studies,* special issue, *Leisure in African History* 35, no. 1 (2002): 11. For recent studies of leisure in Africa, see Paul Tiyambe Zeleza and Cassandra Rachel Veney, eds., *Leisure in Urban Africa* (Trenton, N.J., and Asmara, Eritrea: Africa World Press, 2003).

14. Ken Worpole, "The Age of Leisure," in *Enterprise and Heritage: Crosscurrents of National Culture,* ed. John Corner and Sylvia Harvey (London: Routledge, 1991), 137–161.

15. John Davis, "An Anthropologist's View of Exchange," *Oxford Development Studies* 24, no. 1 (1996): 54 and 47–59; Megan Vaughan, "The Character of the Market: Social Identities in Colonial Economies," *Oxford Development Studies* 24, no. 1 (1996): 61–77; Thomas L. Haskell and Richard F. Teichgraeber, *The Culture of the Market: Historical Essays* (Cambridge: Cambridge University Press, 1993); Roy Dilley, ed., *Contesting Markets: Analyses of Ideology, Discourse and Practice* (Edinburgh: Edinburgh University Press, 1992).

16. Deborah Fahy Bryceson, *Alcohol in Africa: Mixing Business, Pleasure and Politics* (Portsmouth, N.H.: Heinemann, 2002); Justin Willis, *Potent Brews: A Social History of Alcohol in East Africa, 1850–1999* (Oxford: James Currey and the British Institute in East Africa, 2002); Emmanuel Akyeampong, *Drink, Power, and Cultural Change: A Social History of Alcohol in Ghana, c. 1800 to Recent Times* (Portsmouth, N.H. and Oxford: Heinemann and James Currey, 1996); Emmanuel Akyeampong, "What's in a Drink? Class Struggle, Popular Culture and the Politics of *Akpeteshie* (Local Gin) in Ghana, 1930–67," *Journal of African History* 37, no. 2 (1996): 215–236; Michael West, "Liquor and Libido: 'Joint Drinking' and the Politics of Sexual Control in Colonial Zimbabwe, 1920s–1950s," *Journal of Social History* 30, no. 3 (1997): 645–667; Harry F. Wolcott, *The African Beer Gardens of Bulawayo: Integrated Drinking in a Segregated Society* (New Brunswick, N.J.: Rutgers Center of Alcohol Studies, 1974); Susan Diduk, "European Alcohol, History, and the State in Cameroon," *African Studies Review* 36, no. 1 (April 1993): 1–42; Simon Heap, "Before 'Star': The Import Substitution of Western-Style Alcohol in Nigeria, 1870–1970," *African Eco-*

nomic History 24 (1996): 69–89; Simon Heap, "'A Bottle of Gin Is Dangled before the Nose of the Natives': The Economic Uses of Imported Liquor in Southern Nigeria, 1860–1920," *African Economic History* 33 (2005): 69–85; Ilsa M. Glazer, "Alcohol and Politics in Urban Zambia: The Intersection of Gender and Class," in *African Feminism: The Politics of Survival in Sub-Saharan Africa,* ed. Gwendolyn Mikell (Philadelphia: University of Pennsylvania Press, 1997), 142–158.

17. Heap, "Before 'Star,'" 69–89; Emmanuel Akeampong, "The State and Alcohol Revenues: Promoting Economic Development in Gold Coast/Ghana, 1919 to the Present," *Social History* 27, no. 54 (November 1994): 393–411.

18. Bryceson, *Alcohol in Africa*, 8–9.

19. See for example, Justin Willis's discussion of Monica Wilson's work in "'Beer Used to Belong to Older Men': Drink and Authority among the Nyakusa of Tanzania," *Africa* 71, no. 3 (2001): 373–390; Benedict Carton, *Blood from Your Children: The Colonial Origins of Generational Conflict in Africa* (Pietermaritzburg: University of Natal Press, 2002), 73–74.

20. Akyeampong, *Drink, Power, and Cultural Change,* 14.

21. Jim Bailey and Adam Seftel, eds., *Shebeens, Take a Bow! A Celebration of South Africa's Shebeen Lifestyle* (Johannesburg: Bailey's African History Archives, 1994); Michael Chapman, ed., *The Drum Decade: Stories from the 1950s* (Pietermaritzburg: University of Natal Press, 1989); Bloke Modisane, *Blame Me on History,* 2nd ed. (Craighall: Ad. Donker, 1986); Ellen Kuzwayo *Call Me Woman* (Johannesburg: Ravan Press, 1985); Essop Patel, ed., *The World of Nat Nakasa* (Johannesburg: Ravan Press, 1995); Mongane Serote, *To Every Birth Its Blood* (Johannesburg: Ravan Press, 1981); Miriam Tlali, *Footprints in the Quag* (Cape Town: David Philip, 1989); J. M. Lotter and J. J. Schmidt, "The Shebeen in an Urban Bantu Community," *Humanitas* 3, no. 1 (1975): 59–65; Rathnamala Pather, "The Figure of the Shebeen Queen in the Selected Works of Black South African Writers" (MA thesis, University of Natal, Durban, 1992). David B. Coplan has made the case for shebeens as centers of musical performance; see *In Township Tonight: South Africa's Black City Music and Theatre* (Johannesburg: Ravan Press, 1985), 90–112. Ian Edwards has argued that shebeen culture was too tied up with the business of illicit liquor to constitute a locus of cultural endeavor; see "Shebeen Queens: Illicit Liquor and the Social Structure of Drinking Dens in Cato Manor," *Agenda* 3 (1988): 75–97.

22. D. N. Suggs, "'These Young Chaps Think They Are Just Men Too': Redistributing Masculinity in Kgatleng Bars," *Social Science and Medicine* 53, no. 2 (2001): 241–250.

23. Willis, *Potent Brews,* 14.

24. Ivan Karp, "Beer Drinking and Social Experience in an African Society: An Essay in Formal Sociology," in *Explorations in African Systems of Thought,* ed. Ivan Karp and Charles Bird (Washington, D.C.: Smithsonian Institution Press, 1980), 83–119; Juha Partanen, *Sociability and Intoxication: Alcohol and Drinking in Kenya, Africa and the Modern World* (Helsinki: Finnish Foundation for Alcohol Studies, 1991), 219.

25. Karp, "Beer Drinking and Social Experience in an African Society: An Essay in Formal Sociology"; Partanen, *Sociability and Intoxication.*

26. Georg Simmel, *On Individuality and Social Forms: Selected Writings,* ed. and with an intro. by Donald N. Levine (Chicago: University of Chicago Press, 1971), 132.

27. Simmel, *On Individuality,* 134.

28. Karp, "Beer Drinking and Social Experience in an African Society," 97.

29. Ibid., 104.

30. Partanen, *Sociability and Intoxication,* 77.

31. Paul Morris, "Freeing the Spirit of Enterprise: The Genesis and Development of the Concept of Enterprise Culture," in *Enterprise Culture,* ed. Russell Keat and Nicholas Abercrombie (London and New York: Routledge, 1991), 180.

32. Diduk, "European alcohol, History, and the State in Cameroon," 1–42.

33. Juan Scott, designer of Castle Lager advertisements, interview with the author, July 2000.

34. Quoted in Alan Gregor Cobley, *The Rules of the Game: Struggles in Black Recreation and Social Welfare Policy in South Africa* (Westport, Conn.: Greenwood, 1997), 23.

35. Ibid., 24.

36. Andre Odendaal, "South Africa's Black Victorians: Sport and Society in the Nineteenth Century," in *Pleasure, Profit, Proselytism: British Culture and Sport at Home and Abroad, 1700–1914,* ed. James A. Mangan (London: Frank Cass, 1988), 199–200; see also Fredrick Cooper, "Elevating the Black Race: The Social Thought of Black Leaders, 1927–50," *American Quarterly* 24, no. 5 (December 1972): 604–625; Alan Gregor Cobley, *The Rules of the Game: Struggles in Black Recreation and Social Welfare Policy in South Africa* (Westport, Conn.: Greenwood, 1997); Wallace G. Mills, "The Fork in the Road: Religious Separatism versus African Nationalism in the Cape Colony, 1890–1910," *Journal of Religion in Africa* 9, no. 1 (1978): 51–61; Norman Etherington, "An American Errand in the South African Wilderness," *Church History* 39, no. 1 (March 1970): 62–71; David H. Anthony, III, "Max Yergan in South Africa: From Evangelical Pan-Africanist to Revolutionary Socialist," *African Studies Review* 34, no. 2 (September 1991): 27–55; Les Switzer, *Power and Resistance in an African Society: The Ciskei Xhosa and the Making of South Africa* (Madison: University of Wisconsin Press, 1993).

37. Peter Alegi, "'Keep Your Eye on the Ball': A Social History of Soccer in South Africa, 1910–1976 (Ph.D. diss., Boston University, 2000), 119.

38. Ibid., 123.

39. Ibid.

40. Peter Alegi, "Moving the Goal Posts: Playing Styles, Sociability, and Politics in South African Soccer in the 1960s," Working Paper 225, African Studies Center, Boston University, 2000, 17–19.

41. Albert Grundlingh, "Playing for Power? Rugby, Afrikaner Nationalism and Masculinity in South Africa, c. 1900–c. 1970," in *Making Men: Rugby and Masculine Identity,* ed. John Nauright and Timothy J. L. Chandler (London: Frank Cass, 1996), 186–188; John Nauright, "Colonial Manhood and Imperial Race Virility: British Responses to Post–Boer War Colonial Rugby Tours," in Nauright and Chandler, *Making Men,* 122–134.

42. Tony Collins and Wray Vamplew, *Mud, Sweat, and Beers: A Cultural History of Sport and Alcohol* (Oxford: Berg, 2002), 75.

43. Ibid. See also Eric Dunning and Kenneth Sheard, *Barbarians, Gentlemen and Players: A Sociological Study of the Development of Rugby Football* (Oxford: Martin Robertson, 1979), 216–218.

44. Grant Jarvie, "Sport, Nationalism and Cultural Identity," in *The Changing Politics of Sport,* ed. Lincoln Allison (Manchester: Manchester University Press, 1993), 76.

45. Clifford Geertz, *Interpretation of Cultures* (New York: Basic Books, 1973), 433.

46. This generalized distinction does not mean that white men did not play soccer or that black men did not play rugby.

47. Andre W. Miracle, Jr., and C. Roger Rees make this argument for the United States. See *Lessons of the Locker Room: The Myth of School Sports* (New York: Prometheus Books, 1994), 20.

48. Ibid., 18.

49. Joey Burke quoted in Graham Barrett, "Intervarsity: Through the Eyes of Joey Burke, Cheerleader and Chair, 1989–1990," unpublished research project, University of Cape Town, Historical Studies Department, 2005. See also Louis Babrow and R. K. Stent, *The Varsity Spirit: The Story of Rugby Football at the University of Cape Town, 1883–1963* (Cape Town: Johnston and Neville, 1963).

50. Varda Burstyn, *The Rites of Men: Manhood, Politics, and the Culture of Sport* (1999; repr., Toronto: University of Toronto Press, 2000), 95–96.

51. Ibid., 32.

52. Ibid., 101 and 36.

53. Pierre Bourdieu, *Masculine Domination* (Stanford, Calif.: Stanford University Press, California, 1998), 51.

54. Ibid., 52.

55. Ibid., 53.

56. For variants on robust masculinities, see Robert Morrell, "Of Boys and Men: Masculinity and Gender in Southern African Studies," *Journal of Southern African Studies* 24 (1998): 605–630; L. Ouzgane and Robert Morrell, eds., *African Masculinities: Men in Africa from the Late Nineteenth Century to the Present* (New York: Palgrave, 2004); Robert Morrell, ed., *Changing Men in Southern Africa* (Pietermaritzburg/London: University of Natal Press/Zed Books, 2001); Linda Richter and Robert Morrell, eds., *Baba: Men and Fatherhood in South Africa* (Cape Town: Human Sciences Research Council Press, 2006); Graeme Reid and Liz Walker, eds., *Men Behaving Differently: South African Men since 1994* (Cape Town: Double Storey, 2005); Kopano Ratele, "The End of the Black Man," *Agenda* 37 (1998): 60–64.

57. For studies of masculinity in the workplace, see T. Dunbar Moodie with Vivienne Ndatshe, *Going for Gold: Men, Mines, and Migration* (Berkeley: University of California Press, 1994); Patrick Harries, *Work, Culture, and Identity: Migrant Laborers in Mozambique and South Africa, c. 1860–1910* (Portsmouth, N.H.: Heinemann, 1994); and Lisa A. Lindsay, *Working with Gender: Wage Labor and Social Change in Southwestern Nigeria* (Portsmouth, N.H.: Heinemann, 2003).

1. ILLICIT DRINKING, PROHIBITION, AND SOCIABILITY IN APARTHEID'S TOWNSHIPS

1. The word "shebeen" is derived from *sibin,* meaning "bad ale," and was used in Ireland to refer to lowbrow or illicit drinking houses. The term was brought to South Africa by immigrants serving in the colonial police force and soon became part of

the vocabulary of those who lived in the segregated townships adjacent to white cities. See Geoff Hughes, "'Shebeen' Is Actually an Irish Term," *Star*, 27 October 1991.

2. In Zambia, then Northern Rhodesia, Africans were permitted to drink beer and light wine in 1951. Kenyans had been allowed beer since 1948, and in Southern Rhodesia, beer and wine were sold in government beer halls from 1957. See Muriel Horrel, *The Liquor Laws* (Braamfontein: South African Institute of Race Relations, 1960), 32–42.

3. The market value of the merged companies in 1956 was £40 million; Avril Iré Malan, *Report of the Commission of Enquiry into the General Distribution and Selling Prices of Intoxicating Liquor* (Pretoria: Government Printer, 1960), 8; J. A. H. van Niekerk, Brewers Institute of South Africa, to Commission of Enquiry into the General Distribution and Selling Prices of Intoxicating Liquor, Johannesburg, 12 November 1956, Government Publications Department, University of Cape Town.

4. See "Inside Johannesburg's Underworld," in *Shebeens, Take a Bow! A Celebration of South Africa's Shebeen Lifestyle*, ed. Jim Bailey and Adam Seftel (Johannesburg: Bailey's African History Archives, 1994), 14.

5. See Ian Edwards, "Shebeen Queens: Illicit Liquor and the Social Structure of Drinking Dens in Cato Manor," *Agenda* 3 (1988): 75–97, for a description of illicit concoctions.

6. See, for example, Can Themba, "Let the People Drink . . . They Are Drinking Anyway!" in Bailey and Seftel, *Shebeens, Take a Bow!* 24–31.

7. The statistics were collected by *Drum* and published in its May 1955 issue. See "Should Africans Be Allowed Liquor?" in Bailey and Seftel, *Shebeens Take a Bow!* 20.

8. Bloke Modisane, *Blame Me on History*, 2nd ed. (Craighall: Ad. Donker, 1986), 39.

9. Can Themba, "There Is a Yard Where People Have Gone Mysteriously Mad: Boozers Beware of Barberton," in Bailey and Seftel, *Shebeens, Take a Bow!* 38–41.

10. Modisane, *Blame Me on History*, 39.

11. Themba, "Let the People Drink," 24.

12. See Casey Motsisi, "On the Beat," in *The Drum Decade: Stories from the 1950s*, ed. Michael Chapman (Pietermaritzburg: University of Natal Press, 1989), 175–182.

13. Jacky Heyns, "Down the Hatch!" in Bailey and Seftel, *Shebeens, Take a Bow!* 1–13.

14. Peter Magubane's photo is in Casey Motsisi, "One Man's Day of Reckoning," in Bailey and Seftel, *Shebeens, Take a Bow!* 74–75.

15. Rathnamala Pather, "The Figure of the Shebeen Queen in the Selected Works of Black South African Writers" (MA thesis, University of Natal, Durban, 1992), 6.

16. Modisane, *Blame Me on History*, 38.

17. Casey Motsisi, "Casey's Beat: At Sixes and Sevens," *Drum*, October 1976, 71.

18. Heyns, "Down the Hatch!" 11.

19. "I Am a Shebeen Queen," in Bailey and Seftel, *Shebeens Take a Bow!* 103; Modisane, *Blame Me on History*; J. M. Lotter and J. J. Schmidt, "The Shebeen in an Urban Bantu Community," *Humanitas* 3, no. 1 (1975): 59–65.

20. For example, Casey Motsisi, "Miss Prettiful," in Bailey and Seftel, *Shebeens, Take a Bow!* 60–62.

21. Malan, *Report of the Commission of Enquiry into the General Distribution and Selling Prices of Intoxicating Liquor,* 8. See also "Police Raided Langa Single Quarters to Stop Liquor Parties," *Argus,* 26 November 1956; "Policemen Stoned by Sixty Natives," *Star,* 20 November 1956; "Native and Womenfolk Assaulted Police," *Star,* 7 September 1956; "Police Group Attacked by Mob," *Star,* 29 September 1956; "Natives Held after Stoning of Police," *Rand Daily Mail,* 20 November 1956; "Prisoners Released by Native Mob," *Daily Dispatch,* 1 October 1956; "Constable in Lone Liquor Raid: Native Shot Dead in Location Attack," *Natal Daily News,* 5 November 1956; "Native Quotes Bible in His Defence," *Natal Mercury,* 18 February 1956.

22. "They All Go to Cato for a Drink," *Rand Daily Mail,* 1 July 1961.

23. Cape Town City Council, Native Affairs Committee Minutes, 25 September 1961, Cape Town City Council Collection, Western Cape Archives and Records Service, Cape Town; D. L. Smit, 16 June 1961, and Mr. Holland, 19 June 1961, both in South Africa, Parliament, House of Assembly, *Debates of the House of Assembly* (Cape Town: Government Printer, 1961), 8287 and 8441, respectively. See also "Liquor Bill to Crush Illegalities," *Cape Times,* 17 June 1961.

24. Malan, *Report of the Commission of Enquiry into the General Distribution and Selling Prices of Intoxicating Liquor,* 8.

25. Major General C. I. Rademeyer, Commissioner of Police, quoted in "Police Commissioner Pleads for Reasonable Sales of Liquor to Non-Europeans," *Argus,* 1 February 1955.

26. Malan, *Report of the Commission of Enquiry into the General Distribution and Selling Prices of Intoxicating Liquor,* 8.

27. "Police Commissioner Pleads for Reasonable Sales of Liquor to Non-Europeans."

28. See Emmanuel Akeampong, *Drink, Power, and Cultural Change: A Social History of Alcohol in Ghana, c. 1800 to Recent Times* (Portsmouth and Oxford: Heinemann and James Currey, 1996); M. O. West, "Liquor and Libido: 'Joint Drinking' and the Politics of Sexual Control in Colonial Zimbabwe, 1920s–1950s," *Journal of Social History* 30, no. 3 (1997): 645–667; T. R. Gourvish and R. G. Wilson, *The British Brewing Industry, 1830–1980* (Cambridge: Cambridge University Press, 1994); and D. Christian, *Living Water: Vodka and Russian Society on the Eve of Emancipation* (Oxford: Clarendon Press, 1990). For discussion of the character of persons and markets, see Megan Vaughan, "The Character of the Market: Social Identities in Colonial Economies," *Oxford Development Studies* 24, no. 1 (1996): 61–77.

29. Malan, *Report of the Commission of Enquiry into the General Distribution and Selling Prices of Intoxicating Liquor,* 8.

30. Ibid.

31. Minister of Justice, 16 June 1961, in South Africa, Parliament, House of Assembly, *Debates of the House of Assembly,* 8287.

32. Ibid.

33. D. L. Smit, 16 June 1961, in South Africa, Parliament, House of Assembly, *Debates of the House of Assembly,* 8292. South Africa became a republic in 1961.

34. Vaughan, "The Character of the Market," 68–69.

35. D. L. Smit, 16 June 1961, in South Africa, Parliament, House of Assembly, *Debates of the House of Assembly,* 8295; "Effect of Liquor on Violent Bantu Is Feared," *Cape Times,* 20 June 1961; Parliamentary Correspondent, "Thirty Thousand

Coloureds Live Off Illicit Liquor Trade," *Cape Times,* 17 June 1961; Political Correspondent and Staff Reporter, "Hotelier: Good Temperance Man: Evil Bill Surprise," *Rand Daily Mail,* 10 June 1961. For similar white panic elsewhere, see West, "Liquor and Libido," 645–667.

36. Staff Reporter, "Farmers Want Liquor for Africans," *Cape Times,* 24 April 1958.

37. Vaughan, "Character of the Market," 68.

38. H. R. Cocking, National Secretary of Temperance Alliance, letter to *Argus,* 19 September 1958; National Council of Women to Malan Commission, reported about in *Cape Times,* 19 October 1958; Temperance Alliance to *Cape Times,* 29 January 1959.

39. Bantu Administration Boards, established in the terms of the Bantu Affairs Administration Act (1971), removed black townships from white municipalities and brought them under the Department of Bantu Administration and Development; Deborah Posel, *The Making of Apartheid 1948–1961: Conflict and Compromise* (Oxford: Clarendon Press, 1991), 248n78. For comments on government control of liquor distribution, see "Cape Coloureds Get Same Liquor Rights as Whites," *Star,* 8 November 1961; "Reaction to Liquor Sales to Coloured in European Area," *Argus,* 22 November 1961.

40. Staff Reporter, "Liquor a Danger to Coloured," *Argus,* 9 November 1961. See also R. E. van der Ross, "Coloured Access to Liquor," *Cape Times,* 16 November 1961; and "Four Natives in Liquor Bill Protest," *Argus,* 20 June 1961.

41. "Luthuli Attacks Liquor Bill," *Rand Daily Mail,* 18 August 1961; Dr. R. T. Bokwe and Thomas Nkosinkulu, "The Beer Question," *South African Outlook,* November 1941.

42. Vaughan, "Character of the Market," 69.

43. See three letters in South African Institute of Race Relations Collection, AD 1947/38.1, Archives of the Church of the Province of South Africa, University of the Witwatersrand: Bishop A. H. Zulu, Umtata, to SA Institute of Race Relations, 21 February 1961; Federal Council of African Teachers Associations to South African Institute of Race Relations, 4 April 1961; and Mangosutho Buthelezi to South Africa Institute of Race Relations, April 1961. See also "Why Natives Welcome Liquor Bill," *Star,* 24 June 1961; Makgona-Tsotlhe, "Varied Reactions to New Liquor Bill," *Star,* 10 July 1961; and "Africans Clamour for Drink Licences," *Rand Daily Mail,* 6 July 1961.

44. See "Bigger Market for Wines and Brandies," *Rand Daily Mail,* 17 June 1961.

45. C. W. A. Lansdown, *South African Liquor Law* (Cape Town: Juta, 1983), 332–344.

46. M. C. Botha, Deputy Minister of Bantu Administration and Development and Nationalist Member of Parliament for Roodepoort, 7 May 1962, in South Africa, Parliament, House of Assembly, *Debates* (Cape Town: Government Printer, 1962), 5040.

47. J. von S. Moltke, Nationalist Member of Parliament for Karas, 11 May 1962, in South Africa, Parliament, House of Assembly, *Debates* (Cape Town: Government Printer, 1962), 5467.

48. "Bantoebier 'n Groot Bedryf in S.A.," *Vaderland,* 27 July 1966.

49. The brewers at this moment were SAB and the smaller Old Dutch Brewery, which was owned by the Independent Brewers Corporation and the Union Free State Mining and Finance Corporation.

50. The Department of Bantu Administration and Development was the apartheid-era name given to the Department of Native Affairs, a national government department. The Bantu Affairs Administration Boards were established in the 1950s to run black townships and remove this responsibility from white municipalities. See Posel, *The Making of Apartheid 1948-1961*, 232-235.

51. SAB established the South African Brewers Institute in 1956 for the purpose of conducting public relations and government liaison activities; the name was later changed to the South African Breweries Institute.

52. Harold Moulton's interview with Joss van Niekerk, Pretoria, 13 April 1987, SAB Records, South African Breweries Head Office, Johannesburg (hereafter SAB Records).

53. Parliamentere Beriggewer, "Volksraad skerp verdeel oor drank aan nie-blankes," *Vaderland,* 17 June 1961; "Brewers Study Native Liquor Market," *Star,* 25 September 1961.

54. Author's interview with John Seton, 30 October 1997.

55. Municipal Reporter, "Drunken Orgy Threatens SA—Councillor," *Rand Daily Mail,* 28 June 1961.

56. Author's interview with John Seton.

57. Memorandum, Road Safety Council, Pretoria, Cape Town City Council Minutes, 17 July 1962, Cape Town City Council Collection, Western Cape Archives and Records Service, Cape Town. All Cape Town City Council Minutes cited are from this archive.

58. SA Road Safety Notice, Cape Town City Council Minutes, 3 July 1962.

59. "No Liquor Rush by Peninsula Natives," *Argus,* 15 August 1962.

60. Ibid.

61. Memorandum, Road Safety Council 17 July 1962, Cape Town City Council Minutes, September 1961–August 1962.

62. Zambia's Copperbelt was seen as an example to follow. In 1961, the Johannesburg City Council went on a study tour of drinking houses on the Zambian Copperbelt to inform themselves of African drinking habits. See Harold MacCarthy (Johannesburg city councillor), "European Liquor and the African," *Rand Daily Mail,* 19 October 1961. SAB's Mr. Braadtvedt addressed a meeting of Bantu Affairs administrators on liquor consumption patterns in Rhodesia and Zambia in 1965; see Department of Bantu Administration and Development, Institute of Administrators of Non-European Affairs, *Records of Proceedings of 14th Annual Conference 30 August–2 September 1965* (n.p., n.d.), 109–110.

63. Author's interview with John Seton.

64. "No Liquor Rush by Peninsula Natives," *Argus,* 15 August 1962.

65. Ibid.

66. Staff Reporter, "Shebeen Queens Count on Business as Usual," *Star,* 19 July 1961, quoting *Drum* as the source.

67. "New Liquor Laws a Shot in the Arm for the Trade," *Argus,* 17 August 1962.

68. Staff Reporter, "Shebeen Queens Count on Business as Usual."

69. Lennox Mbokoma, letter to *Argus,* 22 August 1962.

70. Makgona-Tsotlhe, "Africans Foresee No Binge on 'L' Day," *Star,* 6 August 1960); Witness Reporter, "Drinking Habits of Africans Improved by New Laws," *Natal Witness,* 1 July 1964.

71. Author's interview with John Seton; see also "Brewers Study Native Liquor Market," *Star,* 25 September 1961.

72. Ibid.

73. Municipal beer halls were first established in Durban in 1908. Johannesburg followed suit in 1937 and by 1965 had made a profit of R18.7 million from the sale of sorghum beer. See Michael Savage, "Bantu Beer," *South African Outlook,* September 1976, 133; and Institute of Administrators of Non-European Affairs, *Records of Proceedings of 12th Annual Conference (9–12 July 1963)* (n.p., n.d.), 123–144.

74. Divisional councils were responsible for the peri-urban areas of all towns and were under provincial rather than local administration.

75. "'Secrecy' Follows Recent Langa Liquor Referendum," *Cape Times,* 26 August 1961.

76. See Posel, *Making of Apartheid,* 90–103.

77. "Bantu Say 'No' to Liquor Sale," *Cape Times,* 1 September 1961; Native Affairs Minutes, 14 September and 7 November 1961, Cape Town City Council, Cape Town City Council Collection, Western Cape and Archives Records Service, Cape Town. All Cape Town Native Affairs Minutes cited are from this collection.

78. "'Secrecy' Follows Recent Langa Liquor Referendum," *Cape Times,* 26 August 1961.

79. Interview with Sister Lydia Mosala, 29 April 1998.

80. Ibid.

81. Cape Town City Council Minutes, 11 June 1962, 113. The delegation included Mrs. B. Stoy, representative of the National Council of Women of South Africa Cape Town Branch; Dr. J. R. L Kingon and Mrs. B. Hermanson of the South African Temperance Alliance and the Women's Christian Temperance Union of the Cape; Mrs. H. Agnew and Mrs. W. Jennings of the Methodist Women's Auxiliaries, Cape District; Rev. N. B. Kok and Rev. E. W. A. Barber of the Methodist Church of South Africa; and Mrs. Lily Mafu of the National Council of African Women, Langa Branch. See also Rev. N. B. Kok, Memorandum to the City Council, 28 May 1962, Cape Town City Council Collection, Western Cape and Archives Records Service, Cape Town.

82. Mr. G. G. Ndzotyana to Cape Town City Council, 18 September 1961, quoted in Cape Town City Council, Native Affairs Minutes, Reports from the Town Clerk, 3 October 1961, 4. See also "Langa Need Is Better Wages—Not Bars—Says Bantu Pastor," *Argus,* 21 August 1962.

83. See Staff Reporter, "Native Liquor: Licence 'Gold Rush' on in SA," *Argus,* 23 October 1961.

84. Cape Town City Council, Native Affairs Minutes, 7 November 1961, 6.

85. C. B. Young, Secretary of Bantu Administration and Development to Town Clerk, Cape Town, 25 May 1962, Cape Town City Council Collection, Western Cape and Archives Records Service, Cape Town. Young's letter is marked "Confidential— Not for publication—Copyright reserved."

86. Native Affairs Agenda, 7 November 1961, Cape Town City Council Minutes. Twenty applications were advertised in the *Cape Argus* and eighteen columns of notices appeared in the *Star;* see "Rush for Licences Has Begun," *Argus,* 31 October 1961.

87. Memorandum from Native Affairs Committee to the Town Clerk, 28 June 1962, Cape Town City Council Minutes, September 1961 to August 1962.

88. "Objections Considered: R1m Beerhall Plan to Go on," *Argus,* 25 September 1963. Protest from African entrepreneurs in Johannesburg was far stronger. See Makgona-Tsotlhe, "Liquor Licences for Individual Africans," *Star,* 25 October 1961; and "Africans Appeal to the Government: 'Let Liquor Be in Hands of Private Enterprise,'" *Rand Daily Mail,* 25 August 1961.

89. Argus Representative, "PE Council Expects R72 000 Profit from Liquor Sold to Natives," *Argus,* 30 August 1961; see also Herald Municipal Reporter, "Sales of Liquor to Africans Soar," *Eastern Province Herald,* 24 November 1964.

90. Bantu Affairs Administration Boards were recommended by the Control Measures Committee of 1967; by 1975, twenty-two boards had been established. See Doug Hindson, *Pass Controls and the Urban African Proletariat in South Africa* (Johannesburg: Ravan Press, 1987), 72.

91. The dry powder for instant beer was supplied by Jabula Foods, which supplied Jabula Instant Bantu Beer Powder to a large number of municipalities. See "Jabula Instant Bantu Beer—List of Users," n.d., attachment to letter from Jabula Foods (Pty) Ltd. to Cape Town City Council, 5 January 1962, Cape Town City Council Collection, Western Cape and Archives Records Service, Cape Town.

92. Chief Reporter, "'Go-Ahead' for Townships Brewery Loan," *Cape Times,* 19 September 1968.

93. Argus Correspondent, "Drink for Natives: 500 Applications Are Approved," *Argus,* 18 April 1962; "Quick Start Planned for Nyanga and Langa Pubs," *Argus,* 25 April 1962. Similar plans were made by the Johannesburg City Council; see South African Institute of Race Relations, "Johannesburg City Council Plans Luxury Bar Lounges for Africans," *News,* November 1961.

94. "Call for Change of Attitude to Native Townships," *Argus,* 15 August 1963.

95. See Francis Wilson, "Migrant Labour: Pros and Cons," *South African Outlook* (January/February 1973): 20–33; Wilson used figures from Cape Town City Council, Department of Bantu Administration. See also Office of the City Treasurer to Chairman and Members of the Bantu Affairs and Finance Committees, D.5/15q, Purchases of Liquor for Bantu Liquor Outlets, City of Cape Town Bantu Affairs Committee Minutes, September 1963 to August 1964, Cape Town City Council Collection, Western Cape and Archives Records Service, Cape Town. This document is marked "Confidential—Not for Publication."

96. Councillor M. B. Luntz, Chair, Bantu Affairs Committee, quoted in "Call for Change of Attitude to Native Townships," *Argus,* 15 August 1963.

97. Ibid.

98. Cape Times Chief Reporter, "Liquor Controls Sought," *Cape Times,* 29 February 1964; Municipal Affairs Reporter, "Townships and Drink Delivery," *Evening Post,* 9 October 1967; Staff Reporter, "Curb on Liquor Sales Sought," *Rand Daily Mail,* 20 May 1967.

99. Author's interview with Councillor Eulalie Stott, 25 October 1997; "Appeal for Pubs in Townships: Provide for Liquor Trade, City Told," *Cape Times,* 7 July 1964; Cape Times Chief Reporter, "Definitely No Liquor, Says Council," *Cape Times,* 10 July 1964.

100. For early accounts of shebeen queens, see Paul la Hause, "Drink and Cultural Innovation in Durban: The Origins of the Beerhall in South Africa, 1902–1916," in

Liquor and Labour in Southern Africa, ed. J. Crush and C. Ambler (Athens: Ohio University Press, 1992), 78–114; and Edwards, "Shebeen Queens," 75–97. For literary accounts of shebeen queens, see Rathnamala Pather, "The Figure of the Shebeen Queen in the Selected Works of Black South African Writers" (MA thesis, University of Natal, Durban, 1992); Nat Nakasa, "And So the Shebeen Lives On," *Rand Daily Mail,* 2 May 1964, reprinted in *The World of Nat Nakasa,* ed. Essop Patel (Johannesburg: Ravan Press, 1995); Mongane Serote, *To Every Birth Its Blood* (Johannesburg: Ravan Press 1981); and Miriam Tlali, *Footprints in the Quag* (Cape Town: David Philip, 1989).

101. *eSpotini,* November 1980, accessed in SAB Records, South African Breweries Head Office, Johannesburg. All issues of *eSpotini* cited in these notes were accessed from this archival collection.

102. *eSpotini,* September 1981.

103. *eSpotini,* September 1980.

104. "Cook-dladla" (eatery) was a popular term for "shebeen" in the Johannesburg area, derived from the mining world's pidgin or "fanagalo"; in referring to food rather than drink, the term disguised the purpose of the establishment. *eSpotini,* April 1980; author's interview with "Big Mike," 8 July 1998.

105. Author's interview with Cooksie Senne, 8 July 1998; "R1,000 Fine for Liquor Offence," *Rand Daily Mail,* 27 June 1964; "Shebeens in Soweto Upset City," *Sunday Times,* 22 January 1967; "Twelve Arrested in Shebeen Raids," *Star,* 21 June 1967. *Tsotsis* were township youths who belonged to gangs; "double-up" was slang for customer service.

106. The Johannesburg City Council reported that while profits on Bantu beer sales were R2.8 million in 1969, sales were declining; see "Africans Switch to White Liquor," *Sunday Times,* 15 February 1970; and "Soweto Liquor Bill—R16m," *Star,* 16 April 1970.

107. *eSpotini,* February 1980.

108. For the demolition of Sophiatown, see Tom Lodge, "The Destruction of Sophiatown," *Journal of Modern African Studies* 19, no. 1 (1981): 107–132.

109. *eSpotini,* February 1980.

110. Simmel quoted in Juha Partanen, *Sociability and Intoxication: Alcohol and Drinking in Kenya, Africa and the Modern World* (Helsinki: Finnish Foundation for Alcohol Studies, 1991), 219.

111. "Beer Is Better Than Brandy in Soweto," *Rand Daily Mail,* 20 October 1964.

112. Confidential Memorandum from the City Treasurer to the Bantu Affairs Committee, Cape Town City Council, 28 January 1965.

113. J. L. Rusburne and H. Hamman, *A Survey of the Liquor Industry in South Africa* (Johannesburg: Statsinform, 1972), iv.

114. Judge J. H. Steyn, "The Alcoholic Offender," *Medical Proceedings* (September 1969): 321; "Crime Wave in Wake of Liquor Freedom," *Sunday Times,* 9 July 1961.

115. "Centre for African Alcoholics," *Natal Mercury,* 3 May 1969; A. L. Becker, "Alcoholism," *Medical Proceedings* (25 September 1966): 487–488; E. Louw, "The Medical Profession and the Rehabilitation of the Alcoholic," *Medical Proceedings* (25 September 1966): 490–493; A. B. Franciscus, "Summary of Reports on Discussions Conducted at Seminars on Alcoholism," *Alpha* 7, no. 10 (November 1969): 26–28.

116. SAB, "Take a Fresh Look at Carling Black Label," *Beer Business: A Quarterly Newsletter to the Liquor Trade from the Southern Transvaal Region of South African Breweries Ltd.* (December 1985): 2.

117. John R. Shorten, *The Johannesburg Saga* (Johannesburg: John R. Shorten [Pty] Ltd., 1970), 1.

118. Author's interview with Cooksie Senne, 8 July 1998; author's interview with "Big Mike," 8 July 1998; "Just Why Shebeens Stay in Business," *Rand Daily Mail,* 20 July 1967; "The Soweto Shebeen Raids Are Necessary," *Star,* 22 July 1967; "Shebeens: Where the Trouble Lies," *Star,* 18 August 1967.

119. "A Night on the Product," *Financial Mail,* supplement on South African Breweries Ltd., 7 December 1973, 46.

120. Ibid.

121. "Africans Switch to White Liquor," *Sunday Times,* 15 February 1970; "African Drinking Habits Change," *Star,* 20 May 1971.

122. "Twee miljoen gelling bantoebier per maand," *Transvaler,* 2 May 1968; "Bantu Beer Is Booming," *Pretoria News,* 29 December, 1964; "Beer Pays for Bantu Sport," *Pretoria News,* 9 May 1964; "Soweto Angry at Shortage of Beer," *Rand Daily Mail,* 31 March 1964.

123. "Bantu Beer Is Booming," *Pretoria News,* 29 December 1964; Rusburne and Hamman, *A Survey of the Liquor Industry in South Africa,* 33–38.

124. The deputy minister of Bantu Administration and Development confirmed that the municipality of Welkom had made a contribution to homeland development from township liquor revenues; see 4 February 1962 in South Africa, Parliament, House of Assembly, *Debates* (Cape Town: Government Printer, 1962), 711.

125. "Surplus" was calculated on the basis of income and expenditure in Bantu Affairs Administration Boards current accounts. In 1971, the surplus for Soweto was R170,000 against an expenditure of R11,222,000; for Pretoria's townships, the surplus was R298,000 against an expenditure of R5,760,000. See "Sales of Bantu Beer Soar," *Star,* 11 January 1971; "Drink Up for Bantustan," *Star,* 8 October 1968; "R1m Beer Profit for Homelands," *Friends,* 31 August 1968.

126. See Posel, *Making of Apartheid,* 231–235.

2. "IF YOU WANT TO RUN WITH THE BIG DOGS"

"If you want to run with the big dogs, you can't piss like a puppy" was a favorite expression of SAB executive Norman Adami, who joined SAB in 1977; Daniel Eisenberg, "Big Brew-Haha! The Battle of the Beers," Time, 12 July 2004.

1. See Frederick Johnstone, "White Prosperity and White Supremacy in South Africa Today," *African Affairs* 19, 275 (April 1970): 124–140; Merle Lipton, "The Debate about South Africa: Neo-Marxists and Neo-Liberals," *African Affairs* 78, no. 310 (1979): 57–80; Martin Legassick, "South Africa: Forced Labour, Industrialisation and Racial Differentiation," in *The Political Economy of Africa,* ed. Richard Harris (Cambridge, Mass.: Schenkman Publishing Co., 1973); Dan O'Meara, *Volkskapitalisme: Class, Capital and Ideology in the Development of Afrikaner Nationalism, 1934–48* (Cambridge, 1983); Merle Lipton, *Capitalism and Apartheid: South Africa 1910–1986* (Aldershot: Ashgate, 1986); Nancy Clark, "The Limits of Industrialization under Apartheid," in *Apartheid's Genesis, 1935–1962,* ed. Philip Bonner, Peter

Delius and Deborah Posel (Johannesburg: Ravan Press, 1993), 65–95; Nicoli Nattrass, "Controversies about Capitalism and Apartheid in South Africa," *Journal of Southern African Studies* 17, no. 4 (December 1991): 654–677.

2. See Alfie Kohn, *No Contest: The Case against Competition* (Boston: Houghton Mifflin, 1992), 116.

3. Typescript of dictation from S. J. Constance, n.d., bearing his signature. The document is labeled "In the SAB 1988 Annual Report" in the section "SAB: A Story of Growth" under the heading "Beer" in SAB Records.

4. Ibid.

5. Ibid.

6. Ibid.

7. Ibid.

8. See *Keeping Pace: The Story of the First Seventy-Five Years of the South African Breweries Group,* 12, pamphlet, "In the SAB 1988 Annual Report" in the section "SAB: A Story of Growth" under the heading "Beer," SAB Records.

9. For details on excise duties, see Table 2 in the appendix.

10. Michael Fridjhon and Andy Murray, *Conspiracy of Giants: The South African Liquor Industry* (Johannesburg: Divaris Stein, 1986), 81–87. See also Teresa da Silva, "The Impact of Multinational Investment on Alcohol Consumption since the 1960s," *Business and Economic History* 28, no. 2 (Winter 1999): 109–122.

11. To do so, SAB formed a partnership with Roberto Moni's Italian-based company Monis, which had interests in sherry, sparkling and fortified wines, and fruit juices and owned the Nederberg Estate near Paarl; see Ebbe Dommisse with the cooperation of Willie Esterhuyse, *Anton Rupert: A Biography* (Cape Town: Tafelberg, 2005), 195.

12. Ibid.

13. Rupert's anger may have been fueled by the fact that Rembrandt chairman Dirk Hertzog had canceled a meeting with Monis for a golf date and had inadvertently sent Monis in the direction of SAB. See Dommisse with the cooperation of Esterhuyse, *Anton Rupert,* 195.

14. South Africa, Competition Board, *Investigation into Restrictive Practices in the Supply and Distribution of Alcoholic Beverages in the Republic of South Africa,* Competition Board Report No. 10 (Pretoria: Government Printer, 1982), 19.

15. Ibid.

16. Stag Brewery was founded by Danish interests in 1907. It closed in 1954 and was reopened in 1962 by Schoeman. Old Dutch was brewed by the Independent Brewers United Corporation. H. Moulton, interview with Dr. Frans Cronje, former chairman of SAB, Johannesburg, n.d., SAB Records.

17. In 1964–1965, SAB contributed R3.5 million in excise. The increase from 51 cents to 74 cents per gallon of beer in 1966 meant that SAB paid an additional R1.35 million in that year. Also, a surcharge calculated on a sliding scale based on volume was slapped on individual breweries. This increased SAB's tax obligation on the large Isando plant by 29 cents to 80 cents per gallon, affecting profits considerably. See "The South African Breweries Limited (1949–1969)," 16, SAB Records.

18. *Data* (December 1968). *Data* is one of SAB's information bulletins. Its publication format is inconsistent over time.

19. In 1967, SAB estimated that the excise tax on alcoholic beverages had increased over the previous year by almost 100 percent. The excise on beer had increased by 27

percent; on wine by 8.5 percent; on spirits by 65 percent; and on sorghum beer by 2 percent. SAB, *Data* (Spring 1968). Figures for 1966 and 1967 show that the market share for natural wine increased from 26.8 percent to 29.7 percent and the market share for beer declined from 18 percent to 15.3 percent. Summary of SAB chairman's report quoted in *Data* (September 1967).

20. For excise and profit details, see "The South African Breweries, Limited, 1949–1969," 21 July 1969, 14, Ref. WWL/PH, SAB Records. In 1966, SAB acquired interests in wine through its purchase of the Stellenbosch Farmers Wine Trust Ltd. and engineering through its purchase of the Barlow Group. See "The South African Breweries Limited (1949–1969)," 15; and *Data* (Spring 1966), both in SAB Records.

21. See SAB, *Data* 9, no. 1 (Autumn 1969); *Data* 9, no. 2 (Winter 1969); *Data* 9, no. 3 (Spring 1969); *Data* 9, no. 4 (Summer 1969); *Data* 9, no. 2 (Winter 1969); *Data* 10, no. 4 (Summer 1970).

22. The expression "uitlander" (foreigner/outsider) was associated with Paul Kruger, president of the Transvaal Republic, who used it to describe British immigrants. P. W. Botha was appointed to the SAB Hop Farms board in the late 1950s and Frans Cronje took over the SAB chairmanship in 1963.

23. South African Breweries, "Keeping Pace: The Story of the First 75 Years of the SAB Group" (1970).

24. Typescript of dictation from S. J. Constance.

25. Ibid.

26. Total liquor expenditure in South Africa in 1971 amounted to approximately R135 million; C. D. H. Parry and A. L. Bennetts, "Country Profile on Alcohol in South Africa," in *Alcohol and Public Health in Eight Developing Countries*, ed. L. Riley and M. Marshall (Geneva: World Health Organization, 1999), 137. See also Rusburne and Hamman, *A Survey of the Liquor Industry in South Africa*.

27. Louis Luyt, *Walking Proud: The Louis Luyt Autobiography* (Cape Town: Don Nelson, 2003), 70.

28. Ibid., 68.

29. Alec Sabbagh quoted in "Breweries Battle Fermenting," *Financial Mail*, 5 November 1971, 49.

30. Ibid.

31. Luyt, *Walking Proud*, 69.

32. Ibid., 77.

33. Ibid., 72.

34. "Breweries Battle Fermenting," *Financial Mail*, 5 November 1971, 49; "Beer— A Storm Brewing," *Business South Africa* (July 1972): 40; "Louis Luyt Getting into His Stride," *Food Industries of South Africa* (December 1972): 15.

35. "Breweries Battle Fermenting," 49.

36. Luyt, *Walking Proud*, 77.

37. South Africa, Competition Board, *Investigation into Restrictive Practices in the Supply and Distribution of Alcoholic Beverages in the Republic of South Africa*, 19.

38. Luyt, *Walking Proud*, 76. Oude Meester was formed in 1965 as the holding company for Anton Rupert's wholesale liquor interests.

39. Luyt, *Walking Proud*, 76.

40. Louis Luyt produced three brands, Luyt Lager, Beck's Kronenbräu 1308, and Heidelberg. See "Beer Brawl Goes Underground," *Liquor Survey*, supplement to *Financial Mail*, 28 November 1975, 23.

41. Dommisse with the cooperation of Esterhuyse, *Anton Rupert*, 224.

42. Luyt, *Walking Proud*, 76.

43. "What's Brewing?" *Business South Africa* (January 1973): 44; author's interview with Richard Midgley, 20 January 2005.

44. "What's Brewing?" 45.

45. "Blowing Their Tops," *Financial Mail*, 22 September 1972, 1083.

46. Luyt, *Walking Proud*, 81–82.

47. "Blowing Their Tops," 1083.

48. Luyt, *Walking Proud*, 80.

49. Rupert applied for the interdiction on 28 August 1972 in the Transvaal Provincial Division of the High Court. See *South African Law Reports* 4 (1973): 145 (E.C.D.).

50. See *Oude Meester Groep Bpk. and Another v. S.A. Breweries Ltd.* and *S.A. Breweries Ltd and Another v Distillers Corporation (S.A.) Ltd. and Another,* both in *South African Law Reports* 4 (1973), 145 (E.C.D.).

51. *Distillers Corporation (S.A.) Ltd. v S.A. Breweries Ltd. and Another* and *Oude Meester Groep Bpk. and Another v. S.A. Breweries Ltd. (1976),* both in *South African Law Reports* 3 (1976), 514 (A.D.).

52. Ibid. See also "Master Brew Case," *Financial Mail*, 13 July 1973, 138–139.

53. "Cheers for German Beers," *Financial Mail*, 26 October 1973, 360. SAB's Keller brand was launched to counter ICB's Culemborg.

54. "Tobacco salesmen" was a reference to the Rembrandt Group's role as a manufacturer of cigarettes. Luyt, *Walking Proud*, 82; see also Max du Preez, *Louis Luyt Unauthorised* (Cape Town: Zebra Press, 2001), 17–18; and "Luyt and Rupert: Seconds Out," *Financial Mail*, 3 August 1973, 429.

55. "Brewers' Droop," *Financial Mail*, 24 January 1975, 255.

56. South Africa, Competition Board, *Investigation into Restrictive Practices in the Supply and Distribution of Alcoholic Beverages in the Republic of South Africa,* 18.

57. "Trouble in Store," *Financial Mail*, 23 November 1973, 816.

58. In 1956, SAB owned 421 houses under management that included mostly uneconomical bottle stores and bars attached to hotels. In 1957, the state abolished the "tied house" system and SAB disposed of most of its assets of houses under management. Fridjhon and Murray, *Conspiracy of Giants,* 180.

59. In November 1973, of the four companies that dominated the retail sector, only two included some public ownership. The two wholly private companies were Anton Rupert's Oude Meester with 180 bottle stores and Gilbeys Distillers and Vintners with 38 bottle stores. Stellenbosch Wine Trust created a public company, John Dwyer Holdings (of which 40 percent was owned by the public, 54 percent by Stellenbosch Wine Trust and 6 percent by SAB), which owned 131 bottle stores. Jan Pickard, owner of Union Wine, established Pichotels as a public company with 23 bottle stores. "Trouble in Store," *Financial Mail*, 23 November 1973, 816.

60. SAB's interests in Coca-Cola were particularly important. See "Guiding SAB through Negative Growth," *Financial Mail*, 12 November 1976, 605; "SA Breweries," *Financial Mail*, 12 November 1976, 645. Interestingly, Coca-Cola was engaged in a bitter battle with Pepsi-Cola at about this time. See J. C. Louis and Harvey Z. Yazjian, *The Cola Wars* (New York: Everest House, 1980); Thomas Oliver, *The Real Coke, the Real Story* (New York: Penguin Books, 1987); and Mark Pendergrast, *For*

God, Country and Coca-Cola: The Definitive History of the Great American Soft Drink and the Company That Makes It (New York: Basic Books, 2000).

61. Anton Rupert quoted in "Trouble in Store," 816.

62. "Beer War—Fresh Moves," *Financial Mail,* 7 December 1973, 1023–1024.

63. "Brewers' Droop," *Financial Mail,* 24 January 1975, 256.

64. "Bottling Up Liquor Sales," *Financial Mail,* 7 March 1975, 807.

65. SAB and Oude Meester were each allocated 2,000 points on a sliding scale: seven points for each bottle store, six points for each management system, three points for each bar, two for each hotel, and one for each restaurant or grocers' wine license; "Winning on Points," *Financial Mail,* 26 November 1976, 23–24.

66. Harold Moulton's interview with Frank Moodie, 8 October 1983, SAB Records.

67. "Time, Gentlemen," *Finance Week,* 16 February 1979, 149.

68. "Price Fixing: The Case Continues," *Financial Mail,* 20 May 1977, 631.

69. By 1976, SAB owned 100 percent of Solly Kramer Limited. See "SA Breweries," *Financial Mail,* 12 November 1976, 645; "What Makes Solly Kramer Tick," *Business South Africa* (April 1977), 15–17; and "Time, Gentlemen," *Finance Week,* 16 February 1979, 149.

70. Fridjhon and Murray, *Conspiracy of Giants,* 182.

71. "Over a Barrel," *Financial Mail,* 6 June 1975, 864.

72. Ibid. In November 1975, SAB controlled 94 percent of beer sales, 76 percent of natural wine, and 70 percent of cane spirits, while Anton Rupert struggled with accumulated losses of R9.2 million on his brewing operation. See "In the Drinkers' Market," *Liquor Survey,* supplement to *Financial Mail,* 23 November 1975, 39–40.

73. The beer market was worth around R530 million in 1978; "The Brewing Scene: Intercontinental Buys a Round," *Financial Mail,* 21 April 1978, 215.

74. "Beer: Stepping Out Litely," *Financial Mail,* 11 November 1977, 502.

75. "Horses for Courses," *Financial Mail,* 29 September 1978, 1169.

76. Author's interview with Peter Savory, 11 July 2000. Savory was SAB's director of marketing at the time.

77. *Carling National Breweries, Inc. and Intercontinental Breweries Ltd v. National Brewing Company (Pty) Ltd and the South African Breweries Ltd.,* Supreme Court of South Africa (Transvaal Provincial Division) (M2813/78), judgment delivered on 28/12/1978. I am grateful to Adams and Adams, patent, trademark, and copyright attorneys, for access to this unpublished judgment.

78. Ibid., 16.

79. Ibid., 18.

80. Author's interview with Peter Savory.

81. "Beer Dispatch: Premature Casualty," *Financial Mail,* 26 January 1979, 241–242.

82. Ibid.; "Liquor Supermarkets: R7m's Worth," *Financial Mail,* 12 January 1979, 87.

83. The Board of Trade and Industries had been given the task of investigating and reporting on monopolistic conditions in the supply and distribution of liquor several months earlier.

84. Hugh Murray, "SAB/Union Wine: Dick Goss v Pretoria," *Financial Mail,* 20 July 1979, 259.

85. Ibid.

86. "Liquor War: Infighting for Outlets," *Financial Mail,* 27 July 1979, 349.

87. Ibid.

88. "Beer War: Blame the Liquor Act," *Financial Mail,* 3 August 1979, 417.

89. Ibid.

90. Ibid.

91. "Dr Rupert's Affidavit," *Financial Mail,* 23 November, 1979.

92. South Africa, Competition Board, *Investigation into Restrictive Practices in the Supply and Distribution of Alcoholic Beverages in the Republic of South Africa,* 19–20 and 47.

93. Dommisse with the cooperation of Esterhuyse, *Anton Rupert,* 233.

94. Michael Coulson, "After the New Dispensation in Liquor: An Industry Still in Ferment," *Management* (October 1980): 54.

95. Ibid.; Fridjhon and Murray, *Conspiracy of Giants,* 183–184.

96. "The Politics of Drink," *Management* (October 1980): 77.

97. Harold Moulton's interview with Peter Savory, Port Elizabeth, 27 February 1987, SAB Records.

98. Ibid.

99. Harold Moulton's interview with Frank Moodie, 8 October 1993, SAB Records.

100. Harold Moulton's interview with Mike Rosholt, 9 November 1992, SAB Records.

101. Coulson, "After the New Dispensation in Liquor," 54.

102. There are no available estimates for the number of illicit dealers in the 1970s and early 1980s. The estimated figure for 1991 is 120,000. See Elisabeth Sidiroplous, "Black Economic Empowerment," *Spotlight* 2, no. 93 (1993), 30.

103. The South African government instructed the Competition Board to undertake the inquiry under the terms of the Maintenance and Promotion of Competition Act (Act 96 of 1979). The Competition Board was replaced in 1999 by the Competition Commission and the Competition Tribunal, which hears appeals against rulings of the commission. See "Investigation Fever," *Finance Week,* 3–9 December 1981, 9.

104. "Liquor Trade: Last Round," *Financial Mail,* 16 November 1979, 691. For more comment on the government's role in the establishment of CWD as a monopoly, see "Pitfalls of Meddling," *Financial Mail,* 27 March 1981, 1293.

105. "Business View," *Financial Mail,* 27 March 1981, 1294.

106. "Structural Nightmare Looms," *Financial Mail,* 24 April 1981, 376–378.

107. South Africa, Competition Board, *Investigation into Restrictive Practices in the Supply and Distribution of Alcoholic Beverages in the Republic of South Africa,* 71–72.

108. Sections 35 (1) and 35 (2) of the Liquor Act were amended to permit "general dealers" to sell wine in October 1981 and were made retrospective to April 1978; "Victory for the Grocers," *Financial Mail,* 23 October 1981, 447.

109. "Government Bends the Rules," *Financial Mail,* 1 April 1983, 67.

110. F. C. van Niekerk Fourie, "Issues and Problems in South African Competition Policy," *South African Journal of Economics* 55, no. 4 (1987): 345, 349, and 352.

111. Fridjhon and Murray, *Conspiracy of Giants,* 188.

112. Coulson, "After the New Dispensation in Liquor," 54.

113. Ibid.

114. "Liquor Trade: Last Round," *Financial Mail,* 16 November 1979, 692.

115. Beer production in South Africa rose from approximately 7.5 million hectoliters in 1980 to over 10 million hectoliters in 1981; South Africa, Department of Statistics, *Census of Manufacturing Statistics* (Pretoria: Government Printer 1981).

116. "King of the Castle," *Management* (October 1980): 65; "Truce in Beer War but New Monopolies Must Be Monitored," *Finance Week,* 8–14 November 1979, 348.

117. SAB subsidiary Southern Associated Maltsters Ltd manufactured malt. SAB held the controlling interest and the South African Central Co-operative Grain Company Ltd and Caledon Riviersonderend Co-operative Ltd owned 45 percent of the shares; South Africa, Competition Board, *Investigation into Restrictive Practices in the Supply and Distribution of Alcoholic Beverages in the Republic of South Africa,* 24.

118. See "A Humble Beginning Led to a Flourishing Industry," *Food Industries of South Africa* (January 1967): 26; and Loanne Sharp, "The South African Breweries Ltd: A Case Study in Monopoly Conditions, Conglomerate Diversification and Corporate Control in the South African Malt Beer Industry" (Master of Commerce thesis, University of Cape Town, 1997), 6.

119. Ivan Deacon, "The South African Liquor Industry—Structure, Conduct, Performance and Strategies for Future Action" (Doctor of Commerce thesis, University of Stellenbosch, 1980), 215.

120. See Table 2 in the appendix.

121. In 1981, the market share by volume of wine and spirits was 14.3 percent, but the market share was 42.6 percent based on alcohol (liters of absolute alcohol). See "Big Boom in Beer," *Liquor Survey,* supplement to *Financial Mail,* 26 March 1982, 11–12; South Africa, Competition Board, *Investigation into Restrictive Practices in the Supply and Distribution of Alcoholic Beverages in the Republic of South Africa,* 74.

122. "Spirit of Rebellion," *Financial Mail,* 25 September 1981, 1559; "Saving Dawie," *Financial Mail,* 11 September 1981, 1290–1293.

123. "King of the Castle," *Management* (October 1980), 64–65.

124. "Big Boom in Beer," 11.

125. "Man of the Year: Dick Goss," *Financial Mail,* 18 December 1981, 1372.

126. Harold Moulton's interview with Dick Goss, 13 February 1985, SAB Records.

127. See "Battle Royal," *Financial Mail,* 10 June 1983, 1311.

128. Harold Moulton's interview with Mike Rosholt.

129. Harold Moulton's interview with Vic Hammond, 10 November 1992; and Harold Moulton's interview with Ken Redfern, 14 April 1986, both in SAB Records.

130. Harold Moulton's interview with Dick Goss.

131. Harold Moulton's interview with Ken Williams, 14 April 1986, SAB Records.

132. Goss attended Rondebosch Boys' High in the Cape; Harold Moulton's interview with Bomber Wells, 9 November 1992, SAB Records.

133. Harold Moulton's interview with Frank Moodie, 8 October 1993; and Harold Moutlon's interview with Gert Goedhals, no date, both in SAB Records. Goedhals was managing director of Indol International.

134. Harold Moulton's interview with Gert Goedhals.

135. Harold Moulton's interview with Dick Goss.

3. BEER ADVERTISING

1. See Naomi Klein, *No Space, No Choice, No Jobs, No Logo: Taking Aim at the Brand Bullies* (London: Flamingo, 2001), 21; and B. Kirshenblatt-Gimblett, *Destination Culture: Tourism, Museums and Heritage* (Berkeley: University of California Press, 1998).

2. Gillian Dyer, *Advertising as Communication* (London: Routledge, 1996), 114–127.

3. Ibid., 123; Robert Goldman, *Reading Ads Socially* (London: Routledge, 1992), 19 and 104; and Judith Williamson, *Decoding Advertisements: Ideology and Meaning in Advertising* (London: Boyars, 1978), 177.

4. For a discussion of how communities are imagined, see Benedict Anderson, *Imagined Communities: Reflections on the Origins and Spread of Nationalism* (London: Verso, 1983), 6.

5. Author's interview with Bruce Starke, 28 April 2000.

6. Author's interview with Peter Savory, 12 July 2000.

7. Ibid.

8. Ibid. In practice, human resource development did not lag behind. Starting in the 1960s, SAB implemented scientific management and personnel development programs and employed more skilled black workers than most other companies.

9. Ibid.

10. Ibid.

11. Author's interview with Bruce Starke.

12. "Packaging Improvement Programme: Notes for Presentation," 7 January 1966, SAB Records.

13. Author's interview with Bruce Starke. For more on Louis Luyt, see chapter 2; and Michael Fridjhon and Andy Murray, *Conspiracy of Giants: The South African Liquor Industry* (Johannesburg: Divaris Steyn, 2000), 183–184.

14. Author's interview with Bruce Starke.

15. Author's interview with Peter Savory.

16. Ibid.

17. Ibid.

18. *Data* (September 1964).

19. *Data* (September 1972).

20. Rafe Howard, "Beer Advertising: Why So Stale and Flat," *Insight,* November 1978, 20.

21. See Varda Burstyn, *The Rites of Men: Manhood, Politics, and the Culture of Sport* (1999; repr., Toronto: University of Toronto Press, 2000), 148.

22. Peter Savory, letter to *Insight,* January 1979, 12.

23. Author's interview with Peter Savory.

24. *Data* (December 1969); SAB, *Data* (June 1972).

25. *Data* (June 1967).

26. See Goldman, *Reading Ads Socially,* 24, for a discussion of the "active agency" of the object of desire.

27. *Data* (December 1968).

28. Ibid.

29. *Data* (September 1967).

30. Ibid.

31. The percentage of women drinking bottled beer rose from 25 percent in 1962 to 77 percent in 1982; see C. van der Burgh and Lee Rocha-Silva, "Drinking in the Republic of South Africa, 1962–1982," *Contemporary Drug Problems* (Fall 1988): Table 2.

32. Author's interview with Bruce Starke.

33. Ibid.

34. Ibid.

35. Author's interview with Peter Savory.

36. Timothy Burke, *Lifebuoy Men, Lux Women: Commodification, Consumption and Cleanliness in Modern Zimbabwe* (Durham, N.C.: Duke University Press, 1996), 129.

37. Author's interview with Bruce Starke.

38. See "New Beer Successfully Launched on the Rand," *Food Industries of South Africa* 19, no. 9 (January 1967): 31. Within two years, Carling Black Label had won 24 percent of the beer market. See "Take a Fresh Look at Carling Black Label," *Beer Business,* December 1985, 21.

39. See "Carling Black Label," *Star,* 28 November 1966.

40. Sorghum beer production, which was responsible for 46.7 percent of market share in 1984, remained a state monopoly. Nontaxable earnings from sorghum beer were R70 million. As a comparison, the earnings from clear beer were only R13 million. See Fridjhon and Murray *Conspiracy of Giants,* 5 and 195.

41. Author's interview with Frank Moodie, 29 April 2000.

42. See Paul la Hause, "Drink and Cultural Innovation in Durban: The Origins of the Beerhall in South Africa, 1902–1916," in *Liquor and Labor in Southern Africa,* ed. Jonathan Crush and Charles Ambler (Athens: Ohio University Press, 1992), 98–105.

43. Author's interview with Frank Moodie; author's interview with Bruce Starke.

44. S. M. Gatley and J. E. Bayley, "A Report on a Research Project on Patterns of Use and Attitudes towards the Use and Misuse of Alcohol, Dagga, Mandrax, and Inhalants in the Black Community of New Brighton, Port Elizabeth," unpublished report, Vista University and SANCA, Port Elizabeth, November 1987, 25.

45. "Big Boom in Beer," *Financial Mail,* 26 March 1982, 15. In 1985, 89 percent of black men and 64 percent of black women drinkers drank clear beer, compared with 29 percent and 25 percent, respectively, in 1976; Lee Rocha-Silva, *Drinking Practices, Drinking-Related Attitudes and Public Impressions of Services for Alcohol and Other Drug Problems in Urban South Africa* (Pretoria: Human Sciences Research Council, 1989), Table 4.

46. For the politics of antiapartheid sports, see Douglas Booth, *The Race Game: Sport and Politics in South Africa* (London: Frank Cass, 1988); John Nautright and David Black, "'Hitting Where It Hurts': Springbok–All Black Rugby, Masculine National Identity and Counter-Hegemonic Struggle, 1959–1992," in *Making Men: Rugby and Masculine Identity,* ed. John Nauright and Timothy Chandler (London: Frank Cass, 1996), 205–226. For the uses of nonverbal advertising in South Africa, see Nick Green and Reg Lascaris, *Communication in the Third World: Seizing Ad-*

vertising Opportunities in the 1990s (Cape Town: Tafelberg, Human and Rousseau, 1990), 65.

47. Green and Lascaris, *Communication in the Third World,* 28.

48. For a social history of alcohol and the gold rush, see Charles van Onselen, "Randlords and Rotgut 1886–1903," *History Workshop* 2, no. 1 (1976): 33–89.

49. Author's interview with Bruce Starke.

50. Ibid.

51. Author's interview with Peter Savory.

52. See advertisement for Castle Lager in *Sowetan,* 10 December 1987. The copy said "My beer will rank with the finest in the world."

53. Eric Rosenthal, *Tankards and Tradition* (Cape Town: Howard Timmins, 1961), 109–110.

54. Full-page advertisement for Castle Lager, *Sowetan,* 15 October 1987. The copy said "Man has five senses."

55. See Jonathan Crush and Charles Ambler, "Introduction," in *Liquor and Labour in Southern Africa,* ed. Jonathan Crush and Charles Ambler (Athens: Ohio University Press, 1992), 1–55.

56. Author's interview with Windsor Shuenyane, 12 July 2000.

57. Author's interview with Bruce Starke.

58. Green and Lascaris, *Communication in the Third World,* 81–82.

59. Julian Stallabras, *Gargantua: Manufactured Mass Culture* (London: Verso, 1996), 66.

60. See the advertisement for Ohlsson's Lager in *Sowetan,* 6 December 1985. The copy said "It goes down singing hymns."

61. See the advertisement for Ohlsson's Lager in *Sowetan,* 24 November 1986. The copy said "How to say goodbye to your old beer."

62. See the advertisement for Ohlsson's Lager in *Sowetan,* 18 December 1986. The copy said "How to introduce your friends to your new beer."

63. See the following advertisements for Ohlsson's Lager: *Sowetan,* 4 November 1988 ("They say my music is too heavy"); *Sowetan,* 11 November 1988 ("I've got a great understanding with the older generation"); and *Sowetan,* 18 November 1988 ("They said I wouldn't make university").

64. For a discussion of how culture shapes the imagining of communities, see Kobena Mercer, "Imagine All the People: Constructing Community Culturally," in *Imagined Communities,* ed. Christian Boltanski, Sofie Calle, Denzil Forrester, Komar and Melamid, Guisepe Penone, Tim Rollins and K.O.S., Yinka Shonibare, Gary Simmons, and Gillian Wearing (London: National Touring Exhibitions, SBC, 1995), 12.

65. Hansa History Reel, Johannesburg, copy dated July 2000, Ogilvy and Mather advertising and marketing agency. Ogilvy and Mather later became Ogilvy South Africa.

66. A premium beer in this context was defined as a brand that "commands a price premium of 10 percent or more to the benchmark mainstream." see "Big Boom in Beef," Liquor Survey, supplement to *Financial Mail,* 26 March 1982, 12.

67. See, for example, the image of a "split cane fly rod with engraved and silvered brass ringed butt" in an advertisement for Amstel Lager in *Sowetan,* 28 November 1986.

68. See, for example, the burnished copper kettles in an advertisement for Amstel Lager in *Sowetan*, 9 November 1987. The copy said "When other beers are already in the bottle store, one beer isn't even in the bottle."

69. Author's interview with Peter Savory.

70. Ibid.

71. Amstel History Reel, July 2000, Ogilvy and Mather advertising and marketing agency.

72. Anderson, *Imagined Communities*, 7.

73. Castle Lager introduced the Castle Cup in 1959, a major football and soccer sponsorship. See G. A. L. Thabe, comp., *It's a Goal! 50 Years of Sweat, Tears, and Drama in Black Soccer* (Johannesburg: Skotaville, 1983), 101–104.

74. Castle Lager History Reel, Sandton, July 2000, Ogilvy and Mather advertising and marketing agency. Bafana Bafana is the name of the South African soccer team. It is a colloquial term derived from the word *abafana* (big boys).

75. Ibid. *Laduma* is a colloquial Xhosa expression derived from the verb *duma* (to make a big noise) and implies a shout of triumph, such as when a player scores a goal.

76. Author's interview with Juan Scott, 9 July 2000. Scott designed advertisements for Castle Lager in the 1990s.

77. *Amaboko-boko* is a colloquial expression that combines a Xhosa plural noun prefix with the Afrikaans *bok* (deer) and so puts an African gloss on Springbok, a name associated with all-white rugby.

78. See Douglas Booth, "Mandela and the Amabokoboko: The Political and Linguistic Nationalism of South Africa?" *Journal of Modern African Studies* 34, no. 3 (September 1996): 459–477.

79. Castle Lager History Reel.

80. Alistair Hewitt, SAB Castle Milk Stout brand manager, interviewed in *The Making of Ndlanu*, dir. Michael Yelseth (Johannesburg: Incha Film Productions, 1996).

81. Dimape Seremanye, strategic director of Herdbouys, interviewed in *Making of Ndlanu*.

82. Ben Horowitz, director of Salamander, interviewed in *Making of Ndlanu*.

83. Kingsley Potter, SAB Castle Milk Stout brand manager, interviewed in *Making of Ndlanu*.

84. Jackie, Soweto Theatre choreographer, interviewed in *Making of Ndlanu*.

85. Paul Gilroy, *The Black Atlantic: Modernity and Double Consciousness* (London: Verso, 1993), 102.

86. Green and Lascaris, *Communication in the Third World*, 80.

87. Ibid.

88. M. L. Roberts, "Review Essay: Gender, Consumption and Commodity Culture," *American Historical Review* 103, no. 3 (June 1998): 817–844.

89. Green and Lascaris, *Communication in the Third World*, 151.

90. Ibid.

91. Author's interview with Juan Scott.

92. Ibid.

93. Marcia Klein, "Alcohol Advertising Adds Froth to the Debate," *Business Day*, 30 April 1991.

94. Ibid.; see also Charles Parry and Anna Bennetts, *Alcohol Policy and Public Health in South Africa* (Cape Town: Oxford University Press, 1998).

95. Maureen Isaacson, "Cronin the Librarian Grapples with History and Transition," *Sunday Independent,* 13 July 1997.

96. See Dr. Chris van der Burgh, "Some Guidelines for Combating the Advertising/Marketing Strategies of the Alcohol Industry in Black Communities," paper prepared for committee workshop, SANCA national office, Johannesburg, 1 October 1988, 5; resolution taken on liquor advertising by the Medical Association of South Africa, in "Minutes of Meeting of the Federal Council of the Medical Association of South Africa, 11–13 May, 1977," *S.A. Medical Journal,* Supplement (17 September 1977), 22–23; C. N. Moodliar, 18 April 1989, in South Africa, Parliament, *Debates of Parliament* (Cape Town: Government Printer, 1989), 5670; and Parry and Bennetts, *Alcohol Policy and Public Health in South Africa,* 143–146.

97. Raymond Williams, *Keywords: A Vocabulary of Culture and Society* (London, 1983), 78.

98. Celia Lury, *Consumer Culture* (New Brunswick, N.J: Rutgers University Press, 1996), 100; Kirshenblatt-Gimblett, *Destination Culture,* 262.

99. M. L. Roberts, paraphrasing Jennifer Jones, "Review Essay: Gender, Consumption, and Commodity Culture," *American Historical Review* 103, no. 3 (June 1998), 823.

100. According to the 1995 October Household Survey, unemployment in South Africa was 29.3 percent; Government of South Africa, Central Statistics, *Statistics in Brief* (Pretoria: Government Printer, 1997), figure 10.2.

101. *SAB International t/a Sabmark International v Laugh It Off Promotions [2003], South African Law Reports* 2 (2003): 454 (Cape of Good Hope Provincial Division); *Laugh It Off Promotions CC v SAB International (Finance) BV t/a Sabmark International and Another (2005),* available at http://www.saflii.org/za/cases/ZACC/2005/7.html. See also Carmel Rickard, "Why Didn't SAB Just Laugh It Off?" *Sunday Times,* 19 September 2004; Marianne Merten, "SAB Won't Laugh It Off," *Mail and Guardian,* 19–25 November 2004; Ann Crotty, "SAB Represents Vexing Face of Corporate SA," *Sunday Business Report,* 3 June 2001; Karyn Maughan, "Victory for T-Shirt Man," *Cape Argus,* 27 May 2005; and Kenneth Chikanga, "Laugh It Off Can Now Guffaw after Ruling," *Sunday Independent,* 29 May 2005.

102. Rickard, "Why Didn't SAB Just Laugh It Off?"

103. Author's interview with Bruce Starke.

4. "TOMORROW WILL ALSO BE A HARD DAY"

1. J. Moser, "WHO and Alcoholism: Alcohol Problems and National Health Planning in Programmes of the World Health Organisation," in *Notes on Alcohol and Alcoholism,* ed. S. Caruana (London: Medical Council on Alcoholism, 1972).

2. J. Lewis, "Patterns of Drinking among the Coloureds of South Africa," paper presented to First National Summer School on Alcoholism, Pretoria, October 1966, 2–5.

3. See Moser, "WHO and Alcoholism," 1–6.

4. See V. Bechman, *Alcohol, Another Trap for Africa* (Sweden: Bokforlaget Libris-Orebro, 1988), 92 and 149–152.

5. E. Bougas, "The Policy on Alcoholism of a Large Industrial Company," *Public Health* 77, no. 7 (1977): 143–149; E. Bougas, "Industrial Alcohol Programmes—Do

They Work?" *Food Industries of South Africa* 9 (1979): 28–29; G. M. du Plessis, "The Treatment of Employees with Drinking Problems by the Social Services Department of the Chamber of Mines of South Africa," paper presented to SANCA Symposium, 3–4 February 1977.

6. For the respectability of disease in American society, see C. Wiener, *The Politics of Alcoholism: Building an Arena around a Social Problem* (London: Transaction Books, 1977), 230.

7. South Africa, *Department of Social Welfare Report on the National Conference on Alcoholism held at Pretoria on 20th and 21st November* (Pretoria: Government Printer, 1951), 51–52.

8. Ibid., 36.

9. Ibid., 12 and 35. The figures for alcoholism were based on admissions to mental hospitals and convictions for drunkenness; in 1950, these totaled 77,966.

10. A. T. Winkler, "Basic Principles Underlying Statutory Measures for the Treatment of Alcoholics in the Republic of South Africa," *Volkswelsyn en Pensioene* (June 1970): 8. See also F. P. Pieterse, "The Role of Social Work in the Treatment of Alcoholism," *Volkswelsyn en Pensioene* (December 1970): 43–46.

11. Government of South Africa, *Commission of Inquiry into Matters Relating to the Coloured Population Group* (Pretoria: Government Printer, 1976).

12. L. S. Gillis, "Summary of the Findings of a Survey of Psychiatric Disturbance and Alcoholism amongst the Coloured People of the Cape Peninsula," unpublished paper, Psychiatry Department, University of Cape Town and Groote Schuur Hospital, 25 October 1965; M. J. Fialkov, "Alcoholics and the Emergency Ward," *S.A. Medical Journal* (1 October 1977), 613–616; "Voorkoming is SANRA se grootste taak," *Vrouevolksdiens* 17, no. 4 (1978): 8.

13. Minister of Health Services and Welfare, 13 June 1988, in South Africa, Parliament, *Debates of Parliament* (Cape Town: Government Printer, 1989), 13844.

14. Author's interview with Henry Fabe, 6 November 1997.

15. N. Slabbert, "Coloureds and the Demon Drink," *Eastern Province Herald,* 27 July 1971.

16. Prof. A. D. Muller of the University of Port Elizabeth, quoted in Slabbert, "Coloureds and the Demon Drink"; Government of South Africa, *Commission of Inquiry into Matters Relating to the Coloured Population Group,* 265. See also Phyllis Martin, *Leisure and Society in Colonial Brazzaville* (Cambridge: Cambridge University Press, 1995), 128, for a discussion of the partial payment of wages in liquor in the Congo.

17. S. J. Terreblanche, "Misuse of Alcohol and Alcoholism as Extremely Important Factors in the Loss Accounts of Employers and the Economy as a Whole," *Social Work* 13, no. 1 (13 March 1977): 40–47.

18. Ibid.

19. "The Way Back via Avalon," *Alpha* (June 1979): 18–19; Government of South Africa, *Commission of Inquiry into Matters Relating to the Coloured Population Group,* 265.

20. See Jonathan Crush and Charles Ambler, "Introduction," in *Liquor and Labor in Southern Africa,* ed. Jonathan Crush and Charles Ambler (Athens: Ohio University Press, 1992), 10 for discussion of racist discourses on liquor.

21. J. T. C. Wolmarans, "Aspects of the Problem of Alcoholism and Drug Dependence among the Bantu," *SANCA Information Bulletin* (29 July 1975): 1–2.

22. J. J. Schmidt and P. A. Botha, "Die drinkpatroon van die Bantoe in 'n stedelike gebied," unpublished paper, Instituut vir Sosiologiese, Demografiese en Kriminologiese Navorsing, Pretoria, 1974, 42.

23. The percentage of sorghum was reduced from 4.9 percent to 0.73 percent. See L. Novelli, "Biological Ennoblement of Kaffir Beer," *Food Technology*, 26 December 1966, 1607–1608; and Deacon, *The South African Liquor Industry*, 38–39.

24. F. Scheigart, H. Vlietstra, and P. van Twisk, "Bantu Beer—A Return to Kaffir Corn?" *Food Industries of South Africa* (March 1972), 27–33.

25. B. I. Frahm, "Aspects in the Marketing of Sorghum Beer in South Africa" (MA thesis, University of Pretoria, 1982), 4–5 and 83.

26. Paul S. Landau, *The Realm of the Word: Language, Gender and Christianity in a Southern African Kingdom* (Portsmouth, N.H.: Heinemann, 1995), 83.

27. For discussion of beer as a reward for labor, see Patrick McAllister, *Building the Homestead: Agriculture, Labour and Beer in South Africa's Transkei* (Leiden and Aldershot, Hampshire: Ashgate, 2001), 159–176; Patrick McAllister, "Indigenous Beer in Southern Africa: Functions and Fluctuations," *African Studies* 52, no. 1 (1993): 71–88; E. Colson and T. Scudder, *For Prayer and Profit: The Ritual, Economic and Social Importance of Beer in Gwembe District, Zambia, 1950–1982* (Stanford, Calif.: Stanford University Press, 1988), 72–79.

28. In 1971, sorghum beer dominated the total alcoholic beverage market at 49 percent. Natural wine followed at 14 percent, brandy at 10 percent, and malt beer at 9 percent. See Charles Parry and Anna Bennetts, "Country Profile on Alcohol in South Africa," in *Alcohol and Public Health in Eight Developing Countries*, ed. L. Riley and M. Marshall (Geneva: World Health Organization, 1999), 137. See also J. L. Rusburne and H. Hamman, *A Survey of the Liquor Industry in South Africa* (Johannesburg: Statsinform Pty. Ltd. 1972).

29. J. K. McNamara, "Social Life, Ethnicity and Conflict in a Gold Mine Hostel" (MA thesis, University of the Witwatersrand, 1978), 56.

30. Ibid.

31. Heavy drinking is defined as the consumption of a minimum of 10 centiliters (3.4 ounces) of absolute alcohol on average per day. See Lee Rocha-Silva, *Attitudes towards Drinking and Drunkenness in the RSA* (Pretoria: Human Sciences Research Council, ca. 1989), 18.

32. See Juha Partanen, *Sociability and Intoxication: Alcohol and Drinking in Kenya, Africa, and the Modern World* (Helsinki: Finnish Foundation for Alcohol Studies, 1991), 39.

33. See Pamela Scully, "Liquor and Labor in the Western Cape, 1870–1900," in *Liquor and Labor in Southern Africa*, ed. Jonathan Crush and Charles Ambler (Athens: Ohio University Press, 1992), 59.

34. H. C. Seftel, "Alcoholism in Johannesburg Africans—Causes and Consequences," unpublished report, Department of Medicine, Johannesburg and Non-European Hospital and University of the Witwatersrand, ca. 1974, 4.

35. Scheigart, Vlietstra and van Twisk, "Bantu Beer—A Return to Kaffir Corn?" 28; Seftel, "Alcoholism in Johannesburg Africans," 5–7.

36. Mrs. A. N. Lekgetha, "A District Nurse Looks at the Problem of Alcohol Abuse and Alcoholism among the Bantu People," *SANCA Information Bulletin* 2, no. 2 (13–17 August 1972): 1–2.

37. H. C. Seftel, senior physician of the Department of Medicine, University of the Witwatersrand, reported in 1972 that fewer township residents presented with alcoholic symptoms at the Johannesburg Non-European Hospital; see H. C. Seftel, "Alcoholism in Johannesburg Africans—Causes and Consequences," *The Leech* 42, no. 3 (1972): 18.

38. H. B. Coetzee, "Die drinkpatroon van die Bantoe in Suid-Afrika" unpublished paper, SANCA ca. 1966, 8; D. R. Mabiletsa, "My Experience in the African Community as a Social Worker with Regard to the Problems of the Abuse of Alcohol and Drug Dependence," paper presented to Bantu Symposium, 18–19 August 1972.

39. Jon Qwelane, "The Good Old Days of the Bad Old South Africa," *Tribute*, November 1992, 64.

40. See Michael Chapman, "Preface," and "Selections from Casey Motsisi, 'On the Beat,'" in Chapman, *The Drum Decade*, vii–ix and 175–182, respectively.

41. Qwelane, "The Good Old Days of the Bad Old South Africa," 62–67.

42. C. Ballantine, "From Marabi to Exile: A Brief History of Black Jazz in South Africa," in Papers Presented at the Sixth Symposium on Ethnomusicology, Music Department, Rhodes University, 1st–3rd October, 1987 (Grahamstown: International Library of African Music, 1988), 2–5; Qwelane, "The Good Old Days of the Bad Old South Africa," 65. For a description of socializing in bars in Brazzaville after 1945, see David Coplan, *In Township Tonight! South Africa's City Music and Theatre* (Johannesburg: Ravan Press, 1985), 101; and Martin, *Leisure and Society in Colonial Brazzaville*, 136–137.

43. Author's interview with Windsor Shuenyane, 12 July 2000; see also Mabiletsa, "My Experiences in the African Community," 5.

44. See E. Linder, Letter to *Cape Times*, 24 November 1971.

45. Seftel, "Alcoholism in Johannesburg Africans," 3.

46. Ibid.

47. Ibid, 2; see also South Africa, *Department of Social Welfare Report on the National Conference on Alcoholism held at Pretoria on 20th and 21st November*, 3.

48. Seftel, "Alcoholism in Johannesburg Africans," 3.

49. See Megan Vaughan, *Curing Their Ills: Colonial Power and African Illness* (Cambridge: Polity Press, 1991), 133.

50. D. H. Reader, "Sociological Aspects of Alcoholism," *Psychologica Africana* 10 (1964): 200.

51. Cape of Good Hope Liquor Laws Commission, *Report of the Liquor Laws Commission*; Tshediso Maloka, "'Khomo lia oela!' Canteens, Brothels and Labour Migrancy in Colonial Lesotho, 1900–1940," *Journal of African History* 38, no. 1 (1997): 101–122; Benedict Carton, *Blood from Your Children: The Colonial Origins of Generational Conflict in South Africa* (Pietermaritzburg: University of Natal Press, 2000), 73.

52. H. A. Luiz, "Facilities for the Treatment of Bantu Alcoholics, and Their Deficiencies," *SANCA Information Bulletin* (30–31 July 1973): 1–2.

53. Ibid., 2.

54. J. T. C. Wolmarans, "Aspects of the Problem of Alcoholism and Drug Dependence among the Bantu," *SANCA Information Bulletin* (29 July 1975): 1.

55. Ibid., 2.

56. "Health Statistics Related to Alcohol," World Health Organization resolution WHA28.81, May 1975, available at http://www.searo.who.int/en/Section1174/Section1199/Section1629_6738.htm (accessed 16 August 2009).

57. "Die S.A. Bantoe en Alkoholisme," *Die Taalgenot,* April 1974, 14. Arrests for male drunkenness increased 114 percent (140 percent for females) between 1963 and 1971. Twenty-two percent of the money blacks spent on alcohol was for spirits in 1971.

58. Lekgetha, "A District Nurse Looks at the Problem," 2–4. In 1973, the various homelands in South Africa enacted their own liquor legislation to circumvent the ban on black ownership of bottle stores and pubs; Deacon, *The South African Liquor Industry,* 46.

59. W. G. Daynes, "The Illness of Alcoholism as It Affects Transkeian Citizens Today," *SANCA Information Bulletin* (13–17 August 1972): 3; "Die S.A. Bantoe en Alkoholisme," 15.

60. Landau, *The Realm of the Word,* 83.

61. Lekgetha, "A District Nurse Looks at the Problem," 1–2.

62. See G. Vaillant, *The Natural History of Alcoholism* (Cambridge, Mass.: Harvard University Press, 1983), 103, for the idea of alcoholism as choice.

63. W. G. Daynes, "The Illness of Alcoholism as It Affects Transkeian Citizens Today," *SANCA Information Bulletin* (13–17 August 1972), 2.

64. Mabiletsa, "My Experience in the African Community," 4–5. For alcoholism among women in Zambia, see Colson and Scudder, *For Prayer and Profit,* 78.

65. Mabiletsa, "My Experience in the African Community," 5; author's interview with Sister Lydia Mosala, 29 April 1998.

66. Twenty percent of women in Transkei drank spirits in 1983. See E. Bradshaw, N. McGlashan, and J. S. Harington, "The Use of Tobacco and Alcoholic Beverages by Male and Female Xhosa in Transkei in Relation to Cancer of the Oesophagus," unpublished paper, Institute of Social and Economic Research, Rhodes University, Grahamstown, 1983, 23–24; and Mabiletsa, "My Experience in an African Community," 3. See also E. Galli, "An Educational Answer via the Family in Connection with the Problem of Drug Dependence," unpublished paper, SANCA, n.d.

67. "Die S.A. Bantoe en Alkoholisme," 15.

68. Mabiletsa, "My Experience in the African Community," 4–5.

69. Reverend Robert de Maar quoted in N. Slabbert, "Coloureds and the Demon Drink," *Eastern Province Herald,* 27 July 1971.

70. See Liquor Act (Act no. 30 of 1928).

71. "Frustrations Are Driving Bright Africans to Drink," *Star,* 21 April 1970; T. Muil, "We Can't Fire Every Teacher Who Drinks," *Natal Mercury,* 2 August 1971; "Nothing to Do So They Drink," *Rand Daily Mail,* 5 February 1969.

72. Alan Cobley, "Liquor and Leadership: Temperance, Drunkenness and the African Petty Bourgeoisie in South Africa," *South African Historical Journal* 31, no. 1 (November 1994): 132–134.

73. Regular advertisements for gin and brandy and a small number of beer advertisements appeared in magazines such as *Drum* after 1962, but alcohol advertising for the black market escalated after 1976. See Nick Green and Reg Lascaris, *Third World Destiny: Recognising and Seizing the Opportunities Offered by a Changing South Africa* (Cape Town: Human and Rossouw, 1988), 31–32.

74. A. Haworth and S. W. Acuda, "Sub-Saharan Africa," in *Alcohol in Emerging Markets,* ed. M. Grant (Philadelphia, Pa.: Brunner, Maize, 1998), 42.

75. From 1976 to 1982, black men's consumption of clear beer increased from 29 percent to 92 percent; their consumption of spirits increased from 16 percent to 48 percent during the same period. See G. Kew, "A Descriptive Study of Alcohol Consumption Patterns on a South African Gold Mine," *Urbanisation and Health Newsletter* (June 1994): 39.

76. See J. J. Schmidt and P. A. Botha, "Die Drinkpatroon van die Bantoe in 'n Stedelike Gebied," unpublished paper, Instituut vir Sosiologiese, Demografiese en Kriminologiese Navorsing, Pretoria, 1974, 42–43.

77. Author's interview with Bruce Starke, 28 April 2000.

78. Ibid.

79. The per capita consumption of malt beer in South Africa rose from 5.41 liters in 1962 to 13.18 liters in 1972 and 22.9 liters in 1979. This growth reflects the increase in the number of black consumers. See Michael Coulson, "After the New Dispensation in Liquor: An Industry Still in Ferment," *Management* (October 1980), 80.

80. Author's interview with Cooksie Senne, 8 July 2000.

81. Author's interview with Sister Lydia Mosala.

82. Author's interview with Mrs. Mabiki Mtshali, 4 July 2000.

83. For a discussion of how young men in Botswana used the symbolic structures of masculine seniority in bars, see D. N. Suggs, "'These Young Chaps Think They Are Just Men, Too': Redistributing Masculinity in Kgatleng Bars," *Social Science and Medicine* 53, no. 2 (2001): 241–250.

84. Annual sales growth rates for beer averaged between 6 percent and 8 percent per annum for the next two decades. See Editorial, *SANCA Forum* (June 1990): 1; R. Morris, *Marketing to Black Townships: Practical Guidelines* (Cape Town: Juta, 1992), 20.

85. John Scott, "Rhubarb Juice for Shebeens," *Cape Times,* 15 October 1976; author's interview with Sister Lydia Mosala.

86. SANCA records a 15.25 percent increase in spending on alcohol advertising from 1984 to 1985, from R32.8 million in 1984 to R37.8 million in 1985. See SANCA information pamphlet, Johannesburg, ca. 1986, SANCA Records, Johannesburg. See also Wiener, *The Politics of Alcoholism,* 245, for opposition to advertisements for alcohol in the United States in the mid-1970s.

87. Robert Goldman, *Reading Ads Socially* (London: Routledge, 1992), 19.

88. Van der Burgh, "Some Guidelines for Combating the Advertising/Marketing Strategies of the Alcohol Industry in Black Communities," 5.

89. Author's interview with Sipho Mathe, 3 July 2000.

90. See resolution on alcohol advertising by the Medical Association of South Africa in "Minutes of Meeting of the Federal Council of the Medical Association of South Africa (11–13 May)," *S.A. Medical Journal,* Supplement (17 September 1977): 22–23; C. N. Moodliar, 18 April 1989, in South Africa, Parliament, *Debates of Parliament,* 5670; Charles Parry and Anna Bennetts, *Alcohol Policy and Public Health in South Africa* (Cape Town: Oxford University Press, 1998), 143–146.

91. See the cartoon "Jo-Jo's World" in the *Sowetan* on the following dates: 2 October 1987, 5 November 1987, 19 November 1987, 23 November 1987, and 30 November 1987.

92. See "Jo-Jo's World" in the *Sowetan* on the following dates: 7 November 1986, 6 October 1987, 18 December 1987, and 28 December 1988.

93. See "Jo-Jo's World" in the *Sowetan* on 27 February 1981 and 4 March 1987.

94. See Duduzile column in the *Sowetan*: Reply to "Worried Mother," *Sowetan*, 11 March 1987; see also Duduzile, reply to "Somebody," *Sowetan*, 23 November 1988, implying an absence of outside support.

95. See Coplan, *In Township Tonight*, 102. Originating in the nineteenth century, these clubs formed a network of associations across the townships of Johannesburg and in other parts of the country.

96. N. Diseko, "Spotlight on Sharpeville," *Sowetan*, 6 November 1985.

97. Author's interview with Mrs. Mabiki Mtshali; Diseko, "Spotlight on Sharpeville," 5.

98. SANCA estimated that in 1985, the number of alcoholics per racial group was as follows: 67,287 Coloured, 10,255 Indian, 202,000 white, and 360,000 African (based on a 6 percent sample of each racial category of the population). See S. Pleming, "R7,5m Spent Daily on Drink," *Star*, 24 October 1985; "Generation of Black Addicts Is SANCA's Fear," *Star*, 19 September 1986.

99. Author's interview with Mrs. Mabiki Mtshali.

100. Gatley and Bayley, "A Report on a Research Project on Patterns of Use and Attitudes towards the Use and Misuse of Alcohol, Dagga, Mandrax, and Inhalants in the Black Community of New Brighton, Port Elizabeth"; see also "Research Survey, New Brighton Township," SANCA, Port Elizabeth Branch, November 1987, 3–5.

101. "Inauguration of Themba Centre," *SANCA Forum* (June 1989), 5.

102. Lee Rocha-Silva, *Alcohol and Other Drug Use by Blacks Resident in Selected Areas in the RSA* (Pretoria: Human Sciences Research Council, 1991), 6.

103. Lee Rocha-Silva, *Drinking Practices, Drinking Related Attitudes and Public Impressions of Services for Alcohol and Other Drug Problems in Urban South Africa*, Report S-193 (Pretoria: Human Sciences Research Council, 1989), 34–35. According to this report, 76 percent of black men and nearly 51 percent of black women approved of "becoming slightly drunk" on New Year's Eve.

104. Author's interview with Sipho Mathe; author's interview with Mrs. Mabiki Mtshali.

105. AA's approach to alcoholism was set out in Patrick D., "Report on Fourth National School 13–17 August," *SANCA Information Bulletin* 2, no. 2 (August 1972).

106. Cobley, "Liquor and Leadership," 140.

107. Patrick D., "Report on Fourth National School."

108. Wiener, *Politics of Alcoholism*, 221.

109. Patrick D., "Report on Fourth National School."

110. Ibid.

111. "Turnabout—A Self-Help Group for the Woman Alcoholic and Drug Dependent," *SANCA Forum* 6 (September 1988), 5.

112. P. I. Devan, Solidarity Party, House of Delegates, 21 March 1989, in South Africa, Parliament, *Debates of the House of Delegates* (Cape Town: Government Printer, 1989), 3804. The House of Delegates was introduced to give Indians a voice in apartheid's tricameral parliament.

113. In 1978, an estimated 150,000 whites were alcoholics; this was 6 percent of the white population. See E. A. van Rooyen, "Drankmisbruik van Ouers as oorsaak van Sorgbehoewendheid van hul kinders," *Rehabilitation in S.A.* (September 1980),

100. See A. Thomas, "Relapse of White Alcoholics in South Africa," *Social Work* 16, no. 4 (October 1980): 222, for an estimate of 40,000 white alcoholics in 1963. SANCA's estimate of 202,000 white alcoholics in 1985 represents 4 percent of the population of over 5,000,000; see S. Pleming, "R7,5m Spent Daily on Drink," *Star* (24 October 1975); and South Africa, *Official Year Book of the Republic of South Africa* (Johannesburg: Chris van Rensburg, 1984), 33. Whites consumed 7.55 liters of alcohol per capita per year, the highest per capita consumption in the world in 1971; see "African Drinking Habits Change," *Star,* 20 May 1971.

114. D. J. de Villiers, Minister of Industries, Commerce and Tourism, 4 May 1983, in South Africa, Parliament, *Debates of the House of Assembly* (Cape Town: Cape and Transvaal Printers, 1983), 6252.

115. S. P. Barnard, Conservative Party, 4 May 1983, in ibid., 6249.

116. Rocha-Silva, *Drinking Practices,* 6.

117. Ibid., 4. See also Lee Rocha-Silva, "Alcohol and Other Drug-Related Risks in Informal Urban Settlements in South Africa: A Comparative Perspective," *Urbanisation and Health Newsletter* (June 1994): 27.

118. While the total number of illicit dealers in the country was estimated at close to 200,000 in 1994, the number of established shebeeners who might seek licensing was a mere 30,000 and only 12,000 obtained licenses in that year. See Gary May, "Licensing as an Alcohol Control Measure within the South African National Control Strategy," *Urbanisation and Health Newsletter* 21 (June 1994): 68.

119. Lulama Mbobo, Charles Parry, and Nosisi Dingani, "Alcohol Use in an Informal Settlement (Noordhoek)," *Urbanisation and Health Newsletter* (June 1994): 9–15.

120. Ibid., 8.

121. Ibid., 7–8.

122. J. van der Spuy, "Home Violence? Some Data from the National Trauma Research Programme, MRC," *Trauma Review* 2, no. 3 (December 1994): 3 and 5. The percentage at rural hospitals was 76 percent; E. Steyn, "Women and Trauma," *Trauma Review* 4, no. 2 (1996): 2.

123. Rocha-Silva, *Attitudes towards drinking,* 5. In Ghana, for example, intoxicated individuals were not held responsible for their actions; see Emmanuel Akyeampong, *Drink, Power and Cultural Change: A Social History of Alcohol in Ghana, c. 1800 to Recent Times* (Portsmouth, N.H. and Oxford: Heinemann and James Currey, 1996), 19.

124. Tribute to Tshepo Seepe, musician and former cocaine addict, on the *Tim Modise Show,* SAFM Radio, 24 October 2001.

125. Mbobo, Parry, and Dingani, "Alcohol Use in an Informal Settlement," 9–15.

5. REMAKING THE OLD ORDER

1. At no stage did the government's reform initiatives envisage the dismantling of apartheid. Rather, efforts were directed at placing African, Coloured, and Asian leaders in separate administrations through an "election" process.

2. The Sullivan Code set out principles for multinationals doing business in South Africa, and the Riekert and Wiehahn commissions made recommendations for regulating the process of urbanization and the labor force. See Charles Feinstein,

An Economic History of South Africa: Conquest, Discrimination and Development (Cambridge: Cambridge University Press, 2005), 200–251; Stephen Gelb, ed., *South Africa's Economic Crisis* (Cape Town: David Philip, 1991). N. E. Wiehahn, *Report of the Commission of Inquiry into Labour Legislation* (Pretoria: Government Printer, 1979); Government of South Africa, *Report of the Commission of Inquiry into Legislation Affecting the Utilization of Manpower (Excluding the Legislation Administered by the Departments of Labour and Mines)* (Pretoria: Commission of Inquiry into Legislation Affecting the Utilization of Manpower, 1979).

3. SAB moved to make use of this opportunity. It set aside capital for its brewery in Transkei in 1977, pending political developments. The government granted Southern Sun Hotel Holdings Limited, a subsidiary of SAB headed by Sol Kerzner, exclusive rights to casinos in the homelands in 1978. See SAB Board minutes, ca. May 1978, SAB Records. Kerzner arranged for prominent blacks to be granted ownership of 49 percent of Southern Sun's Transkei operations.

4. "Shebeens Must Go," *Argus,* 9 October 1976.

5. "Casey's Beat: Raining Cats and Dogs," *Drum,* November 1976, 77.

6. "A Man Is Entitled to Have His Drink," *Weekend Argus,* 16 October 1976.

7. Ibid.

8. "Casey's Beat: Live Fast, Die Young," *Drum,* January 1977, 47.

9. "Shebeens 'Must Go,'" *Argus,* 9 October 1976.

10. "Drive to Clean Up Shebeens," *Argus,* 3 January 1977.

11. Bootleggers or runners bought bulk supplies of alcohol from white-owned bottle stores at a discount and supplied shebeeners. See Ric Turner, "The Bootlegger: On the Soweto Booze Run for a Cool R2 000 a Month," *Sunday Tribune,* 23 May 1982; and figures in "Soweto, a Survey," *Financial Mail,* 25 March 1983, supplement, 3 and 59.

12. The Western Cape Taverners' Association and the Natal and KwaZulu Taverners' Association as well as the STA and other Transvaal-based taverners' associations affiliated with the NTA. The STA affiliated with the Foundation for African Business and Consumer Services, which was formed in 1989. In 1991, members of the STA formed the United Taverners' Association of South Africa and broke away from the STA. See Ivan Deacon, "The Black Liquor Market—Some Implications, Size and Potential," *eSpotini,* June 1982, 1; Elizabeth Sidiropolous, "The Politics of Black Business," *Spotlight* 3, no. 94 (1994): 18–21; and Elizabeth Sidiropolous, "Black Economic Empowerment," *Spotlight* 2, no. 93 (1993): 29.

13. "National Taverners Association Educational Fund," *eSpotini,* February 1980.

14. "Soweto, a Survey," *Financial Mail,* 25 March 1983, supplement, 58.

15. Ibid.

16. "Peggy Bel-Air: A Shebeen Sheikh," *Financial Mail,* 18 September 1981, 1405.

17. *eSpotini,* March 1980.

18. "We're the Best Business People Says Shebeen King," *Daily Dispatch,* 24 June 1983.

19. Bob Connell, "Masculinity, Violence and War," in *Men's Lives,* ed. Michael S. Kimmel and Michael A. Messner (Boston: Allyn & Bacon, 1995), 130.

20. "Cutting the Red Tape," *Financial Mail,* 18 September 1981, 1368.

21. "The Big Booze Drink-Up," *Sowetan,* 3 March 1981; "ECAB View on Govt Liquor Sales Move," *Evening Post,* 28 July 1985.

22. SAB conducted training courses for alcohol retailers in the homelands. For example, in 1980–1981, SAB ran a four-module course attended by thirty-two people from Lebowa and two from Venda; see "Report on S.A. Breweries Bottle Store Course," *Black Business,* August 1980, 16–20; "Bottle Store Course," *Black Business,* November 1980, 19–23; "Bottle Store Course: A Successful Finale," *Black Business,* February 1981, 4–15. Tseke Mphahlele, an established businessman in Lebowa, obtained a bottle-store license in 1970; see "Black Business News 'Spotlights': Tseke Lehlaga Mphahlele," *Black Business News,* July 1979, 24–25.

23. Colin McCarthy, "Apartheid Ideology and Economic Development Policy," in *The Political Economy of South Africa,* ed. Nicoli Nattrass and Elisabeth Ardington (Cape Town: Oxford University Press, 1990), 43–54.

24. Michael Fridjohn and Andy Murray, *Conspiracy of Giants: The South African Liquor Industry* (Johannesburg: Divaris Stein, 1986), 294.

25. "Shebeens Hit Back," *Financial Mail,* 1 May 1981, 528–529.

26. Author's interview with Sis Cooksie Senne, 8 July 1998.

27. Ibid.

28. Len Kalane, "Big Indaba over Booze Boycott," *Sowetan,* 3 April 1981; Sam Mabe, "WRAB Won't Sell Bottle Stores to STA," *Sowetan,* 16 April 1981; "Money Down the Drain," *Rand Daily Mail,* 11 June 1982.

29. In 1976, the Department of Bantu Administration and Development was renamed first as the Department of Plural Relations and thereafter as the Department of Co-operation and Development. See A. J. Christopher, *The Atlas of Apartheid* (London: Routledge and Johannesburg: Witwatersrand University Press, 1994), 52.

30. Community councils, established by the Community Councils Act (1977), were ostensibly elected by residents to assist with township administration. Electoral turnout was small, however, because the councils were perceived to be puppets of the apartheid government.

31. "Vicious War Brews for Control of Township Liquor Industry," *Sowetan,* 9 November 1983.

32. "Cutting the Red Tape," *Financial Mail,* 18 September 1981, 1369; "Bottlestore Row: ERUCA to Meet Deputy Minister," *Sowetan,* 15 January 1985. ERUCA was the East Rand Urban Councils Association.

33. "Cutting the Red Tape," *Financial Mail,* 18 September 1981, 1369.

34. "Shebeens: More Brewing," *Financial Mail,* 7 May 1982, 647; Willie Bokala, "Row over Tycoon's Booze Store Licence," *Evening Post,* 26 January 1982; Mzikayise Edom and Len Maseko, "Vicious War Brews for Control of Township Liquor Industry: Bottle Stores," *Sowetan,* 9 November 1983.

35. "High Prices Halt the Great Liquor Outlet Sale: R1m Price Tag on Soweto Bottlestores," *Sunday Times,* 22 December 1985.

36. Author's interview with Chris Mhlongo, South African Liquor Stores Association (SALSA) chairman and former International Business Machines (IBM) manager, 8 July 1998.

37. "Blacks in Shebeen Shock," *Sowetan,* 8 March 1985.

38. Author's interview with Sis Dolly Malunga, 8 July 1998.

39. Author's interview with Lucky Michaels, 7 July 1998.

40. Author's interview with Wandie Ndala, 7 July 1998.

41. Ibid. See also "Shebeen Shebang," *Sawubona,* July 1998, 58–61, for an account of Wandie's success.

42. Author's interview with Sis Dolly Malunga.

43. Author's interview with Sis Cooksie Senne.

44. Author's interview with Wandie Ndala.

45. Elliott Makhaya, "Cothoza Makes Our Day," *Sowetan,* 19 December 1988.

46. Elliot Makhaya, "Amajita Boggle the Mind," *Sowetan,* 28 November 1988; Elliot Makhaya, "The Molls Get Sizzled in Mixed Company," *Sowetan,* 3 November 1986.

47. Dorothy Driver, "*Drum* Magazine (1951–59) and the Spatial Configurations of Gender," in *Text, Theory, Space: Land, Literature and History in South Africa and Australia,* ed. Kate Darian-Smith, Liz Gunner, and Sarah Nuttall (London: Routledge, 1996), 233.

48. Stokvels were an adaptation of harvest-time parties in which a shebeener would invite a dozen or more other similarly ranked shebeeners and their friends to a party that could last three days. The hostess sold food and drink to the guests, who pooled a specified sum of money that she pocketed. Next time around, it would be someone else's turn. The key rule was never to break the chain. "Stokvel Night," *Rand Daily Mail,* 7 June 1982.

49. "The First in Daveyton," *Beer Business: A Quarterly Newsletter to the Liquor Trade from the Southern Transvaal Region of the South African Breweries Ltd* (Winter 1989): 6.

50. Author's interview with Bra Boysie, 8 May 1998.

51. Author's interview with Bra Bys, 8 May 1998.

52. Author's interview with Sis Fanny Mokoena, 7 July 1998.

53. Author's interview with Sis Cooksie Senne; see also Elizabeth Sidropolous, "Black Economic Empowerment" in *Spotlight* 2, no. 93 (1993): 31.

54. Peter Savory quoted in "Cutting the Red Tape," *Financial Mail,* 18 September 1981, 1369.

55. See *African Business,* July/August 1991. The NTA's figures were below the 2,855 quoted by the KWV; see Sidropolous, "Black Economic Empowerment," 30.

56. Nat Nakasa, "And So the Shebeen Lives On," in *The World of Nata Nakasa,* ed. Essop Patel (Johannesburg: Ravan Press, 1995), 15.

57. The volume of beer produced in South Africa increased from over 5.3 million hectoliters per year in 1976 to over 13.7 million hectoliters in 1986; see Appendix, Table 1. SAB produced over 95 percent of this volume.

58. "Special Survey on SAB Beer Division," *SA Food Review,* December 1977, 7–74.

59. Ibid., 87–89.

60. Both the Wiehahn and the Riekert commissions made recommendations for reform. See Wiehahn, *Report of the Commission of Inquiry into Labour Legislation,* paragraph 1.2; and Government of South Africa, *Report of the Commission of Inquiry into Legislation Affecting the Utilization of Manpower,* paragraph 6.4.

61. While SFAWU was based exclusively in the Transvaal and Natal and did not have the capacity to service workers in Cape Town, the union organized several breweries in these provinces. FAWU agreed that it was best that workers at the Newlands plant belong to SFAWU. E-mail communication from Jan Theron, 16 March 2009. At the same time, workers at Newlands Brewery rejected the advances of the white-dominated Liquor and Catering Workers Union.

62. E-mail communication from Jan Theron, 16 March 2009; *Food and Allied Workers Union v SA Breweries Ltd* (1990) in *Industrial Law Journal* 11 (1990): 413 (A.R.B.). The initial arbitration was conducted by Clive Thompson on 20 January 1988.

63. The first national recognition agreement between the union and SAB, which was signed in 1987, provided for annual wage negotiations at a national level and marked the beginning of a new era in labor relations for workers and SAB. The agreement was thrashed out between Jan Theron as general secretary of the Food and Allied Workers Union and SAB's Graham Mackay and Rob Childs (then human resources manager for the SAB Group).

64. Moore, *A Passion for Difference,* 50.

65. "Much Ado about Nothing," *Financial Mail,* 3 July 1987, 41.

66. *Food and Allied Workers Union v SA Breweries Ltd.* (1990).

67. Ibid.; *SA Breweries v Food and Allied Workers Union and Others* (1988), in *Industrial Law Journal* 9 (1988): 244–730; *SA Breweries v Food and Allied Workers Union and Others* (1990), in *South African Law Reports* 1 (1990): 92–100; author's interview with Whitey Maphanga, 15 November 2006.

68. *Food and Allied Workers Union v SA Breweries Ltd* (1990).

69. Hearings by the Conciliation Board were provided for by the Wage Act (No. 5 of 1957); the legality of the strike was determined in terms of the Labour Relations Act (No. 28 of 1956).

70. *SA Breweries v Food and Allied Workers Union and Others* (1988); *SA Breweries v Food and Allied Workers Union and Others* (1990).

71. *SA Breweries v Food and Allied Workers Union and Others* (1990), 99.

72. Jeff Hearn, *Men in the Public Eye* (London: Routledge, 1992), 3.

73. "SAB's A-Truck-Tive Offer," *Financial Mail,* 18 March 1988, 111.

74. Author's interview with Whitey Maphanga; see also Nndateni Ndou, "The Changing Nature of Employment Relationship: The South African Breweries (SAB) Owner-Driver Scheme" (Bachelor of Social Science Honours thesis, University of Cape Town, November 2002).

75. See, for example, P. Cappelli, *The New Deal at Work: Managing the Market-Driven Workforce* (Boston: Harvard Business School Press, 1999).

76. Workers in retail companies such as Edgars, which was owned by the SAB Group, were paid considerably less; e-mail communication from Jan Theron, 16 March 2009. Theron, the longtime general secretary of FAWU, was on sabbatical leave at this time.

77. "Edging Closer," *Financial Mail,* September 1989, 53–54.

78. See Jeremy Baskin, *Striking Back: A History of COSATU* (Johannesburg: Raven Press, 1991), 417.

79. "A Dry Season," *Financial Mail,* 20 October 1989, 45; "Thirst for Trust," *Financial Mail,* 27 October 1989, 50; author's interview with Whitey Maphanga.

80. Author's interview with Whitey Maphanga.

81. The National Stokvels Association of South Africa was established in 1988, bringing together thousands of informal credit unions with an estimated membership of 108,000 of the approximately 1.3 million *stokvel* members in South Africa. These credit unions encompassed three major types: burial societies, investment syndicates, and *imigalelo* groups for purchase of major items. For detail on how *stokvels* operated in this period, see Andrew Lukhele, *Stokvels in South Africa* (Johannesburg:

Amagi Books, 1990); see also Sidropolous, "Black Economic Empowerment," 20; and "Digging In," *Financial Mail,* 10 November 1989, 60.

82. "Digging In."

83. "Loyal to the Last Drop," *Financial Mail,* 27 October 1989, 92; "No Surrender Yet," *Financial Mail,* 17 November 1989, 54–55.

84. "Frothy Tussle," *Financial Mail,* 3 November 1989, 83.

85. Staff reporter, "Labour Action," *South African Labour Bulletin* 14, no. 5 (February 1990): 4–5.

86. Peter Alegi, "'Moving the Goalposts': Playing Styles, Sociability, and Politics in South African Soccer in the 1960s," working paper 225, African Studies Center, Boston University, 2000, 4.

87. Sponsorship for black soccer amounted to approximately R3,000 per season in the early 1970s. See "Rands Pour into Soccer," in *Thirty Years of South African Soccer,* ed. Thami Mazwai (Johannesburg: Mafube, 2002), 50.

88. Much has been written about the politics of sport in South Africa. For example, see Douglas Booth, *The Race Game: Sport and Politics in South Africa* (London: Frank Cass, 1998); Grant Jarvie, *Sport, Racism and Ethnicity* (London: Falmer, 1991); Grant Jarvie, *Class, Race and Sport in South Africa's Political Economy* (London: Routledge, 1985); John Nauright, *Sport, Cultures and Identities in South Africa* (Cape Town: David Philip, 1997); Cheryl Roberts, *SACOS, 1973–1988: Fifteen Years of Resistance* (Durban: Natal University Press); Cheryl Roberts, *Against the Grain: Women and Sport in South Africa* (Cape Town: CT Publishing Co-op, 1992); David Black and John Nauright, *Rugby and the South African Nation* (Manchester: Manchester University Press, 1998); Robert Archer, *The SA Game: Sport and Racism in South Africa* (London: Zed Press, 1982); Joan Brickhill, *Race against Race: South Africa's Multinational Sport Fraud* (London: IDAF, 1976); Thomas Oliver Newnham, *Apartheid Is Not a Game: NZ vs Apartheid Sport* (Auckland: Graphic Public, 1975); and Peter Alegi, *"Laduma!" Soccer, Politics and Society in South Africa* (Scottsville: University of KwaZulu Natal Press, 2004).

89. Author's interview with Bruce Starke, 28 April 2000.

90. See Joan Brickhill, *Race against Race: South Africa's "Multinational" Sport Fraud* (London: International Defence and Aid Fund for Southern Africa, 1976), 44–52; see also Douglas Booth, *The Race Game: Sport and Politics in South Africa* (London and Portland, Ore.: Frank Cass, 1998).

91. The rebel tours of 1979 cost SAB over R1 million; the cost in 1978 was approximately R600,000; see "The Great Race," *Financial Mail,* 24 March 1978, 907.

92. Tony Collins and Wray Vramplew, *Mud, Sweat, and Beers: A Cultural History of Sport and Alcohol* (Oxford: Berg, 2002), 69.

93. One newspaper reported that South Africa had appointed a roving sports ambassador; see *Sunday Express,* 25 April 1982, 11. See also Adrian Guelke, "Sport and the End of Apartheid," in *The Changing Politics of Sport,* ed. Lincoln Allison (Manchester: Manchester University Press, 1993), 151–170.

94. Sy Lerman's receipt of the SAB award is confirmed in Government of South Africa, *South Africa 1984: Official Yearbook of the Republic of South Africa* (Johannesburg: Chris van Rensburg, ca. 1985), 824.

95. Sy Lerman, "Top SA Soccer Sides Face Their Moment of Truth against Tourists," *Rand Daily Mail,* 14 July 1982, 26.

96. Burstyn, *Rites of Men,* 136.

97. Lerman, "Top SA Soccer Sides Face Their Moment of Truth against Tourists."

98. "Error in Soccer 'Teaser' Ads," *Rand Daily Mail,* 15 July 1982.

99. Ian Hobbs, "Ardiles Warned: Don't Play, as Row Hots Up," *Rand Daily Mail,* 15 July 1982.

100. Ibid.

101. "FA Get Tough as UK Slams 'Phoney' Tour," *Rand Daily Mail,* 23 July 1982.

102. "Ardiles Forced Out of SA Tour," *Rand Daily Mail,* 17 July 1982.

103. Chris Olckers and Anne Sacks, "Tour Game Flops as Pirates Refuse to Play," *Rand Daily Mail,* 19 July 1982.

104. Sy Lerman, "Withdrawal Has Harmed SA Soccer," *Rand Daily Mail,* 19 July 1982.

105. Sy Lerman, "Signs That Swallows May Yet Rescue SA Soccer," *Rand Daily Mail,* 20 July 1982; "Tour Ends as Thabe Concedes Defeat," *Rand Daily Mail,* 21 July 1982.

106. Lerman, "Tour Ends as Thabe Concedes Defeat." George Thabe did not discuss this fiasco in George Andries Lesitsi Thabe assisted by M. Mutloatse, *It's a Goal: 50 Years of Sweat, Tears and Drama in Black Soccer* (Johannesburg: Skotaville, 1983).

107. Lerman, "Tour Ends as Thabe Concedes Defeat."

108. Chris Freimond, "What Really Sank the Soccer Tour," *Rand Daily Mail,* 23 July 1982.

109. "More Than a Hiccup?" *Financial Mail,* 23 July 1982, 439.

110. Freimond, "What Really Sank the Soccer Tour."

111. Chris Olckers and Anne Sacks, "Tour Game Flops as Pirates Refuse to Play," *Rand Daily Mail,* 19 July 1982.

112. Ducky Tankiso oa Mohokare, letter to *Rand Daily Mail,* 30 July 1982; Mashabaile F. Mohlala, letter to *Rand Daily Mail,* 11 August 1982.

113. Stable Heads, Lenasia, letter to *Rand Daily Mail,* 28 July 1982; black referee, letter to *Rand Daily Mail,* 30 July 1982.

114. Letter from Rosettenville, *Rand Daily Mail,* 27 July 1982.

115. "Deon Erasmus of the SAB Responds to Letters," *Rand Daily Mail,* 27 July 1982.

116. Rodney Hartman, "Costly Collapse of Tour Hasn't Deterred Biggest Sponsor," *Rand Daily Mail,* 24 July 1982.

117. Author's interview with Peter Savory, 11 July 2000.

118. "Brickbats and Bouquets: Not a Very Good Year," *Financial Mail,* 24 December 1982, 1384.

119. G. D. May, SAB public affairs manager, letter to *Financial Mail,* 21 January 1983.

120. Editorial, *Rand Daily Mail,* 23 July 1982.

121. Varda Burstyn, *The Rites of Men: Manhood, Politics, and the Culture of Sport* (1999; repr., Toronto: University of Toronto Press, 2000), 32.

122. Albert Grundlingh, "Playing for Power? Rugby, Afrikaner Nationalism and Masculinity in South Africa, c. 1900–c. 1970," in *Making Men: Rugby and Masculine Identity,* ed. John Nauright and Timothy J. L. Chandler (London: Frank Cass, 1996), 182. See also John Nauright, "Colonial Manhood and Imperial Race Virility: British Responses to Post–Boer War Colonial Rugby Tours," in Nauright and Chandler, *Making Men,* 122–134.

123. See Louis Babrow and R. K. Stent, *The Varsity Spirit: The Story of Rugby Football at the University of Cape Town, 1883–1963* (Cape Town: Johnston and Neville, 1963); Felicity Swanson, "Die SACS kom terug": Intervarsity Rugby, Masculinity and White Identity at the University of Cape Town, 1960s–1970s," in *Imagining the City: Memories and Cultures in Cape Town,* ed. Sean Field, Renate Meyer, and Felicity Swanson (Pretoria: Human Sciences Research Council, 2007), 207–227.

124. Author's interview with Joey Burke, 22 January 2008.

125. Ibid.

126. In a down-down, a drinker swallows large quantities of beer while onlookers chant "Down, down, down."

127. Ibid.

128. Ibid.

129. "Bacchus Unseen at Pig," *Varsity* 47, no. 7 (3 August 1988), accessed at Manuscripts and Archives, University of Cape Town.

130. Pierre Bourdieu, *Masculine Domination* (Stanford, Calif.: Stanford University Press, 1998), 40; Robert A. Rhoads, "Whales Tales, Dog Piles, and Beer Goggles: An Ethnographic Case Study of Fraternity Life," *Anthropology and Education Quarterly* 26, no. 3 (September 1995): 314.

131. Dave Marrs, "Moves to Cut Intervarsity Thuggishness," *Cape Times,* 31 July 1990.

132. Author's interview with Joey Burke.

133. Bourdieu, *Masculine Domination,* 51.

134. Ibid., 52.

135. "Buddy Up," *Rag News* (April 1988), accessed at Manuscripts and Archives, University of Cape Town.

136. "'No-Booze' Message for Intervarsity," *Cape Times,* 3 August 1988.

137. "Talking to SATISCO," *Varsity* 48, no. 1 (February 1989); "Ikeys Facing the Maties," *Varsity* 47, no. 8 (17 August 1988). Both accessed at Manuscripts and Archives, University of Cape Town.

138. "Beer Makes Vote Unanimous," *Varsity* 48, no. 5 (30 May 1989), accessed at Manuscripts and Archives, University of Cape Town.

139. Ibid.

140. Clifford Geertz, *Interpretation of Cultures* (New York: Basic Books, 1973), 433.

141. Author's interview with Joey Burke.

142. Michael Owen-Smith, "Province Must Follow UCT's Stirring Example," *Cape Times,* 14 August 1990.

143. Ken Gardner, letter to editor, *Cape Times,* 20 August 1990.

144. Willem van de Putte, "Never-Say-Die Ikeys Deserve a Monument," *Cape Times,* 13 August 1990.

145. "Burke Wows Out," *Varsity* 49, no. 7 (no month, 1990), accessed at Manuscripts and Archives, University of Cape Town.

146. Author's interview with Joey Burke.

147. "Anderson Cup Competition Re-Introduced: Farewell Intervarsity," *Monday Paper* 14, no. 13 (May 1995).

148. Sello S. Alcock, "Classical Genius," *Mail and Guardian,* February 28–06 March 2008.

6. HERITAGE AND BEER TOURISM

1. See Benedict Anderson, *Imagined Communities: Reflections on the Origin and Spread of Nationalism* (London: Verso, 1983) for a discussion of nation as an imagined community; and Homi Bhabha, ed., *Nation and Narration* (London: Routledge, 1990), for how nations must be narrated into existence.

2. M. Lane Bruner, *Strategies of Remembrance: The Rhetorical Dimensions of National Identity Construction* (Columbia: University of South Carolina Press, 2002), 10.

3. Annie E. Coombes, *History after Apartheid: Visual Culture and Public Memory in a Democratic South Africa* (Durham, N.C.: Duke University Press, 2003), 23. See also Bill Nasson, "Commemorating the Anglo-Boer War in Post-Apartheid South Africa," *Radical History Review* 78 (2000): 149–165; Ciraj Rassool and Leslie Witz, "The 1952 Jan van Riebeeck Tercentenary Festival: Constructing and Contesting Public National History in South Africa," *Journal of African History* 34 (1993): 447–468; and Nigel Worden, "Signs of the Times: Tourism and Public History at Cape Town's Victoria and Alfred Waterfront," *Cahiers d'Etudes africaines* 141, no. 2 (1996): 215–236. Gold Reef City is a prime example of a postapartheid theme park, and Robben Island is the nation's premier world heritage site. See Leslie Witz, *Apartheid's Festival: Contesting South Africa's National Pasts* (Bloomington: Indiana University Press and David Philip, 2003), 249, for a discussion of heritage policy; and Nigel Worden, "The Changing Politics of Slave Heritage in the Western Cape, South Africa," *Journal of African History* 50, no. 1 (2009): 23–40, for a discussion of conflicts around the concepts of heritage and identity in postapartheid South Africa.

4. Patrick Wright, *On Living in an Old Country* (London: Verso, 1985), 69.

5. Craig Colhoun, *Nationalism* (Minneapolis: University of Minnesota Press, 1997), 34.

6. J. E. Tunbridge and E. J. Ashworth, *Dissonant Heritage: The Management of the Past as a Resource in Conflict* (Chichester: John Wiley 1996), 8.

7. P. H. Mooney, "The Practice of History in Corporate America: Business Archives in the United States," in *Public History: An Introduction,* ed. B. J. Howe and E. L. Kemp (Florida: Robert Krieger, 1988), 438.

8. Paul la Hause, "Drink and Cultural Innovation in Durban: The Origins of the Beerhall in South Africa, 1902–1916," in *Liquor and Labour in Southern Africa,* ed. Jonathan Crush and Charles Ambler (Athens: Ohio University Press, 1992), 78–114.

9. See "Proposal for the Kwa Muhle Museum," unpublished paper, Local History Museum, Durban, 26 September 1991.

10. Author's interview with Bruce Starke, 28 May 2000.

11. "Three Cheers for Capitalism," *Financial Mail,* 13 July 1990, reprinted in "Did You Notice What the *FM* Said about Us?" *Beer Business* (Spring 1990): 4.

12. Ibid.

13. The term socioscapes is akin to Francaviglia's "lived heritage landscapes"; see Richard Francaviglia, "Selling Heritage Landscapes," in *Preserving Cultural Landscapes in America,* ed. Arnold R. Alanen and Robert Z. Melnick (Baltimore, Md.: Johns Hopkins University Press, 2000), 48–67.

14. See chapter 2.

15. Barbara Kirshenblatt-Gimblett, *Destination Culture: Tourism, Museums and Heritage* (Berkeley: University of California Press, 1998), 137; Tony Bennett, *The Birth of the Museum: History, Theory, Politics* (London: Routledge, 1995), 20; Wolfhard Weber, "The Political History of Museums of Technology in Germany since the Nineteenth Century," in *Industrial Society and Its Museums 1890–1990: Social Aspirations and Cultural Politics,* ed. B. Schroeder-Gudehus (Chur, Switzerland: Harwood Academic Publishers, 1993), 13–25; David J. Rhees, "Corporate Advertising, Public Relations and Popular Exhibits: The Case of Du Pont," in Schroeder-Gudehus, ed., *Industrial Society and Its Museums,* 67–75; John M. Staudenmaier, "Clean Exhibits, Messy Exhibits: Henry Ford's Technological Aesthetic," in Schroeder-Gudehus, ed., *Industrial Society and Its Museums,* 55–65; Corinne A. Kratz and Ivan Karp, "Wonder and Worth: Disney Museums in World Showcase," *Museum Anthropology* 17, no. 3 (October 1993): 38.

16. Tunbridge and Ashworth, *Dissonant Heritage,* 233.

17. Consumer preference in the region was shifting away from Ohlsson's Lager, and SAB's strategy of increasing its advertising budget for this brand could not halt the shift. It discontinued the brand in 1998.

18. Ted Friedman, "Receiving Information . . . the World of Coca-Cola," *Communication Research* 19, no. 5 (October 1992): 643. Secrecy surrounding the Coca-Cola recipe created mystery but also limited what there was to tell.

19. Author's interview with Robert Staples and Barbara Charles, 25 April 2003.

20. Ibid. SAB increased the budget for the design of the tourist center from $7,000 to nearly $14,000.

21. Author's interview with Frank Johnson, 20 July 2000.

22. See Patrick McAllister, *Agriculture, Labour and Beer in South Africa's Transkei* (Aldershot: Ashgate, 2001), 148–176, for an account of the changing meanings of "traditional beer"; and Juha Partanen, *Sociability and Intoxication: Alcohol and Drinking in Kenya, Africa, and the Modern World* (Helsinki: Finnish Foundation for Alcohol Studies, 1991), 39.

23. A mash tun is a copper kettle in which maize and malt are mixed in the process of beer brewing.

24. Francaviglia, "Selling Heritage Landscapes," 64.

25. Sophiatown, a freehold township where shebeen culture flourished in the 1950s, was demolished in 1959 to make way for the white suburb of Triomf.

26. Author's interview with Sue Birch, 8 September 1998.

27. Francaviglia, "Selling Heritage Landscapes," 64.

28. See McAllister, *Agriculture, Labour and Beer,* 148–176, for an account of the changing meanings of "traditional beer" in new contexts.

29. R. Hewison, "Commerce and Culture," in *Enterprise and Heritage: Crosscurrents of National Culture,* ed. J. Corner and S. Harvey (London: Routledge, 1991), 175.

30. See chapter 3.

31. For a discussion of how museums might represent different viewpoints, see Tony Bennett, "Contesting Times: Conflicting Histories in Post-Colonial Contexts," in *Social Change,* ed. Tim Jordan and Steve Pile (Oxford: Blackwell for the Open University, 2002), 50–77.

32. SAB's turnover rose from R1.24 billion in 1985 to R1.6 billion in 1995. See Michael Fridjhon and Andy Murray, *Conspiracy of Giants: The South African Liquor Industry* (Johannesburg: Divaris Steyn, 1986), 185. See Wright, *On Living in an Old Country,* 65.

33. Author's interview with Bruce Starke.

34. "Speech by President Nelson Mandela at the Opening of the South African Breweries Centenary Centre," Johannesburg, 15 May 1995, available at http://www.anc.org.za/ancdocs/history/mandela/1995/sp950515.html.

35. SAB's conference facilities are at the Centenary Centre and its training facilities are at the SAB Heritage Center, Newlands.

36. Barbara Fahs Charles to Julian Doods, SAB Beer Division, 12 July 1995, personal collection of Robert Staples and Barbara Charles, Alexandria, Virginia, United States.

37. Author's interview with Windsor Shuenyane, 12 July 2000.

38. Author's interview with John Eastwood, 25 September 2003.

39. Ibid.

40. *Ohlsson's Cape Breweries: Brewers since 1889,* SAB pamphlet, SAB Records. The first successful malt brewery in Newlands was established by Willem Menssink in the 1690s; see Nigel Penn, *Rogues, Rebels, and Runaways: Eighteenth-Century Cape Characters* (Cape Town: David Philip, 1999), 9–72.

41. SAB Heritage Centre, which encompassed the malt house and the Mariendahl brewery, was declared a national monument by the National Monuments Council, created in 1969. When this council was replaced by the South African Heritage Resources Agency in 1999 under the revised Heritage Act, provinces became responsible for maintaining existing monuments.

42. Francaviglia, "Selling Heritage Landscapes," 53.

43. Author's interview with Etienne de Kock, 6 November 2003.

44. Author's interview with Gabriel Fagan, 18 April 2000.

45. Cape Town artist Sue Williamson produced the collage in 1995.

46. The six breweries were Cannon, Newlands, Montebello, Montrose, Anneberg, and Mariendahl.

47. *Ohlssons Cape Breweries,* ca. 1968, SAB pamphlet, SAB Records.

48. Ibid.

49. See chapter 2.

50. Tim Barringer and Tom Flynn, eds., *Colonialism and the Object: Empire, Material Culture and the Museum* (London: Routledge, 1998), 2.

51. See chapter 1.

52. Author's interview with Gwendoline Fagan.

53. Ibid. Nigel Penn told "the slave story" in his account of Willem Menssink's love affair with Trijntje of Madagascar, a passion that led to the ruin of "the Cape's foremost brewer of malt beer" in the seventeenth century. The chapter is evocatively titled, "The Fatal Passion of Brewer Menssink: Sex, Beer and Politics in a Cape Family, 1694–1722." See Penn, *Rogues, Rebels and Runaways,* 9–72.

54. Author's interview with Gabriel Fagan. See also Gabriel Fagan, "Review of the Current State of Affairs," ca. 1972, manuscript, archives of South African Heritage Resources Agency (SAHRA), Cape Town, South Africa.

55. Author's interview with John Eastwood.

56. Doreen Massey, "Power Geometry and a Progressive Sense of Place," in *Mapping the Futures: Local Cultures, Global Change*, ed. J. Bird, B. Curtis, T. Putnam, G. Robertson, and L. Tickner (London: Routledge, 1993), 66.

57. See chapter 3.

58. See Tony Bennett, "Exhibition, Difference and the Logic of Culture," in *Museum Frictions: Public Cultures, Global Transformations*, ed. Ivan Karp, Corinne Kratz, Lynn Szwaja, and Tomás Gbarra-Frausto (Durham, N.C.: Duke University Press, 2006), 25.

59. Speech by Jabu Moleketi, member of Executive Committee for Economic Affairs, South African Liquor Stores Association Conference, World Trade Center, 7 May 1995.

60. See Christian M. Rogerson, "Tourism-Led Local Economic Development: The South African Experience," *Urban Forum* 13, no. 1 (January 2002): 95–119.

61. See Philip Bonner and Lauren Segal, *Soweto: A History* (Cape Town: Maskew Miller, Longman, 1998).

62. Seekings and Nattrass calculate the rate of unemployment among Africans in 1999 as 44 percent; Jeremy Seekings and Nicoli Nattrass, *Class, Race and Inequality in South Africa* (New Haven, Conn.: Yale University Press, 2005), Table 9.11, 319.

63. Author's interview with Sis Fanny Mokoena, 7 July 1998; author's interview with Lucky Michaels, 8 July 1998.

64. Author's interview with Chris Mhlongo, 7 July 1998.

65. Okechukwu Iheduru, "The Development of Black Capitalism in South Africa and the United States," in *Black Business and Economic Power*, ed. Alusine Jallon and Toyin Falola (Rochester, N.Y.: University of Rochester Press, 2002), 573.

66. Author's interview with Chris Mhlongo.

67. Ibid.

68. Howard Green, "A Critique of the Professional Public History Movement," in *Public History Readings*, ed. P. K. Leffler and J. Brent (Malabar, Florida: Kruger, 1992), 121.

69. For discussion of a critically engaged tourism, see Mitsuhiro Yoshimoto, "Images of Empire: Tokyo Disneyland and Japanese Cultural Imperialism," in *Disney Discourse: Producing the Magic Kingdom*, ed. Eric Smoodin (London: Routledge), 1994, 181–199; and Aviad Raz, *Riding the Black Ship: Japan and Tokyo Disneyland* (Cambridge, Mass.: Harvard University Asia Center, 1999), 12.

7. GLOBAL COMPETITION, WORLD CLASS MANUFACTURING, AND NATIONAL ECONOMIC RESTRUCTURING

1. For a debate on industrial policy strategy in postapartheid South Africa, see Nicoli Nattrass, "Economic Restructuring in South Africa: The Debate Continues," *Journal of Southern African Studies* 20, no. 4 (December 1994): 517–531; and Raphael Kaplinsky, "'Economic Restructuring in South Africa: The Debate Continues': A Response," *Journal of Southern African Studies* 20, no. 4 (December 1994): 533–537.

2. Jeremy Baskin and Vishwas Satgar, "South Africa's New LRA," *South African Labour Bulletin* 19, no. 5 (November 1995): 46–55; see also Paul Benjamin, "LRA-Organisational Rights," *South African Labour Bulletin* 19, no. 5 (November 1995): 56–59; Norma Craven and David Cartwright, "Labour Relations Act Ten Years On," *South African Labour Bulletin* 27, no. 5 (October 2003): 42–43.

3. Elizabeth Sidiroplous, "Black Economic Empowerment," *Spotlight* 2, no. 93 (September 1993): 3.

4. See Roger Southall, "Black Empowerment and Corporate Capital," in *State of the Nation South Africa 2004–2005,* ed. John Daniel, Roger Southall, and Jessica Lutchman (Cape Town: Human Sciences Research Council, 2005), 455–478; Roger Southall, "Black Empowerment and Present Limits to a More Democratic Capitalism in South Africa," in *State of the Nation South Africa 2005–2006,* ed. Sakhela Buhlungu, John Daniel, Roger Southall, and Jessica Lutchman (Cape Town: Human Sciences Research Council, 2006), 175–201; Roger Southall, "The ANC and Black Capitalism in South Africa," *Review of African Political Economy* 31 (2004): 313–328; Sidiroplous, "Black Economic Empowerment"; Okechukwu C. Iheduru, "Black Economic Power and Nation-Building in Post-Apartheid South Africa," *Journal of Modern African Studies* 42, no. 1 (2004): 1–30; Cyril Ramaphosa, "Black Economic Empowerment: Changing the South African Business Landscape," in *South Africa: The Good News,* ed. Brett Bower and Steuart Pennington (Hyde Park, Johannesburg: South Africa—The Good News [Pty] Ltd., 2002), 161–166; Danisa Baloyi, "Black Economic Empowerment: Progress Will Lead to Prosperity," in *South Africa: More Good News,* ed. Brett Bower and Steuart Pennington (Hyde Park, Johannesburg: South Africa—The Good News [Pty] Ltd., 2003), 173–178; Ndaba Ntsele, "Empowerment Makes Good Business Sense" in *The Story of Our Future South Africa 2014,* ed. Brett Bower and Steuart Pennington (Hyde Park, Johannesburg: South Africa—The Good News [Pty] Ltd., 2004), 177–179; Andrea Brown, "BEE, a Model for Global Economic Empowerment," in Bower and Pennington *The Story of Our Future South Africa,* 183–185.

5. The Black Management Forum was established in 1977 as a business association to represent the voice of black professionals and businesspeople. In 1989, the members of the forum opened its membership to all who supported their nonracial agenda. For more information, see the forum's Web site at http://www.bmfonline.co.za.

6. See Black Economic Empowerment Commission, *A National Integrated Black Economic Empowerment Strategy* (Johannesburg: Skotaville Press, 2001), available at http://www.capegateway.gov.za/Text/2004/5/beecomreport.pdf.

7. SAB's trade magazine *Beer Business* provides advice, exposure, and positive reinforcement for retailers and distributors and creates a sense of camaraderie for the "SAB community."

8. See South Africa, Competition Board, *Investigation into Restrictive Practices in the Supply and Distribution of Alcoholic Beverages in the Republic of South Africa,* Competition Board Report No. 10 (Pretoria: Government Printer, 1982), 70.

9. "The South African Breweries Limited, Submission to the Truth and Reconciliation Commission," October 1997, 43, National Archives and Records Service of South Africa, Pretoria.

10. See "Consolidation Is Brewing among Beer Producers as Market Leaders Seek Global Brands," *Business Day,* 12 November 1998; Charlotte Matthews, "Interbrew Says It Has Looked at SA Breweries," *Business Day,* 29 November 2001; "Building Castles in the Air?" *Business Day,* 29 November 2001; "More than Froth?" *Business Day,* 30 November 2001; "Sounds Good after Beers," *Business Day,* 5 December 2001.

11. SAB, *The F97 Annual Report to Employees of the SAB Beer Division,* 50, SAB Records. Anheuser-Busch Inc. topped the list at 110.6 million hectoliters per

annum, followed by Heineken (70.6 million), Miller Brewing Co (52.8 million), and SAB (38.8 million); see "SA Breweries: Milestone Equity Offering," *Financial Mail,* 18 October 1996, 136. Between 1994 and 2006, SAB acquired substantial brewing interests in Asia, including in China, India, and Vietnam; in Eastern Europe, including in Poland, Romania, Hungary, Slovakia, and the Czech Republic; and in Latin America, including in Colombia, Honduras, El Salvador, and Peru. It also had interests in Russia and Italy. These interests were augmented by its ventures in the United States in 2002 and North Africa in 2004. At the same time, SAB consolidated interests in established markets in Africa. "Fundamentals: SABMiller plc" provided this information; accessed at http://www.sainvestor.com/SDT/data/00/125/Notes .asp on 28 July 2006.

12. The notion of world class manufacturing is derived from the strategies of flexibility, quality control, elimination of waste, and increased productivity adopted by leading Japanese manufacturers. See Michael H. Best, *The New Competition: Institutions of Industrial Restructuring* (Cambridge, Mass., Harvard University Press, 1990); W. Edwards Deming, *Out of the Crisis* (Cambridge, Mass.: Massachusetts Institute of Technology, Centre for Advanced Engineering Study, 1986); Peter Cappelli, *The New Deal at Work: Managing the Market-Driven Workforce* (Boston: Harvard Business Scholl Press, 1999).

13. For discussion of the ways the notion of "frontier" has been used in the social sciences, see Kerwin Lee Klein, "Reclaiming the 'F' word, or Being and Becoming Postwestern," *Pacific Historical Review* 65, no. 2 (May 1996): 179–215.

14. Robert D. Nixon, Michael A. Hitt, and Joan E. Ricart i Costa, "New Managerial Mindsets and Strategic Change in the New Frontier," in *New Managerial Mindsets: Organizational Transformation Strategy Implementation,* ed. Michael A. Hitt, Robert D. Nixon, and Joan E. Ricart i Costa (Chichester, N.Y.: John Wiley and Sons, 1998), 1–12.

15. Stephen King, "Brand Building in the 1990s," *Journal of Marketing Management* 7 (1991): 3–13.

16. See John Scott, *Corporate Business and Capitalist Classes* (Oxford: Oxford University Press, 1997), 207–220.

17. Nixon, Hitt, and Ricart i Costa, "New Managerial Mindsets and Strategic Change," 2. The authors acknowledge Sifonis and Goldberg for their use of Ali's metaphor of the butterfly and the bee.

18. Premium beer is a general term for brands that sell at prices significantly higher than other beers because of their quality and good image. See also ch. 3, fn. 66. Marketing is key to maintaining the distinction between premium and mainstream brands; green bottles are usually associated with premium lager and brown bottles with mainstream lager. See Jabulani Sikhakhane, "Major Players Jostle for Space at the Bar," *Financial Mail,* 15 October 1999, 58–60.

19. "Frothy Tussle," *Financial Mail,* 3 November 1989, 83.

20. Lucienne Field, "Namibia Shoots Down SAB Plan," *Sunday Times,* 3 August 1997.

21. Robert Gordon, "Inside the Windhoek Lager: Liquor and Lust in Namibia," in *Drugs, Labor and Colonial Expansion,* ed. W. Jankowick and D. Bradburd (Tucson: Arizona University Press, 2003), 117–134; Lucienne Field, "Namibia Shoots Down SAB Plan," *Sunday Times,* 3 August 1997. The reference to South African black empowerment is probably meant as a criticism of the rush of hastily stitched

together empowerment deals that collapsed within a few years. See Southall, "Black Empowerment and Corporate Capital," 466.

22. See Letter from Nairobi, *Times Literary Supplement,* 14 April 2000, 19. See also Willis, *Potent Brews,* 246–248. SAB did build a brewery in Kenya in 1998 but was forced to close it down in 2002. The company retreated to Tanzania and Uganda, where it had joint ventures in Tanzanian Breweries and Nile Breweries, respectively; see Charlotte Mathews, "Breweries' Deal 'Was Collusion,'" *Business Day,* 23 May 2002. Kenya Breweries secured support from Guinness plc, and after four years, SAB conceded that the market was indeed too small to sustain two breweries. It is also the case that the politics were no doubt too hot for external players. In 1997, SAB's African interests included breweries in Botswana, Swaziland, Lesotho, Zimbabwe, Zambia, Mozambique, Tanzania, Uganda, Ghana, and Ethiopia and a non-alcoholic beverage plant in Angola. SAB's external holdings provided SAB International with earnings of R159 million for the year ending 31 March 1998. This figure was 41 percent higher than earnings of the previous year. See SAB, *Annual Report, 31 March 1998,* SAB Records.

23. Tabby Moyo, "Brewers Try to Protect Markets from SAB," *Cape Times,* 13 October 1997.

24. For discussion of elite versus broad-based empowerment strategies, see Southall, "Black Empowerment and Present Limits to a More Democratic Capitalism in South Africa," 176–179.

25. "Fundamentals: SABMiller plc."

26. In the Reinheitsgebot of 1516, Duke William IV of Bavaria went beyond his intention of ensuring that there were sufficient supplies of wheat for bread to establish the principle of purity for beer brewing.

27. See Lucienne Field, "Namib Beer a Healthy Flea in SAB's Ear," *Sunday Times,* 15 June 1997.

28. Kevin Laner Keller and David A. Aaker, "The Impact of Corporate Marketing on a Company's Brand Extensions," in *Revealing the Corporation: Perspectives on Identity, Image, Reputation, Corporate Branding, and Corporate-Level Marketing,* ed. John M. T. Balmer and Stephen A. Greyser (London and New York: Routledge, 2003), 278.

29. Alistair Hewitt, marketing director for Castle Brewing Namibia, quoted in Tabby Moyo, "SAB Loses Beer Battle, but the War Continues," *Namibian,* 12 May 2000.

30. Tabby Moyo, "It's Bottoms Up, Advert Down for SA Breweries," *Namibian,* 11 May 2000.

31. Tabby Moyo, "Beer War Froths—Windhoek Lager or Windhoek's Lager," *Namibian,* 9 May 2000.

32. See Don Robertson, "Trouble Brewing for 'Arrogant' SA Breweries," *Business Times,* 30 November 1997; see also "Bavaria Namibia Challenge Monopoly," *Business Times,* 16 November 1997; "SAB Breaks the Great Wall of Competition," *Business Times,* 16 November 1997.

33. Department of Trade and Industry, *Study of the Liquor Industry in South Africa* (Pretoria: Department of Trade and Industry, March 2004), 42, 44, 53; available at http://www.thedti.gov.za/nla/LiquorIndustryStudyReport1832004.pdf.

34. Jabulani Sikhakhane, "Guinness: Upsetting the Beer Cart," *Financial Mail,* 2 April 1999, 24.

35. Gordon, "Inside the Windhoek Lager," 117–134.

36. See "Spinning in the Rumour Mill," *Financial Mail,* 18 October 1996, 131.

37. SAB plc acquired a 44 percent share of the Czech market through Pilsner Urquell and became a major player in Europe. In May 2002, SAB acquired Miller Brewing from Philip Morris. Miller became a wholly owned subsidiary of SAB and the new entity was registered as SABMiller plc.

38. NBL fought back; in April 2004, Heineken, Diageo, and NBL formed a 3-billion-rand-a-year liquor company to market Heineken, Windhoek Lager, Becks, and Guinness as well as various spirits.

39. Evidence of Denise Smith (a training controller who was then a human resources consultant at Alrode) for SAB in *Food and Allied Workers Union and 33 Others v South African Breweries Ltd in the Labour Court of South Africa,* Case C363/2002 and C1008/2001, Court Record, vol. 1, 174. I am grateful to attorney Glynn Williams at the law firm Chennells Albertyn for providing access to unpublished transcripts that make up the Court Record for this case.

40. See John Pendlebury, "Creating a Manufacturing Strategy to Suit Your Business," in *Making Strategic Planning Work in Practice,* ed. Basil Denning (Oxford: Pergamon Press, 1989), 84.

41. See Huib Ernste and Verena Meier, eds., *Regional Development and Contemporary Industrial Response: Extending Flexible Specialisation* (London: Belhaven Press, 1992), 29.

42. Ibid., 68.

43. SAB, *The F97 Annual Report to Employees of SAB Beer Division,* 51, SAB Records.

44. Evidence of Denise Smith in *Food and Allied Workers Union and 33 Others v South African Breweries Ltd,* Court Record, vol. 1, 73.

45. Ibid., 64.

46. Nixon, Hitt, and Ricart i Costa, "New Managerial Mindsets and Strategic Change," 2.

47. Norman Adami grew up in Kroonstad, joined SAB in 1979, and was appointed managing director of the company's Beer Division in 1994. He became chairman of SAB in 2000 and CEO of SABMiller Americas in 2006. He resigned for family reasons in mid-2008 and resurfaced as CEO of SAB Ltd a few months later.

48. See evidence of Denise Smith, *Food and Allied Workers Union and 33 Others v South African Breweries Ltd,* Court Record, vol. 1, 174.

49. See evidence of SAB industrial relations manager Jacobus Joubert Burger in *Food and Allied Workers Union and 33 Others v South African Breweries Ltd,* Court Record, vol. 2, 347. The study group included, among others, SAB human resources director Richard Davies, SAB industrial relations manager J. J. Joubert, FAWU general secretary Ernst Buthulezi, chairman of the National Shop Stewards Mthunzi Neville, shop steward (Whitey) Maphanga of the Newlands plant, Daniel Letsoalo from Rosslyn, and Vusumzi Phandle from the Eastern Cape.

50. Ibid., 351.

51. Ernst Buthelezi quoted by Advocate Jeremy Gauntlett, senior counsel for SAB, in *Food and Allied Workers Union and 33 Others v South African Breweries Ltd,* Court Record, vol. 2, 357.

52. See evidence of SAB Industrial Relations Manager Jacobus Joubert Burger, in *Food and Allied Workers Union and 33 Others v South African Breweries Ltd,* Court Record, vol. 2, 362.

53. Evidence of Denise Smith, *Food and Allied Workers Union and 33 Others v South African Breweries Ltd,* Court Record, vol. 1, 75 and 239.

54. ILO Department of Communication, "Socially Sensitive Enterprise Restructuring: Swimming Together or Sinking Separately," available at http://www.ilo.org/public/english.bureau/inf/features/05/restructuring.htm (accessed 5 December 2006).

55. Between 1997 and 1999, 181 registered small businesses were set up with help from Project Noah. By 2003, the number of businesses with Project Noah support reached 398. Of the 1,500 retrenched workers who took up skills training, only 120 found jobs through Project Noah. SAB invested R2 million in the project. See evidence of SAB Industrial Relations Manager Jacobus Joubert Burger, in *Food and Allied Workers Union and 33 Others v South African Breweries Ltd,* Court Record, vol. 2, 368–369, and Court Record, vol. 3, 404–405.

56. Author's interview with Whitey Maphanga, 15 November 2006.

57. See evidence of Denise Smith, in *Food and Allied Workers Union and 33 Others v South African Breweries Ltd,* Court Record, vol. 1, 77.

58. See evidence of Manager of SAB Newlands Brewery Ingmar Boesenberg, in *Food and Allied Workers Union and 33 Others v South African Breweries Ltd,* Court Record, vol. 3, 679.

59. Evidence of Felicity Miller, SAB human resources practitioner, in *Food and Allied Workers Union and Others v SA Breweries Ltd (2004),* in *Industrial Law Journal* 25 (2004), 2008 (Labour Court). When quotes I have used have been published, I have cited the published record rather than the verbatim transcripts in the Court Record.

60. See evidence of Denise Smith, *Food and Allied Workers Union and 33 Others v South African Breweries Ltd,* Court Record, vol. 1, 154.

61. Ibid., 247.

62. The shop stewards had learned from their visit to the Heineken plant that it was possible to insist on a moratorium on retrenchments, as the Amsterdam workers had done; author's interview with Whitey Maphanga.

63. See evidence of Jacobus Joubert Burger, in *Food and Allied Workers Union and 33 Others v South African Breweries Ltd,* Court Record, vol. 3, 517.

64. Evidence of Ingmar Boesenberg, in *Food and Allied Workers Union and 33 Others v South African Breweries Ltd,* Court Record, vol. 3, 829.

65. Newlands Brewery produced brands across SAB's product range—mainstream, premium, and alcoholic fruit beverages (also known as alco-pops).

66. See evidence of Ingmar Boesenberg, manager of Newlands Brewery, in *Food and Allied Workers Union and 33 Others v South African Breweries Ltd,* Court Record, vol. 3, 691.

67. *Food and Allied Workers Union and Others v SA Breweries Limited (2004), Industrial Law Journal* 25 (2004): 1979 (Labour Court).

68. Ibid., 2003.

69. Ibid., 2025.

70. Ibid., 2023.

71. Ibid.

72. The Labour Court replaced the apartheid-era Industrial Court following the Labour Relations Act (no. 66) of 1995.

73. *Food and Allied Workers Union and Others v SA Breweries Limited (2004), Industrial Law Journal* 25 (2004): 2024.

74. Cross-examination of J. J. Burger by Advocate Colin Kahanovitz, counsel for FAWU, in *Food and Allied Workers Union and 33 Others v South African Breweries Ltd,* Court Record, vol. 2, 573.

75. *Food and Allied Workers Union and others v SA Breweries Ltd (2004), Industrial Law Journal* 25 (2004): 1997–2005; see also cross-examination of J. J. Burger by Colin Kahanovitz, Counsel for FAWU, in *Food and Allied Workers Union and 33 Others v South African Breweries Limited,* 449. See also Ronnie Morris, "Laid-Off SAB Workers to Speak," *Cape Times,* 6 October 2003; Andisiwe Makinana, "Fired Workers Take SAB to Court," *Argus,* 22 July 2003.

76. *Food and Allied Workers Union and Others v SA Breweries Limited (2004), Industrial Law Journal* 25 (2004): 2015.

77. Ibid., 2016–2017.

78. Ibid., 2031.

79. Ibid., 2012.

80. Ibid., 2017.

81. Similar restructuring that had occurred at the Rosslyn and Prospecton plants had resulted in workers' litigation, but these cases did not set a precedent. See Settlement Agreement between South African Breweries Limited and Food and Allied Workers Union and Individual Members of FAWU Signed at Sandton (24 October 2005). I am grateful to the Food and Allied Workers Union for access to this document.

82. For press reports on the judgment, see "Court Finds SAB's Retrenchments at Cape Plant Unfair," *Sunday Independent,* September 2004.

83. *Food and Allied Workers Union and Others v SA Breweries Limited, Industrial Law Journal* 25 (2004): 2033.

84. Ibid., 2032.

85. Denise Smith, SAB's organizational design expert, acknowledged in court that she had written a report edited and published by the ILO on the SAB experience. This case was susequently rewritten as International Labour Organization, "Supporting Workplace Learning for High Performance Working: High Performance Work Research Project Compensation and Benefits: South African Breweries.plc," available at www.ilo.org/public/english/employment/skills/workplace/case/topi_8.htm (accessed 8 December 2006). See also Nikolai Rogovsky, *Restructuring for Corporate Success: A Socially Sensitive Approach* (Geneva: ILO, 2005), 97. Denise Smith was called from SAB's Czech brewery to provide evidence in this case. After 2002, Smith moved to SABMiller in the United States.

86. See "Agreement between South African Breweries Limited and Food and Allied Workers Union and Individual Members of FAWU."

87. Author's interview with Vusi Landu, 3 November 2006.

88. *M. Mhlongo and Others v. Food and Allied Workers Union and Another* (D1684/2000) [2006] ZALC 94 (1 November 2006), available at http://www.saflii.org/za/cases/ZALC/2006/94.html.

89. For similar developments in other industries, see Anthony Black, "Globalisation and Restructuring in the South African Automotive Industry," *Journal of International Development* 13, no. 6 (2001): 779–796; see also William Freund, "Organised Labor in the Republic of South Africa: History and Democratic Transition," in *Trade Unions and the Coming of Democracy in Africa,* ed. Jon Kraus (Basingstoke, Hampshire, 2007), 220.

90. The Ibhayi plant, which has a capacity of 230 million liters, was built at a cost of R750 million. In November 2000, it employed 127 people and bottled fourteen quarts per second. "Fundamentals: SABMiller plc"; "The Technology behind Ibhayi Brewery: SAB's Latest and Arguably Most Advanced in the World," *Science in Africa* (September 2001), available at http://www.scienceinafrica.co.za/2001/september/sab .htm (accessed 19 August 2007).

91. SAB Limited's brewing capacity in 2007 was 31.4 million hectoliters. Beer was produced in seven breweries: Alrode (8.3 million), Rosslyn (7.2 million), Chamdor (2.2 million), Polokwane (1.5 million), Prospecton (5.3 million), Ibhayi (2.4 million), and Newlands (4.5 million). Information accessed at www.sabreweries.com/ SABLtd on 19 August 2007.

92. Caroline White, "Breaking out of the Laager," *Siyaya* 2 (Winter 1998): 38.

93. Caroline White, "South African Breweries Beer Division," in *Making Affirmative Action Work* (Cape Town: Institute for Democracy in South Africa, 1995), 20.

94. White, "Breaking out of the Laager," 37.

95. White, "South African Breweries Beer Division," 20.

96. Ibid. SAB dismissed several black supervisors for participating in the 1989 strike.

97. Ibid.

98. *Ntai and Others v South African Breweries Limited* (J4476/99) [2000] ZALC 134 (16 November 2000), *Industrial Law Journal* 22 (2001): 214 (Labour Court). This case has also been published at http://www.saflii.org/za/cases/ZALC/2000/134 .html.

99. Ibid.

100. One of the challenges for BEE was the fact that the pool of skilled black managers in the country was small; SAB complained that because very few companies invested in training black managers, SAB managers were sought after and ended up benefiting the broader economy. For example, Fandeso left SAB to become managing director of the Land Bank in 2001. See "Black Managers Could Be Real Pathfinders," *Business Day,* 18 December 2006.

101. Ferial Haffajee, "Move Over Charles Glass!" *Siyaya* 2 (Winter 1998): 39.

102. Surveys leading to these awards were conducted by the Corporate Research Foundation in association with the Black Management Forum and *City Press,* the *Financial Mail* and Deloitte and Touche, Ask Afrika, University of Witwatersrand MBA students, BusinessMap, and others. See "Best Companies to Work for: Ale to the Chief! Breweries Is SA's Best Employer," *Financial Mail,* 16 November 2001, 42.

103. Adami quoted in David Furlonger, "Talent Brewing in the Barrels," *Financial Mail,* 1 November 2002, 38.

104. Author's interview with Whitey Maphanga.

105. Sidiroplous, "Black Economic Empowerment," 15.

106. The excise on sorghum, which was introduced in 1991, rose to two cents per liter in 1992. See SAB, *98th Annual Report for Year Ended 31 March 1993,* SAB Records. Sorghum sales declined by 50 percent in the period 1990–1999; see "Sorghum Deal Ban Will 'Kill the Industry,'" *Sunday Times,* 9 January 2000.

107. "National Sorghum: Giving SAB the Bird," *Financial Mail,* 30 June 1995, 66.

108. See "SA's Competition Watchdog Has Thwarted SA Breweries (SAB) Sorghum Beer Expansion Plans by Rejecting National Sorghum Breweries (NSB) Pro-

posed Acquisition of SAB Subsidiary Traditional Beer Investments," *Business Day*. 18 December 2006. In 2000, TBI's market share was approximately 21 percent and NSB's 72 percent.

109. See Michael Fridjhon and Caroline Pool, *Research Report on the Liquor Industry* (Randburg: Who Owns Whom, 2004), 53.

110. Robin McGregor, "Deconglomerate—or Decay," *Financial Mail,* 24 August 1990; Brian Thompson, "Time, Gentlemen, Please," *Financial Mail,* 17 April 1992, 20. See also C. K. Prahalad and G. Hamel, "The Core Competence of the Corporation," *Harvard Business Review* 68, no. 3 (1990): 79–91.

111. See Stuart Rutherford, "SAB Fails Simple Test in Salesmanship," *Financial Mail,* 17 July 1998, 57.

112. Wiphold was established in 1994 and in 2005 acquired 15 percent of Distell shares.

113. SAB began consolidating its Coca-Cola interests internationally; in 2004, Amalgamated Beverage Industries became a wholly owned subsidiary of SAB.

114. See John Fraser, "Put the Cork on Bottle-Top Merger, Says Commission," *Business Day,* 17 January 2003.

115. The Competition Act of 1998 set up the Competition Commission, the Competition Tribunal, and the Competition Appeal Court. The Competition Commission investigated competition matters and made recommendations; if the commission's recommendations were disputed, the matter came before the tribunal. The Competition Appeal Court heard appeals arising from tribunal decisions.

116. *Coleus Packaging (Pty) Ltd and Rheem Crown Plant (a Division of Highveld Steel and Vanadium Corporation Limited)* (75/LM/Oct02) [2003] ZACT 7 (11 February 2003), available at http://www.saflii.org/za/cases/ZACT/2003/7.html.

117. Southall, "Black Empowerment and Present Limits," 181–188.

118. Miranda Strydom, "Black Empowerment: Is There Really More to It than Equity?" *Business Report,* 10 October 1997.

119. See Larry Nelson, "SAB Prepares for Tomorrow," *Brewers' Guardian,* 3 June 2005, 20.

120. Ibid.

121. *South African Liquor Traders Association and Others v Chairperson Gauteng Liquor Board and Others* (CCT57/05) [2006] ZACC 7; 2009 (1) SA 565 (CC); 2006 (8) BCLR 901 (CC) (2 June 2006), available at http://www.saflii.org/za/cases/ZACC/2006/7.html.

122. Ibid.

123. "Black Empowerment: Leading the Charge," *Financial Mail,* 11 March 1994, 51; "Outsourcing Innovations: BEE Made Easy," *Business Day,* 21 June 2005; "Project Creates Entrepreneurs," *Business Day,* 6 December 2006; Wendy Hall, "SAB to Put R312m into Owner-Driver Network," *Business Day,* 6 December 2006; Nndateni Ndou, "The Changing Nature of Employment Relationship: The South African Breweries (SAB) Owner-Driver Scheme" (BA Honours thesis, Department of Sociology, University of Cape Town, November 2002).

124. Mike Holmes, "SAB Puts Staff into Their Own Businesses," *Business Day,* 6 December 2006.

125. Of SAB's fifty-three distribution centers in 2005, forty-one were owned by SAB, two were newly franchised, and eight were independently owned. See Wendy

Hall, "SAB Farms out Distribution Centres to BEE Franchises," *Business Day,* 6 December 2006.

126. The Southern Cape Barley Farmers' Association was once represented by P. W. Botha, then a National Party Member of Parliament; "Black Empowerment: Leading the Charge," *Financial Mail,* 11 March 1994, 48–49.

127. For a discussion of corporate branding, see Stephen King, "Brand Building in the 1990s," in *Revealing the Corporation: Perspectives on Identity, Image, Reputation, Corporate Branding, and Corporate-Level Marketing,* ed. John T. Balmer and Stephen A. Greyser (London: Routledge, 2003), 265–270; and Constantinos Markides and Vassils M. Papadakis "What Constitutes an Effective Mission Statement? An Empirical Investigation," in *New Managerial Mindsets: Organisational Transformation Strategy Implementation,* ed. Michael A. Hitt, Robert D. Nixon, and Joan E. Ricart i Costa (Chichester, N.Y.: John Wiley and Sons, 1998), 35–54.

128. Mtutuzeli Matshoba, *Call Me Not a Man* (Harlow: Longman, 1987) captures the emasculation of unemployment in the 1970s.

EPILOGUE

1. For mergers and acquisitions in the global brewing industry at the turn of the century, see H. Donald Hopkins, Raj Chaganti, Maasaki Kotabe, and co-editors, "Cross-Border Mergers and Acquisitions: Global and Regional Perspectives," *Journal of International Management* 5, no. 3 (Autumn 1999): 207–239; Richard Benson-Armer, Joshua Leibowitz, and Deepak Ramachandran, "Global Beer: What's on Tap?" *McKinsey Quarterly* 1 (1999): 110–121; "Beer Sales Flat but Malt News Arounds," *Beverage Industry* 90, no. 7 (July 1999): 28–30; and Andrea Foote, "At What Cost, Growth?" *Beverage World International* 19, no. 2 (March/April 2001): 11–15.

2. For speculation about SAB's merger strategy, see Charlotte Matthews, "Interbrew Says It Has Looked at SA Breweries," *Business Day,* 29 November 2001; "Building Castles in the Air?" *Business Day,* 29 November 2001; "More than Froth?" *Business Day,* 30 November 2001; "Sounds Good After Beers," *Business Day,* 5 December 2001.

3. Brent Shearer, "Miller Acquisition May Force Responses in Global Consolidation of Breweries," *Mergers and Acquisitions: The Dealmakers Journal* 37, no. 8 (August 2002): 29–30.

4. Richard Tomlinson, "Is Miller's Time Up?" *Fortune International* (Europe) 148, no. 12 (12 August 2003): 32–36.

5. Denise Smith had been a key player on SAB's world class manufacturing team in South Africa (see chapter 7). See also Chris Gilmour, "It's Miller Time," *Financial Mail,* 15 October 2004, 20–22.

6. Bernard Simon, "Defying Conventional Beer Wisdom, Miller Lite Is Making a Comeback," *New York Times,* 18 March 2004; Tony van Kralingen, managing director of SAB Limited, said in March 2003 that SAB had sent 130 SAB-trained people abroad. This figure included some of those sent to Milwaukee; see "SAB Success Story Looks to Write Up New Challenges," *Business Day,* 15 December 2006.

7. "Stormin' Norman," *Financial Mail,* 18 October 2004.

8. Sales apparently dropped by 2.5 percent while the advertisements were running. Christopher Lawton, "Miller, Coors Still Bet Sex Sells Beer," *Wall Street*

Journal, 6 June 2003; Suzanne Vranica, "Sirius Ad Is Best Bet for Most Sexist," *Wall Street Journal*, 1 April 2004; Bob Cook, "Miller Lite's 'Catfight' Ad," *Flak Magazine*, n.d., available at www.flakmag.com/tv/catfight.html (accessed 29 September 2008).

9. Nat Ives, "After a Wild Period, Beer Ads Sober Up and Put Some Clothes On," *New York Times*, 31 July 2003.

10. See chapter 3.

11. Richard Tomlinson, "Is Miller's Time Up?" *Fortune International* (Europe) 148, no. 12 (12 August 2003): 32–36.

12. Stuart Elliott, "Battling Ads Pit 'The King of Beers' against 'The Queen of Carbs.' As for Taste? Fuhgeddaboutit," *New York Times*, 21 May 2004.

13. Competition for the Chinese beer market was intense. While only 200 million Chinese could afford to drink Western brands in 2005, the facts that China had a beer culture, a population of 1.2 billion, and a growing economy had the global players competing hard for a share of the market. See Chris Buckley, "Battle Shaping Up for Chinese Brewery," *New York Times*, 6 May 2004; Solly Samuel, "Brewers for Chinese Puzzle," *Marketing*, 15 June 2005, 17.

14. Quoted in "Anheuser-Busch Wins China Brewer," *Wall Street Journal*, 4 June 2004, A3.

15. Ibid.

16. See Ann Crotty, "Anheuser-Busch's Message to US Beer Drinkers Lacks Taste," *Business Report*, 1 June 2005.

17. Daniel Eisenberg, "Big Brew-Haha! The Battle of the Beers," *Time*, 12 July 2004.

18. "Bud Must Drop Anti-Miller Ad as Brewery Battle Goes to Court," *New York Times*, 31 May 2004; "Miller Sues Anheuser-Busch over Ads," *New York Times*, 29 May 2004.

19. Elliott, "Battling Ads Pit 'The King of Beers' against 'The Queen of Carbs.'"

20. Comment attributed to Michael Watrous, president of Straightline International in New York, in ibid.

21. Datamonitor, *Beer in the United States—Industry Profile*, (New York: Datamonitor, October 2005), 14.

22. Ibid.

23. Simon, "Defying Conventional Beer Wisdom, Miller Lite Is Making a Comeback."

24. Ibid.; Reuters, "Brewer of Miller Beer Says Its First Half Earnings Were Up 28 Percent," *New York Times*, 19 November 2004.

25. Patricia Sellers, "SAB Brews Up Big Trouble for Bud," *Fortune* 152, no. 4 (22 August 2005), 26.

26. The expression was used in Tomlinson, "Is Miller's Time Up?"

27. Sellers, "SAB Brews up Big Trouble for Bud," 26.

28. Datamonitor, "Company Spotlight: SABMiller," *MarketWatch: Drinks* (November 2007), 27.

29. Perhaps the comment was self-interested, but Graham Mackay said in 2005 that Anheuser-Busch was making a mistake by using price discounts to restore growth momentum. See Sellers, "SAB Brews Up Big Trouble for Bud," 26.

30. Andrew Ross Sorkin, "Anheuser-Busch Agrees to Be Sold to InBev," *New York Times,* 14 July 2008. By the end of 2008, InBev accounted for 25 percent of the world's beer.

31. Datamonitor, "Global Roundup, Drinks Industry Update," *MarketWatch* (August 2008), 30; Tom Strenk, "Battle of the Brewsters," *Beverage World* (April 2008), 84.

32. Comments following Sorkin, "Anheuser-Busch Agrees to Be Sold to InBev," *New York Times,* 14 July 2008, available at http://dealbook.blogs.nytimes .com/2008/07/14/anheuser-busch-agrees-to-be-sold-to-inbev/ (accessed 24 September 2008).

33. "Anheuser-Busch First to Sign Up as FIFA World Cup Sponsor from 2007–2014," FIFA Media Release, 27 April 2006, available at http://www.fifa.com/world cup/organisation/media/newsid=104026.html (accessed 7 August 2009).

34. *Finance Week,* 6 August 2005, 8.

35. Steve Miller, "Migrating Your Brands to Future Markets for Sustained Profitability," speech at Adfocus 2003 Conference, 23 May 2003, available at www.adfocus .co.za/speeches2003/spmiller.htm (accessed 4 March 2007). Miller was marketing development manager for SABMiller.

36. Marcia Klein, "Returning Brewery Boss Needs a Thirst for Challenge," *Sunday Times,* 1 February 2009.

Bibliography

MANUSCRIPT SOURCES

Western Cape Archives and Records Service, Cape Town
    Cape Town City Council Minutes, 1960–1965
Archives of South African Heritage Resources Agency, Cape Town
    Gabriel Fagan Architects, notes pertaining to Ohlssons' Breweries site restoration
Archives of the Church of the Province of South Africa, University of the Witwatersrand
    South African Institute of Race Relations Collection
South African Breweries Records (SAB Records), Johannesburg
    Transcripts of interviews conducted by Harold Moulton
        Interview with Dr. Frans Cronje, no date
        Interview with Gert Goedhals, no date
        Interview with Dick Goss, 13 February 1985
        Interview with Vic Hammond, 10 November 1992
        Interview with Frank Moodie, 8 October 1993
        Interview with Ken Redfern, 14 April 1986
        Interview with Mike Rosholt, 9 November 1992
        Interview with Peter Savory, 27 February 1987
        Interview with Joss van Niekerk, Pretoria, 13 April 1987
        Interview with Ken Williams, 14 April 1986
    SAB annual reports, 1969–2004
    SAB Records
Chennells Albertyn, Attorneys
    FAWU and 33 Others v South African Breweries Ltd in the Labour Court of South Africa, unpublished court record including transcript of court proceedings and witness documents
    Mhlongo and Others v. Food and Allied Workers Union and South African Breweries Ltd, Labour Court D 1684/200 and D1214/2002.
Adams and Adams, Patent, Trademark and Copyright Attorneys
    Carling National Breweries, Inc. and Intercontinental Breweries Ltd v. National Brewing Company (Pty) Ltd and the South African Breweries Ltd, Case no.

M.2813/78, Supreme Court of South Africa, Transvaal Provincial Division. Judgment delivered on 12/28/1978.

      Carling National Breweries, Inc. and Intercontinental Breweries Ltd v. National Brewing Company (Pty) Ltd and the South African Breweries Ltd, Case no. A.7/79, Supreme Court of South Africa, Transvaal Provincial Division. Judgment delivered by full bench 9/28/1979.

Staples and Charles Ltd, Architects

      Records related to the design of The SAB World of Beer

Newspapers and Periodicals

African Gender Institute Newsletter
Beverage Industry
Business Day
Business South Africa
Cape Argus (Argus)
Cape Times
Die Burger
Die Taalgenot
Die Vaderland
eSpotini
Finance Week
Financial Mail
Flak Magazine
Food Industries of South Africa
Fortune
Humanitas
Mail and Guardian
Rand Daily Mail
SAB Data

SANCA Forum
SANCA Information Bulletin
Sawubona
South African Outlook
Sowetan
Star
Sunday Independent
Sunday Times
The Leech
Trauma Review
Tribute
UNISA Psychologica
Urbanisation and Health Newsletter
Volkswelsyn en Pensioene
Vrouevolksdiens
Wall Street Journal
Washington Post
Weekend Post

PRINTED PRIMARY SOURCES

Government Documents

Cape of Good Hope Liquor Laws Commission. *Report of the Liquor Laws Commission.* Series no. G.1-90. (Cape Town: Government Printer, 1890), including the Minority Report (Appendix 1).

Competition Tribunal. Republic of South Africa. *In the Large Merger between Coleus Packaging (Pty) Ltd and Rheem Crown Plant, a Division of Highveld Steel and Vanadium Corporation Limited.* Case no. 75/LM/Oct02. Available at http://www.saflii.org.za/za/cases/ZACT/2003/7.html.

Competition Tribunal. Republic of South Africa. *In the Large Merger between Distillers Corporation (SA) Limited (Primary Acquiring Firm) and Stellenbosch Farmers Winery Group Ltd (Primary Target Firm).* Case no. 08/LM/Feb02. Reasons for Tribunal Decision: Non-Confidential. Available at http://www.saflii.org.za/za/cases/ZACT/2003/15.html.

Department of Foreign Affairs and Information. *South Africa 1984: Official Yearbook of the Republic of South Africa.* Johannesburg: Chris van Rensburg Publications, 1984.

Department of Trade and Industry of South Africa. *Study of the Liquor Industry in South Africa.* Pretoria: Reality Research Africa, 2004.

Government of South Africa. Department of Social Welfare. *Report on the National Conference on Alcoholism Held at Pretoria on 20th and 21st November 1951.* Pretoria: Government Printer, 1951.

Government of South Africa. *Report of the Commission of Inquiry into Matters Relating to the Coloured Population Group.* Pretoria: Government Printer, 1976.

Malan, Avril Iré. *Report of the Commission of Enquiry into the General Distribution and Selling Prices of Intoxicating Liquor.* Pretoria: Government Printer, 1960.

South Africa. Commission of Inquiry into Legislation Affecting the Utilisation of Manpower. *Report of the Commission of Inquiry into Legislation Affecting the Utilisation of Manpower (Excluding the Legislation Administered by the Departments of Labour and Mines).* Pretoria: The Commission, 1979.

South Africa. Competition Board. *Investigation into Restrictive Practices in the Supply and Distribution of Alcoholic Beverages in the Republic of South Africa.* Competition Board Report No.10. Pretoria: Government Printer, 1982.

Wiehahn, N. E. *Report of the Commission of Inquiry into Labor Legislation.* Pretoria: Government Printer, 1979.

Court Cases

Distillers Corporation (S.A.) Ltd. v S.A. Breweries Ltd. and Another and *Oude Meester Groep Bpk. and Another v. S.A. Breweries Ltd.* (1976), both in *South African Law Reports* 3 (1976): 514–554.

Food and Allied Workers Union and Others v South African Breweries Limited (2004), in *Industrial Law Journal* 25 (2004): 1979–2035 and available online at http://www.saflii.org/za/cases/ZALC/2004/65.html.

Food and Allied Workers Union v South African Breweries Ltd (1990), in *Industrial Law Journal* 11 (1990): 413–428. (ARB) Arbitration by Clive Thompson (20 January 1988).

Ntai and Others v South African Breweries Limited (J4476/99) [2000] ZALC 134 (16 November 2000), in *Industrial Law Journal* 22 (2001): 214–231 and available at http://www.saflii.org/za/cases/ZALC/2000/134.html.

S.A. Breweries Ltd. and Another v. Distillers Corporation (S.A.) Ltd. and Another (1973), in *South African Law Reports* 4 (1973): 145–163.

S.A. Breweries Ltd v Food and Allied Workers Union and Others, Witwatersrand Local Division (6–7 October 1987) before Goldstone J [1987] *South African Law Reports* 2 (1988): 723–730. Also published as *S.A. Breweries Ltd v Food and Allied Workers Union and Others,* Witwatersrand Local Division (7 October and 17 November 1987) before Goldstone J [1987] *Industrial Law Journal* 9 (1988): 244–252.

SA Breweries v Food and Allied Workers Union and Others, Appellate Division (21 August and 26 September 1989), in *South African Law Reports* 1 (1989): 92–100.

SAB International t/a Sabmark International v Laugh It Off Promotions [2003] volume 2, *All South African Law Reports* 2 (2003): 454–463 (Cape of Good Hope Provincial Division).

Laugh It Off Promotions CC v SAB International (Finance) BV t/a Sabmark International and Another (2005), in *Butterworths Constitutional Law Reports* 8 (2005): 743–782 and available at http://www.saflii.org/za/cases/ZACC/2005/7.html.

AUTHORS' INTERVIEWS

Interviews with SAB Personnel
John Eastwood, 25 September 2003
Henry Fabe, 6 November 1997
Frank Johnson, 9 July 2000
Frank Moodie, 29 April 2000
Peter Savory, 11 July 2000
John Seton, 30 October 1997
Windsor Shuenyane, 12 July 2000
Bruce Starke, 28 April 2000

Interviews with City Councillors and with Shebeeners, Distributors, and Others in the Liquor Industry
"Big Mike" Sedikwe, 8 July 1998
Sue Birch, 8 September 1998
Bra Boysie, 8 May 1998
Bra Bys, 8 May 1998
Sis Dolly Malunga, 7 July 1998
Chris Mhlongo, 8 July 1998
Lucky Michaels, 7 July 1998
Sis Fanny Mokoena, 7 July 1998
Wandie Ndala, 7 July 1998
Sis Cooksie Senne, 8 July 1998
Eulalie Stott, 25 October 1997

Interviews with Designers, Artists, and Architects
Gabriel Fagan, 18 April 2000
Gwendoline Fagan, 18 April 2000
Etienne de Kock, 6 November 2003
Juan Scott, 9 July 2000
Robert Staples and Barbara Charles, 25 April 2003

Interviews with Community Workers
Sipho Mathe, 3 July 2000
Sister Lydia Mosala, 29 April 1998
Mrs Mabiki Mtshali, 4 July 2000

Interviews with Trade Unionists
Vusi Landu, 13 November 2006
Whitey Maphanga, 15 November 2006

Interviews with Former University Students

Joey Burke, 22 January 2008
Richard Midgley, 20 January 2005

AUDIOVISUAL MATERIAL

Hansa television commercial. Hansa History Reel. Produced by Ogilvy and Mather, Sandton, July 2000. Accessed at Ogilvy and Mather, Sandton.

Ndlanu television commercial. Produced by Herdbouys, Johannesburg, 1996. Accessed at Herdbouys, Johannesburg.

The Making of Ndlanu. Directed by Michael Yelseth. Johannesburg, Spring Studios. Incha Film Productions, 1996.

"Tribue to Tshepo Seepe." *Tim Modise Show,* SAFM radio, 24 October 2001.

SECONDARY SOURCES

Books and Articles

Abrahams, Peter. *Tell Freedom.* Boston: Faber, 1981.

Akyeampong, Emmanuel. *Drink, Power, and Cultural Change: A Social History of Alcohol in Ghana, c. 1800 to Recent Times.* Portsmouth, N.H., and Oxford: Heinemann and James Currey, 1996.

———. "The State and Alcohol Revenues: Promoting Economic Development in Gold Coast/Ghana, 1919 to the Present." *Social History* 27, no. 54 (November 1994): 393–411.

———. "What's in a Drink? Class Struggle, Popular Culture and the Politics of *Akpeteshie* (Local Gin) in Ghana, 1930–67." *Journal of African History* 37, no. 2 (1996): 215–236.

Alegi, Peter. *Laduma! Soccer, Politics and Society in South Africa.* Scottsville: UKZN Press, 2004.

Anderson, Benedict. *Imagined Communities: Reflections on the Origin and Spread of Nationalism.* London: Verso, 1983.

Anthony, David H., III. "Max Yergan in South Africa: From Evangelical Pan-Africanist to Revolutionary Socialist." *African Studies Review* 34, no. 2 (September 1991): 27–55.

Archer, Robert. *The SA Game: Sport and Racism in South Africa.* London: Zed Press, 1982.

Babrow, Louis, and R. K. Stent. *The Varsity Spirit: The Story of Rugby Football at the University of Cape Town, 1883–1963.* Cape Town: Johnston and Neville, 1963.

Bailey, Jim, and Adam Seftel, eds. *Shebeens Take a Bow! A Celebration of South Africa's Shebeen Lifestyle.* Johannesburg: Bailey's African History Archives, 1994.

Baloyi, Danisa. "Black Economic Empowerment: Progress Will Lead to Prosperity." In *South Africa: More Good News,* ed. Brett Bower and Steuart Pennington, 173–178. Hyde Park, Johannesburg: South Africa—The Good News (Pty) Ltd., 2003.

Barringer, Tim, and Tom Flynn, eds. *Colonialism and the Object: Empire, Material Culture and the Museum.* London: Routledge, 1998.

Baskin, Jeremy, and Vishwas Satgar. "South Africa's New LRA." *SA Labour Bulletin* 19, no. 5 (November 1995): 46–55.

———. *Striking Back: A History of COSATU.* Johannesburg: Ravan Press, 1991.

Bechman, V. *Alcohol, Another Trap for Africa.* Sweden: Bokforlaget Libris-Orebro, 1988.

Becker, A. L. "Alcoholism." *Medical Proceedings* (25 September 1966): 487–488.

Benjamin, Paul. "LRA—Organizational Rights." *SA Labour Bulletin* 19, no. 5 (November 1995): 56–59.

Bennett, Tony. *The Birth of the Museum: History, Theory, Politics.* London and New York: Routledge, 1995.

———. "Contesting Times: Conflicting Histories in Post-Colonial Contexts." In *Social Change,* ed. Tim Jordan and Steve Pile, 50–77. Oxford: Blackwell for the Open University, 2002.

———. "Exhibition, Difference and the Logic of Culture." In *Museum Frictions:Public Cultures, Global Transformations,* ed. Ivan Karp, Corinne Kratz, Lynn Szwaja, and Tomás Gbarra-Frausto, 46–69. Durham, N.C.: Duke University Press, 2006.

Benson-Armer, Richard, Joshua Leibowitz, and Deepak Ramachandran. "Global Beer: What's on Tap?" *McKinsey Quarterly* 1 (1999): 110–121.

Best, Michael H. *The New Competition: Institutions of Industrial Restructuring.* Cambridge, Mass.: Harvard University Press, 1990.

Bhabha, Homi, ed. *Nation and Narration.* London and New York: Routledge, 1990.

Black, Anthony. "Globalisation and Restructuring in the South African Automotive Industry." *Journal of International Development* 13, no. 6 (2001): 779–796.

Black, David, and John Nauright. *Rugby and the South African Nation.* Manchester: Manchester University Press, 1998.

Bonner, Philip, and Lauren Segal. *Soweto: A History.* Cape Town: Maskew Miller, Longman, 1998.

Booth, Douglas. "Mandela and the Amabokoboko: The Political and Linguistic Nationalism of South Africa?" *Journal of Modern African Studies* 34, no. 3 (September 1996): 459–477.

———. *The Race Game: Sport and Politics in South Africa.* London: Frank Cass, 1998.

Bougas, E. "Industrial Alcohol Programmes—Do They Work?" *Food Industries of South Africa* 9 (1979): 28–29.

———. "The Policy on Alcoholism of a Large Industrial Company." *Public Health* 77, no. 7 (1977): 143–149.

Bourdieu, Pierre. *Masculine Domination.* Stanford, Calif.: Stanford University Press, 1998.

Brennan, T. *Public Drinking and Popular Culture in Eighteenth-Century Paris.* Princeton, N.J.: Princeton University Press, 1988.

Brickhill, Joan. *Race against Race: South Africa's Multinational Sport Fraud.* London: IDAF, 1976.

Brown, Andrea. "BEE, A Model for Global Economic Empowerment." In *The Story of Our Future South Africa 2014,* ed. Brett Bower and Steuart Pennington, 183–185. Hyde Park, Johannesburg: South Africa—The Good News (Pty) Ltd., 2004.

Bruner, Michael Lane. *Strategies of Remembrance: The Rhetorical Dimensions of National Identity Construction*. Columbia: University of South Carolina Press, 2002.

Bryceson, Deborah Fahy. *Alcohol in Africa: Mixing Business, Pleasure and Politics*. Portsmouth: Heinemann, 2002.

Burke, Timothy. *Lifebuoy Men, Lux Women: Commodification, Consumption and Cleanliness in Modern Zimbabwe*. Durham, N.C., and London: Duke University Press, 1996.

Burstyn, Varda. *The Rites of Men: Manhood, Politics, and the Culture of Sport*. 1999; repr., Toronto: University of Toronto Press, 2000.

Cappelli, Peter. *The New Deal at Work: Managing the Market-Driven Workforce*. Boston: Harvard Business School Press, 1999.

Carton, Benedict. *Blood from Your Children: The Colonial Origins of Generational Conflict in South Africa*. Pietermaritzburg: University of Natal Press, 2000.

Chapman, Michael, ed. *The "Drum" Decade: Stories from the 1950s*. Pietermaritzburg: University of Natal Press, 1989.

Christian, D. *Living Water: Vodka and Russian Society on the Eve of Emancipation*. Oxford: Clarendon Press, 1990.

Clark, Nancy. "The Limits of Industrialization under Apartheid." In *Apartheid's Genesis, 1935–1962,* ed. Philip Bonner, Peter Delius, and Deborah Posel, 65–95. Johannesburg: Ravan Press, 1993.

Cobley, Alan. "Liquor and Leadership: Temperance, Drunkenness and the African Petty Bourgeoisie in South Africa." *South African Historical Journal* 31 (November 1994): 128–148.

Cobley, Alan Gregor. *The Rules of the Game: Struggles in Black Recreation and Social Welfare Policy in South Africa*. Westport, Conn.: Greenwood, 1997.

Colhoun, Craig. *Nationalism*. Minneapolis: University of Minnesota Press, 1997.

Collins, Tony, and Wray Vamplew. *Mud, Sweat, and Beers: A Cultural History of Sport and Alcohol*. Oxford: Berg, 2002.

Colson, E., and T. Scudder. *For Prayer and Profit: The Ritual, Economic, and Social Importance of Beer in Gwembe District, Zambia, 1950–1982*. Stanford, Calif.: Stanford University Press, 1988.

Connell, Bob. "Masculinity, Violence and War." In *Mens' Lives,* ed. Michael S. Kimmel and Michael A. Messner, 125–130. Boston, Mass.: Allyn and Bacon, 1995.

Coombes, Annie E. *History after Apartheid: Visual Culture and Public Memory in a Democratic South Africa*. Durham, N.C., and London: Duke University Press, 2003.

Cooper, Fredrick. "Elevating the Black Race: The Social Thought of Black Leaders, 1927–50." *American Quarterly* 24, no. 5 (December 1972): 604–625.

Coplan, David B. *In Township Tonight: South Africa's Black City Music and Theatre*. Johannesburg: Ravan Press, 1985.

COSATU Policy Unit. "Foreign Investment, the Record." *SA Labour Bulletin* 26, no. 4 (August 2002): 33–34.

Craven, Norma, and David Cartwright. "Labour Relations Act Ten Years On." *SA Labour Bulletin* 27, no. 5 (October 2003): 42–43.

Crush, Jonathan, and Charles Ambler, eds. *Liquor and Labor in Southern Africa*. Athens: Ohio University Press, 1992.

da Silva, Teresa. "The Impact of Multinational Investment on Alcohol Consumption since the 1960s." *Business and Economic History* 28, no. 2 (Winter 1999): 109–122.

Davis, John. "An Anthropologist's View of Exchange." *Oxford Development Studies* 24, no. 1 (1996): 47–59.

Deming, W. Edwards. *Out of the Crisis.* Cambridge: Massachusetts Institute of Technology, Center for Advanced Engineering Study, 1986.

Denning, Basil. *Making Strategic Planning Work in Practice: The Best of Long Range Planning No.3.* Oxford: Pergamon Press, 1989.

Diduk, Susan. "European Alcohol, History, and the State in Cameroun." *African Studies Review* 36, no. 1 (April 1993): 1–42.

Dilley, Roy, ed. *Contesting Markets: Analyses of Ideology, Discourse and Practice.* Edinburgh: Edinburgh University Press, 1992.

Dommisse, Ebbe, with the cooperation of Willie Esterhuyse. *Anton Rupert: A Biography.* Cape Town: Tafelberg, 2005.

Driver, Dorothy. "*Drum* Magazine (1951–9) and the Spatial Configurations of Gender." In *Text, Theory, Space: Land, Literature and History in South Africa and Australia,* ed. Kate Darian Smith, Liz Gunner, and Sarah Nuttall, 231–242. London: Routledge, 1996.

du Preez, Max. *Louis Luyt Unauthorised.* Cape Town: Zebra Press, 2001.

Dunning, Eric, and Kenneth Sheard. *Barbarians, Gentlemen and Players: A Sociological Study of the Development of Rugby Football.* Oxford: Martin Robertson, 1979.

Dyer, Gillian. *Advertising as Communication.* London: Routledge, 1996.

Edwards, Ian. "Shebeen Queens: Illicit Liquor and the Social Structure of Drinking Dens in Cato Manor." *Agenda* 3 (1988): 75–97.

Ernste, Huib, and Verena Meier, eds. *Regional Development and Contemporary Industrial Response: Extending Flexible Specialisation.* London and New York: Belhaven Press, 1992.

Etherington, Norman. "An American Errand in the South African Wilderness." *Church History* 39, no. 1 (March 1970): 62–71.

Feinstein, Charles. *An Economic History of South Africa: Conquest, Discrimination and Development.* Cambridge: Cambridge University Press, 2005.

Fialkov, M. J. "Alcoholics and the Emergency Ward." *S.A. Medical Journal* (1 October 1977): 613–616.

Foote, Andrea. "At What Cost, Growth?" *Beverage World International* 19, no. 2 (March/April 2001): 11–15.

Francaviglia, Richard. "Selling Heritage Landscapes." In *Preserving Cultural Landscapes in America,* ed. Arnold R. Alanen and Robert Z. Melnick, 48–67. Baltimore, Md.: Johns Hopkins University Press, 2000.

Freund, William. "Organised Labor in the Republic of South Africa: History and Democratic Transition." In *Trade Unions and the Coming of Democracy in Africa,* ed. Jon Kraus, 199–227. New York: Palgrave Macmillan, 2007.

Fridjhon, Michael, and Andy Murray. *Conspiracy of Giants: The South African Liquor Industry.* Johannesburg: Divaris Stein, 1986.

Fridjhon, Michael, and Caroline Pool. *Research Report on the Liquor Industry for Who Owns Whom.* Randburg: Who Owns Whom, 2004.

Geertz, Clifford. *Interpretation of Cultures.* New York: Basic Books, 1973.

Gelb, Stephen, ed. *South Africa's Economic Crisis.* Cape Town: David Philip, 1991.

Gindin, Sam. "International Competitiveness and the Democratic Development of Capacities." *SA Labour Bulletin* 19, no. 3 (July 1995): 37–44.

Glazer, Ilsa M. "Alcohol and Politics in Urban Zambia: The Intersection of Gender and Class." In *African Feminism: The Politics of Survival in Sub-Saharan Africa,* ed. Gwendollyn Mikell, 142–158. Philadelphia: University of Pennsylvania Press, 1997.

Goldman, Robert. *Reading Ads Socially.* London: Routledge, 1992.

Gordon, Robert. "Inside the Windhoek Lager: Liquor and Lust in Namibia." In *Drugs, Labor and Colonial Expansion,* ed. W. Jankowick and D. Bradburd, 117–134. Tucson: Arizona University Press, 2003.

Gourvish, T. R., and R. G. Wilson. *The British Brewing Industry, 1830–1980.* Cambridge: Cambridge University Press, 1994.

Grant, M., E. Houghton, and J. Kast. "Introduction: Drinking Patterns and Policy Development." In *Alcohol and Emerging Markets: Patterns, Problems, and Responses,* ed. M. Grant, 1–17. Philadelphia, Pa.: Brunner/Mazel, 1998.

Green, Howard. "A Critique of the Professional Public History Movement." In *Public History Readings,* by P. K. Leffler and J. Brent, 121–126. Malabar, Fla.: Kruger, 1992.

Green, Nick, and Reg Lascaris. *Communication in the Third World: Seizing Advertising Opportunities in the 1990s.* Tafelberg, Cape Town: Human and Rousseau, 1990.

———. *Third World Destiny: Recognising and Seizing the Opportunities Offered by a Changing South Africa.* Cape Town: Human and Rossouw, 1988.

Greising, David. *I'd Like the World to Buy a Coke: The Life and Leadership of Roberto Goizueta.* New York: John Wiley and Sons, 1998.

Grundlingh, Albert. "Playing for Power? Rugby, Afrikaner Nationalism and Masculinity in South Africa, c. 1900–c. 1970." In *Making Men: Rugby and Masculine Identity,* ed. John Nauright and Timothy J. L. Chandler, 178–196. London: Frank Cass, 1996.

Guelke, Adrian. "Sport and the End of Apartheid." In *The Changing Politics of Sport,* ed. Lincoln Allison, 151–170. Manchester: Manchester University Press, 1993.

Harries, Patrick. *Work, Culture, and Identity: Migrant Laborers in Mozambique and South Africa, c. 1860–1910.* Portsmouth, N.H.: Heinemann, 1994.

Haskell, Thomas L., and Richard F. Teichgraeber. *The Culture of the Market: Historical Essays.* Cambridge: Cambridge University Press, 1993.

Haworth, A., and S. W. Acuda. "Sub-Saharan Africa." In *Alcohol in Emerging Markets,* ed. M. Grant, 19–90. Philadelphia: Brunner, Maize, 1998.

Hays, Constance L. *Truth and Power at the Coca-Cola Company.* London: Hutchinson, 2004.

Heap, Simon. "Before 'Star': The Import Substitution of Western-Style Alcohol in Nigeria, 1870–1970." *African Economic History* 24 (1996): 69–89.

———. "'A Bottle of Gin Is Dangled before the Nose of the Natives': The Economic Uses of Imported Liquor in Southern Nigeria, 1860–1920." *African Economic History* 33 (2005): 69–85.

Hearn, Jeff. *Men in the Public Eye.* London and New York: Routledge, 1992.

Hewison, R. "Commerce and Culture." In *Enterprise and Heritage: Crosscurrents of*

National Culture, ed. J. Corner and S. Harvey, 162–177. London: Routledge, 1991.

Heyns, Jacky. "Down the Hatch!" In *Shebeens Take a Bow! A Celebration of South Africa's Shebeen Lifestyle,* ed. Jim Bailey and Adam Seftel, 1–13. Johannesburg: Bailey's African History Archives, 1994.

Hindson, Doug. *Pass Controls and the Urban African Proletariat in South Africa.* Johannesburg: Ravan Press, 1987.

Hopkins, H. Donald, Raj Chaganti, Maasaki Kotabe, and co-editors. "Cross-Border Mergers and Acquisitions: Global and Regional Perspectives." *Journal of International Management* 5, no. 3 (Autumn 1999): 207–239.

Horrell, Muriel. *The Liquor Laws.* Braamfontein: South African Institute of Race Relations, 1960.

Iheduru, Okechukwu. "Black Economic Power and Nation-Building in Post-Apartheid South Africa." *The Journal of Modern African Studies* 42, no. 1 (2004): 1–30.

———. "The Development of Black Capitalism in South Africa and the United States." In *Black Business and Economic Power,* ed. Alusine Jallon and Toyin Falola, 572–603. Rochester, N.Y.: University of Rochester Press, 2002.

"Indigenous Australians and Liquor Licensing Restrictions." *Addiction* 95, no. 10 (2000): 1469–1472.

International Labour Organization. "Supporting Workplace Learning for High Performance Working: High Performance Work Research Project Compensation and Benefits: South African Breweries.plc." www.ilo.org/public/english/employment/skills/workplace/case/topi_8.htm (accessed 8 December 2006).

Jarvie, Grant. *Class, Race and Sport in South Africa's Political Economy.* London: Routledge, 1985.

———. *Sport, Racism and Ethnicity.* London: Falmer, 1991.

Johnstone, Frederick. "White Prosperity and White Supremacy in South Africa Today." *African Affairs* 19, no. 275 (April 1970): 124–140.

Kaplinsky, Raphael. "'Economic Restructuring in South Africa: The Debate Continues': A Response." *Journal of Southern African Studies* 20, no. 4 (December 1994): 533–537.

Karp, Ivan. "Beer Drinking and Social Experience in an African Society: An Essay in Formal Sociology." In *Explorations in African Systems of Thought,* ed. Ivan Karp and Charles Bird, 83–119. Washington: Smithsonian Institution Press, 1980.

King, Stephen. "Brand Building in the 1990s." *Journal of Marketing Management* 7 (1991): 3–13.

———. "Brand Building in the 1990s." In *Revealing the Corporation: Perspectives on Identity, Image, Reputation, Corporate Branding, and Corporate-Level Marketing,* ed. John T. Balmer and Stephen A. Greyser, 265–270. London and New York: Routledge, 2003.

Kirshenblatt-Gimblett, Barbara. *Destination Culture: Tourism, Museums and Heritage.* Berkeley: University of California Press, 1998.

Klein, Kerwin Lee. "Reclaiming the 'F' Word, or Being and Becoming Postwestern." *Pacific Historical Review* 65, no. 2 (May 1996): 179–215.

Klein, Naomi. *No Space, No Choice, No Jobs, No Logo: Taking Aim at the Brand Bullies.* London: Flamingo, 2001.

Kohn, Alfie. *No.Contest: The Case against Competition.* Boston: Houghton Mifflin, 1992.

Kratz, Corinne A., and Ivan Karp. "Wonder and Worth: Disney Museums in World Showcase." *Museum Anthropology* 17, no. 3 (October 1993): 32–42.

Kuzwayo, Ellen. *Call Me Woman.* Johannesburg: Ravan Press, 1985.

la Hause, Paul. "Drink and Cultural Innovation in Durban: The Origins of the Beerhall in South Africa, 1902–1916." In *Liquor and Labour in Southern Africa,* ed. Jonathan Crush and Charles Ambler, 78–114. Athens: Ohio University Press, 1992.

———. "Drinking in a Cage: The Durban System and the 1929 Riots." *Africa Perspective* 20 (1982): 63–75.

Labour Bulletin Staff. "Labour Action." *South African Labour Bulletin* 14, no. 5 (February 1990): 4–5.

Laidlaw, Chris. *Mud in Your Eye: A Worm's Eye View of the Changing World of Rugby.* Cape Town: Howard Timmins, 1974.

Landau, Paul S. *The Realm of the Word: Language, Gender and Christianity in a Southern African Kingdom.* Cape Town and London: Portsmouth, N.H.: Heinemann, 1995.

Lansdown, C. W. A. *South African Liquor Law.* Cape Town: Juta, 1983.

Legassick, Martin. "South Africa: Forced Labour, Industrialisation and Racial Differentiation." In *The Political Economy of Africa,* ed. Richard Harris, 227–270. Cambridge, Mass.: Schenkman Publishing Co., 1975.

Lindsay, Lisa A. *Working with Gender: Wage Labor and Social Change in Southwestern Nigeria.* Portsmouth, N.H.: Heinemann, 2003.

Lipton, Merle. *Capitalism and Apartheid: South Africa, 1910–1986.* Aldershot: Ashgate, 1986.

———. "The Debate about South Africa: Neo-Marxists and Neo-Liberals." *African Affairs* 78, no. 310 (January 1979): 57–80.

Louis, J. C., and Harvey Z. Yazijian. *The Cola Wars.* New York: Everest House, 1980.

Louw, E. "The Medical Profession and the Rehabilitation of the Alcoholic." *Medical Proceedings* (25 September 1966): 490–493.

Lukhele, Andrew. *Stokvels in South Africa.* Johannesburg: Amagi Books, 1990.

Lury, Celia. *Consumer Culture.* New Brunswick, N.J.: Rutgers, 1996.

Luyt, Louis. *Walking Proud: The Louis Luyt Autobiography.* Johannesburg: Don Nelson, 2003.

Magubane, Peter. *Soweto: Portraits of a City.* London: Holland House Publishers, 1990.

Maloka, Tshediso. "'Khomo lia oela!' Canteens, Brothels and Labour Migrancy in Colonial Lesotho, 1900–1940." *Journal of African History* 38 (1997): 101–122.

Markides, Constantinos, and Vassils M. Papadakis. "What Constitutes an Effective Mission Statement? An Empirical Investigation." In *New Managerial Mindsets: Organisational Transformation Strategy Implementation,* ed. Michael A. Hitt, Robert D. Nixon, and Joan E. Ricart i Costa, 35–54. Chichester, N.Y.: John Wiley and Sons), 1998.

Martin, Phyllis. *Leisure and Society in Colonial Brazzaville*. Cambridge: Cambridge University Press, 1995.

Massey, Doreen. "Power Geometry and a Progressive Sense of Place." In *Mapping the Futures: Local Cultures, Global Change*, ed. J. Bird, B. Curtis, T. Putnam, G. Robertson, and L. Tickner, 59–69. London: Routledge, 1993.

Matshoba, Mtutuzeli. *Call Me Not a Man*. Harlow: Longman, 1987.

Mazwai, Thami, ed. *Thirty Years of South African Soccer*. Johannesburg: Mafube, 2002.

McAllister, Patrick. *Agriculture, Labour and Beer in South Africa's Transkei*. Aldershot: Ashgate, 2001.

———. *Building the Homestead: Agriculture, Labour and Beer in South Africa's Transkei*. Leiden and Aldershot: Ashgate, 2001.

———. "Indigenous Beer in Southern Africa: Functions and Fluctuations." *African Studies* 52, no. 1 (1993): 71–88.

McGahan, A. M. "The Emergence of the National Brewing Oligopoly: Competition in the American Market, 1933–1958." *Business History Review* 65 (Summer 1991): 229–284.

Mercer, Kobena. "Imagine All the People: Constructing Community Culturally." In *Imagined Communities*, ed. Christian Boltanski, Sofie Calle, Denzil Forrester, Komar and Melamid, Guiseppe Penone, Tim Rollins and K.O.S., Yinka Shonibare, Gary Simmons, and Gillian Wearing, 12–17. London: National Touring Exhibitions, SBC, 1995.

Mills, Wallace G. "The Fork in the Road: Religious Separatism versus African Nationalism in the Cape Colony 1890–1910." *Journal of Religion in Africa* 9, no. 1 (1978): 51–61.

Miracle, Andre W., Jr., and C. Roger Rees. *Lessons of the Locker Room: The Myth of School Sports*. New York: Prometheus Books, 1994.

Modisane, Bloke. *Blame Me on History*. 2nd ed. Craighall: Ad. Donker, 1986.

Moodie, T. Dunbar, with Vivienne Ndatshe. *Going for Gold: Men, Mines, and Migration*. Berkeley: University of California Press, 1994.

Mooney, P. H. "The Practice of History in Corporate America: Business Archives in the United States." In *Public History: An Introduction*, ed. B. J. Howe and E. L. Kemp, 427–452. Florida: Robert Krieger, 1988.

Moore, Henrietta. *A Passion for Difference*. Cambridge: Polity Press, 1994.

Morrell, Robert, ed. *Changing Men in Southern Africa*. Pietermaritzburg and London: University of Natal Press and Zed Books, 2001.

———. "Of Boys and Men: Masculinity and Gender in Southern African Studies." *Journal of Southern African Studies* 24 (1998): 605–630.

Morris, Paul. "Freeing the Spirit of Enterprise: The Genesis and Development of the Concept of Enterprise Culture." In *Enterprise Culture*, ed. Russell Keat and Nicholas Abercrombie, 21–37. London and New York: Routledge, 1991.

Morris, R. *Marketing to Black Townships: Practical Guidelines*. Cape Town: Juta, 1992.

Moser, J. "WHO and Alcoholism: Alcohol Problems and National Health Planning in Programmes of the World Health Organisation." In *Notes on Alcohol and Alcoholism*, ed. S. Caruana, 1–3. London: Medical Council on Alcoholism, 1972.

Motsisi, Casey. "Miss Prettiful." In *Shebeens Take a Bow! A Celebration of South Africa's Shebeen Lifestyle*, ed. Jim Bailey and Adam Seftel, 60–62. Johannesburg: Bailey's African History Archives, 1994.

———. "On the Beat." In *The Drum Decade: Stories from the 1950s*, ed. Michael Chapman, 175–182. Pietermaritzburg: University of Natal Press, 1989.

———. "One Man's Day of Reckoning." With photos by Peter Magubane. In *Shebeens Take a Bow! A Celebration of South Africa's Shebeen Lifestyle*, ed. Jim Bailey and Adam Seftel, 74–75. Johannesburg: Bailey's African History Archives, 1994.

Mphahlele, Ezekiel. *Down Second Avenue*. London: Faber, 1959.

Nakasa, Nat. "And So the Shebeen Lives On." In *The World of Nat Nakasa*, ed. Essop Patel, 16. 2nd ed. Johannesburg: Ravan Press, 1995.

Nasson, Bill. "Commemorating the Anglo-Boer War in Post-Apartheid South Africa." *Radical History Review* 78 (2000): 149–175.

Nattrass, Nicoli. "Controversies about Capitalism and Apartheid in South Africa." *Journal of Southern African Studies* 17, no. 4 (December 1991): 654–677.

———. "Economic Restructuring in South Africa: The Debate Continues." *Journal of Southern African Studies* 20, no. 4 (December 1994): 517–531.

———. "The Truth and Reconciliation Commission on Business and Apartheid: A Critical Evaluation." *African Affairs* 98 (1999): 373–391.

Nauright, John. "Colonial Manhood and Imperial Race Virility: British Responses to Post-Boer War Colonial Rugby Tours." In *Making Men: Rugby and Masculine Identity*, ed. John Nauright and Timothy J. L. Chandler, 122–143. London: Frank Cass, 1996.

———. *Sport, Cultures and Identities in South Africa*. Cape Town: David Phillip, 1997.

Nauright, John, and David Black. "'Hitting Where It Hurts': Springbok–All Black Rugby, Masculine National Identity and Counter-hegemonic Struggle, 1959–1992." In *Making Men: Rugby and Masculine Identity*, ed. John Nauright and Timothy J. L. Chandler, 205–226. London: Frank Cass, 1996.

Newnham, Thomas Oliver. *Apartheid Is Not a Game: NZ vs Apartheid Sport*. Auckland: Graphic Public, 1975.

Nixon, Robert D., Michael A. Hitt, and Joan E. Ricart i Costa. "New Managerial Mindsets and Strategic Change in the New Frontier." In *New Managerial Mindsets: Organisational Transformation Strategy Implementation*, ed. Michael A. Hitt, Robert D. Nixon, and Joan E. Ricart i Costa, 1–12. Chichester, N.Y.: John Wiley and Sons, 1998.

Ntsele, Ndaba. "Empowerment Makes Good Business Sense." In *The Story of Our Future South Africa 2014*, ed. Brett Bower and Steuart Pennington, 177–179. Hyde Park, Johannesburg: South Africa—The Good News (Pty) Ltd., 2004.

Odendaal, Andre. "South Africa's Black Victorians: Sport and Society in the Nineteenth Century." In *Pleasure, Profit, Proselytism: British Culture and Sport at Home and Abroad, 1700–1914*, ed. James A. Mangan, 193–214. London: Frank Cass, 1988.

Oliver, Thomas. *The Real Coke, The Real Story*. New York: Penguin Books, 1987.

O'Meara, Dan. *Volkskapitalisme: Class, Capital and Ideology in the Development of Afrikaner Nationalism, 1934–48*. Cambridge, 1983.

Ouzgane, L., and Robert Morrell, eds. *African Masculinities: Men in Africa from the Late 19th Century to the Present*. New York: Palgrave, 2004.

Parry, Charles D. H., and Anna L. Bennetts. *Alcohol Policy and Public Health in South Africa*. Cape Town: Oxford University Press, 1998.

———. "Country Profile on Alcohol in South Africa." In *Alcohol and Public Health in Eight Developing Countries,* ed. L. Riley and M. Marshall, 135–175. Geneva: World Health Organization, 1999.

Partanen, Juha. *Sociability and Intoxication: Alcohol and Drinking in Kenya, Africa and the Modern World.* Helsinki: Finnish Foundation for Alcohol Studies, 1991.

Patel, Essop, ed. *The World of Nat Nakasa.* 2nd ed. Johannesburg: Ravan Press, 1995.

Pather, Rathnamala. "The Figure of the Shebeen Queen in the Selected Works of Black South African Writers." M.A. thesis, University of Natal, Durban, 1992.

Pendergrast, Mark. *For God, Country and Coca-Cola: The Definitive History of the Great American Soft Drink and the Company That Makes it.* New York: Basic Books, 2000.

Pendlebury, A. John. "Creating a Manufacturing Strategy to Suit Your Business." In *Making Strategic Planning Work in Practice,* ed. Basil Denning, 81–90. Oxford: Pergamon Press, 1989.

Penn, Nigel. *Rogues, Rebels, and Runaways: Eighteenth-Century Cape Characters.* Cape Town: David Philip, 1999.

Prahalad, C. K., and G. Hamel. "The Core Competence of the Corporation." *Harvard Business Review* 68, no. 3 (1990): 79–91.

Ramaphosa, Cyril. "Black Economic Empowerment: Changing the South African Business Landscape." In *South Africa: The Good News,* ed. Brett Bower and Steuart Pennington, 161–166. Hyde Park, Johannesburg: South Africa—The Good News (Pty) Ltd., 2002.

Rassool, Ciraj, and Leslie Witz. "The 1952 Jan van Riebeeck Tercentenary Festival: Constructing and Contesting Public National History in South Africa." *Journal of African History* 34 (1993): 447–468.

Ratele, Kopano. "The End of the Black Man." *Agenda: Empowering Women for Gender Equity* 37 (1998): 60–64.

Raz, Aviad. *Riding the Black Ship: Japan and Tokyo Disneyland.* Cambridge, Mass.: Harvard University Asia Center, 1999.

Reader, D. H. "Sociological Aspects of Alcoholism." *Psychologica Africana* 10 (1964): 197–205.

Reid, Graeme, and Liz Walker, eds. *Men Behaving Differently: South African Men since 1994.* Cape Town: Double Storey, 2005.

Rocha-Silva, Lee. *Alcohol and Other Drug Use by Blacks Resident in Selected Areas in the RSA.* Pretoria: Centre for Alcohol and Drug-Related Research, Human Sciences Research Council, 1991.

———. *Attitudes towards Drinking and Drunkenness in the RSA.* Pretoria: Institute of Sociological and Demographic Research, Human Sciences Research Council, ca. 1989.

———. *Drinking Practices, Drinking-Related Attitudes and Public Impressions of Services for Alcohol and Other Drug Problems in Urban South Africa.* Pretoria: Human Sciences Research Council, 1989.

Rogerson, Christian. "The Survival of the Informal Sector: The Shebeens of Black Johannesburg." *GeoJournal* 12 (1986): 153–166.

———. "Tourism-Led Local Economic Development: The South African Experience." *Urban Forum* 13, no. 1 (January 2002): 95–119.

Rogovsky, Nikolai, ed. *Restructuring for Corporate Success: A Socially Sensitive Approach.* Geneva: ILO, 2005.

Rojek, Chris. *Decentring Leisure: Rethinking Leisure Theory.* London: Sage 1995.

Rosenthall, Eric. *Tankards and Tradition.* Cape Town: Howard Timmins, 1961.

Rusburne, J. L., and H. Hamman. *A Survey of the Liquor Industry in South Africa.* No. 7. Johannesburg: Statsinform Pty Ltd, 1972.

Scott, John. *Corporate Business and Capitalist Classes.* Oxford: Oxford University Press, 1997.

Sidiropolous, Elizabeth. "Black Economic Empowerment." *South African Institute of Race Relations Spotlight* 2, no. 93 (September 1993): 1–50.

———. "The Politics of Black Business." *South African Institute of Race Relations Spotlight* 3, no. 94 (June 1994): 1–55.

Scully, Pamela. "Liquor and Labor in the Western Cape, 1870–1900." In *Liquor and Labour in Southern Africa,* ed. Jonathan Crush and Charles Ambler, 56–77. Athens: Ohio University Press, 1992.

Seekings, Jeremy, and Nicoli Nattrass. *Class, Race and Inequality in South Africa.* New Haven, Conn.: Yale University Press, 2005.

Serote, Mongane. *To Every Birth Its Blood.* Johannesburg: Ravan Press, 1981.

Shearer, Brent. "Miller Acquisition May Force Responses in Global Consolidation of Breweries." *Mergers and Acquisitions: The Dealmakers Journal* 37, no. 8 (August 2002): 29–30.

Shorten, John R. *The Johannesburg Saga.* Johannesburg: John R. Shorten (Pty) Ltd., 1970.

Simmel, Georg. *On Individuality and Social Forms: Selected Writings,* edited and with an introduction by Donald N. Levine. Chicago: University of Chicago Press, 1971.

Southall, Roger. "The ANC and Black Capitalism in South Africa." *Review of African Political Economy* 31 (2004): 313–328.

———. "Black Empowerment and Corporate Capital." In *State of the Nation South Africa 2004–2005,* ed. John Daniel, Roger Southall, and Jessica Lutchman, 455–478. Cape Town: Human Sciences Research Council, 2005.

———. "Black Empowerment and Present Limits to a More Democratic Capitalism in South Africa." In *State of the Nation South Africa 2005–2006,* ed. Sakhela Buhlungu, John Daniel, Roger Southall, and Jessica Lutchman, 175–201. Cape Town: Human Sciences Research Council, 2006.

Stallabras, Julian. *Gargantua: Manufactured Mass Culture.* London: Verso, 1996.

Staudenmaier, John M. "Clean Exhibits, Messy Exhibits: Henry Ford's Technological Aesthetic." In *Industrial Society and Its Museums 1890–1990: Social Aspirations and Cultural Politics,* ed. B. Schroeder-Gudehus, 55–65. Geneva: Harwood Academic Publishers, 1993.

Steyn, J. H. "The Alcoholic Offender." *Medical Proceedings* (September 1969): 321.

Suggs, D. N. "'These Young Chaps Think They Are Just Men Too': Redistributing Masculinity in Kgatleng Bars." *Social Science and Medicine* 53, no. 2 (2001): 241–250.

Swanson, Felicity. "'Die SACS Kom Terug': Intervarsity Rugby, Masculinity and White Identity at the University of Cape Town, 1960s–1970s." In *Imagining the City: Memories and Cultures in Cape Town,* ed. Sean Field, Renate Meyer, and Felicity Swanson, 207–227. Pretoria: HSRC Press, 2007.

Switzer, Les. *Power and Resistance in an African Society: The Ciskei Xhosa and the Making of South Africa.* Madison: University of Wisconsin Press, 1993.

Terreblanche, S. J. "Misuse of Alcohol and Alcoholism as Extremely Important Factors in the Loss Accounts of Employers and the Economy as a Whole." *Social Work* 13, no. 1 (13 March 1977): 40–47.

Thabe, George, and Andries Letsisi, assisted by M. Mutloatse. *It's a Goal! 50 Years of Sweat, Tears, and Drama in Black Soccer.* Johannesburg: Skotaville, ca. 1983.

Themba, Can. "Let the People Drink . . . They're Drinking Anyway." In *Shebeens Take a Bow! A Celebration of South Africa's Shebeen Lifestyle,* ed. Jim Bailey and Adam Seftel, 24–31. Johannesburg: Bailey's African History Archives, 1994.

———. "There Is a Yard Where People Have Gone Mysteriously Mad: Boozers Beware of Barberton." In *Shebeens Take a Bow! A Celebration of South Africa's Shebeen Lifestyle,* ed. Jim Bailey and Adam Seftel, 38–41. Johannesburg: Bailey's African History Archives, 1994.

Thomas, A. "Relapse of White Alcoholics in South Africa." *Social Work* 16, no. 4 (October 1980): 222–228.

Tlali, Miriam. *Footprints in the Quag: Stories and Dialogues from Soweto.* Cape Town: David Philip Publishers, 1989.

Tomlinson, Richard. "Is Miller's Time Up?" *Fortune International* (Europe) 148, no. 12 (2003): 32–36.

Tucker, B. A. "Interaction Behaviour and Locational Change in the South African Brewing Industry." *South African Geographical Journal* 67, no. 1 (1985): 62–85.

Tunbridge, J. E., and E. J. Ashworth. *Dissonant Heritage: The Management of the Past as a Resource in Conflict.* Chichester: John Wiley, 1996.

Vaillant, G. *The Natural History of Alcoholism.* Cambridge, Mass.: Harvard University Press, 1983.

Van der Burgh, C., and Lee Rocha-Silva. "Drinking in the Republic of South Africa, 1962–1982." *Contemporary Drug Problems* (Fall 1988): 447–470.

van der Spuy, J. "Home Violence? Some Data from the National Trauma Research Programme, MRC." *Trauma Review* 2, no. 3 (1994): 3–5.

van Onselen, Charles. "Randlords and Rotgut 1886–1903." *History Workshop* 2, no. 1 (1976): 33–89.

van Rooyen, E. A. "Drankmisbruik van Ouers as Oorsaak van Sorgbehoewendheid van hul Kinders." *Rehabilitation in S.A.* (September 1980): 99–102.

Vaughan, Megan. "The Character of the Market: Social Identities in Colonial Economies." *Oxford Development Studies* 24, no. 1 (1996): 61–77.

———. *Curing Their Ills: Colonial Power and African Illness.* Cambridge: Polity Press, 1991.

Weber, Wolfhard. "The Political History of Museums of Technology in Germany since the Nineteenth Century." In *Industrial Society and Its Museums 1890–1990: Social Aspirations and Cultural Politics,* ed. B. Schroeder-Gudehus, 13–25. Geneva: Harwood Academic Publishers, 1993.

West, Michael O. "Liquor and Libido: 'Joint Drinking' and the Politics of Sexual Control in Colonial Zimbabwe, 1920s–1950s." *Journal of Social History* 30, no. 3 (1997): 645–667.

White, Caroline. *South African Breweries Beer Division: Making Affirmative Action Work.* Cape Town: Institute for Democracy in South Africa, 1995.

Wiener, C. *The Politics of Alcoholism: Building an Arena around a Social Problem.* London: Transaction Books, 1977.

Williams, Raymond. *Keywords: A Vocabulary of Culture and Society.* Rev. and exp. ed. London: Fontana, 1988.

Williamson, J. *Decoding Advertisements: Ideology and Meaning in Advertising.* London: Boyars, 1978.

Willis, Justin. "'Beer Used to Belong to Older Men': Drink and Authority among the Nyakusa of Tanzania." *Africa* 71, no. 3 (2001): 373–390.

———. *Potent Brews: A Social History of Alcohol in East Africa, 1850–1999.* Oxford: James Currey and the British Institute in East Africa, 2002.

Winkler, A. T. "Basic Principles Underlying Statutory Measures for the Treatment of Alcoholics in the Republic of South Africa." *Volkswelsyn en Pensioene* (June 1970): 4–11.

Witz, Leslie. *Apartheid's Festival: Contesting South Africa's National Pasts.* Bloomington: Indiana University Press and David Philip, 2003.

Wolcott, Harry F. *The African Beer Gardens of Bulawayo: Integrated Drinking in a Segregated Society.* New Brunswick, N.J.: Rutgers Center of Alcohol Studies, 1974.

Worden, Nigel. "Signs of the Times: Tourism and Public History at Cape Town's Victoria and Alfred Waterfront." *Cahiers d'Etudes Africaines* 141–142 (1996): 215–236.

Worpole, Ken. "The Age of Leisure." In *Enterprise and Heritage: Crosscurrents of National Culture,* ed. John Corner and Sylvia Harvey, 137–161. London: Routledge, 1991.

Wright, Patrick. *On Living in an Old Country.* London: Verso, 1985.

Yoshimoto, Mitsuhiro. "Images of Empire: Tokyo Disneyland and Japanese Cultural Imperialism." In *Disney Discourse: Producing the Magic Kingdom,* ed. Eric Smoodin, 181–199. London and New York: Routledge, 1994.

Young, Robert. *Colonial Desire: Hybridity in Theory, Culture and Race.* London: Routledge, 1995.

Zeleza, Paul Tiyambe, and Cassandra Rachel Veney, eds. *Leisure in Urban Africa.* Trenton, N.J. and Asmara, Eritrea: Africa World Press, 2003.

Unpublished Papers and Theses

Alegi, Peter. "Moving the Goal Posts: Playing Styles, Sociability, and Politics in South African Soccer in the 1960s." Working Paper 225, African Studies Center, Boston University, 2000.

Ballantine, C. "From Marabi to Exile: A Brief History of Black Jazz in South Africa." In *Papers Presented at the Sixth Symposium on Ethnomusicology, Music Department, Rhodes University, 1st–3rd October, 1987.* Grahamstown: International Library of African Music, 1988.

Barrat, Graham. "Intervarsity: Through the Eyes of Joey Burke, Cheerleader and Chair, 1989–1990." Unpublished Research Project, Historical Studies Department, University of Cape Town, 2005.

Bradshaw, E., N. McGlashan, and J. S. Harington. "The Use of Tobacco and Alcoholic Beverages by Male and Female Xhosa in Transkei in Relation to Cancer of the Oesophagus." Unpublished paper. Institute of Social and Economic Research, Rhodes University, Grahamstown, 1983.

Deacon, Ivan. "The South African Liquor Industry—Structure, Conduct, Performance and Strategies for Future Action." Doctor of Commerce thesis. University of Stellenbosch, 1980.

du Plessis, G. M. "The Treatment of Employees with Drinking Problems by the Social Services Department of the Chamber of Mines of South Africa." Paper presented to a South African National Council on Alcoholism and Drug Abuse Symposium, 3–4 February 1977.

Frahm, B. I. "Aspects in the Marketing of Sorghum Beer in South Africa." M.A. thesis, University of Pretoria, 1982.

Galli, E. "An Educational Answer via the Family in Connection with the Problem of Drug Dependence." Unpublished Paper, n.d., SANCA archives, Johannesburg.

Gatley, S. M., and J. E. Bayley. "A Report on a Research Project on Patterns of Use and Attitudes towards the Use and Misuse of Alcohol, Dagga, Mandrax, and Inhalants in the Black Community of New Brighton, Port Elizabeth." Vista University and SANCA Port Elizabeth, November 1987.

Gillis, L. S. "Summary of the Findings of a Survey of Psychiatric Disturbance and Alcoholism amongst the Coloured People of the Cape Peninsula." Paper presented at the Psychiatry Department, University of Cape Town & Groote Schuur Hospital, 25 October 1965.

Lewis, J. "Patterns of Drinking among the Coloureds of South Africa." Unpublished paper presented to First National Summer School on Alcoholism, Pretoria, October 1966.

McNamara, J. K. "Social Life, Ethnicity and Conflict in a Gold Mine Hostel." M.A. thesis, University of the Witwatersrand, 1978.

Ndou, Nndateni. "The Changing Nature of Employment Relationship: The South African Breweries (SAB) Owner-Driver Scheme." Bachelor of Social Science Honours thesis, University of Cape Town, 2002.

Schmidt, J. J., and P. A. Botha. "Die Drinkpatroon van die Bantoe in 'n Stedelike Gebied." Unpublished paper, Instituut vir Sosiologiese, Demografiese en Kriminologiese Navorsing, Pretoria, 1974.

Seftel, H. C. "Alcoholism in Johannesburg Africans—Causes and Consequences." Unpublished report, Department of Medicine, Johannesburg and Non-European Hospital and University of the Witwatersrand, ca. 1974.

Sharp, Loanne. "The South African Breweries Ltd: A Case Study in Monopoly Conditions, Conglomerate Diversification and Corporate Control in the South African Malt Beer Industry." Master of Commerce thesis, University of Cape Town, 1997.

Van der Burgh, C., and Lee Rocha-Silva. "Some Guidelines for Combating the Advertising/Marketing Strategies of the Alcohol Industry in Black Communities." Paper prepared for committee workshop, SANCA national office, Johannesburg, 1 October 1988.

Index

Anne Kelk Mager is Associate Professor of Historical Studies at the University of Cape Town. She is author of *Gender and the Making of a South African Bantustan: A Social History of the Ciskei, 1945–1959* and has published in journals including *Past and Present, Social Science and Medicine, Business History, The Journal of African History,* and the *Journal of Southern African Studies.*